Coordinates of Anglo-American Romanticism

Coordinates of Anglo-American Romanticism

WESLEY, EDWARDS, CARLYLE & EMERSON

Richard E. Brantley

UNIVERSITY PRESS OF FLORIDA
Gainesville Tallahassee Tampa Boca Raton Pensacola Orlando Miami Jacksonville

Library of Congress Cataloging-in-Publication Data

Brantley, Richard E.
Coordinates of Anglo-American romanticism: Wesley, Edwards, Carlyle, and Emerson / Richard E. Brantley.
p. cm.
Includes bibliographical references and index.
ISBN 0-8130-1169-8 (acid-free paper)
1. English prose literature—19th century—History and criticism.
2. American prose literature—19th century—History and criticism.
3. Philosophy, American—19th century. 4. Philosophy, English—19th century. 5. Romanticism—Great Britain. 6. Romanticism—United States. 7. Literature—Philosophy. I. Title.
PR778.R65B7 1993
828'.80809—dc20 92-22954

Frontispiece: John Wesley (Museum of Methodism at Wesley's Chapel, London); Jonathan Edwards, portrait by Joseph Badger (Yale University Art Gallery, bequest of Eugene Phelps Edwards, 1938); Thomas Carlyle, portrait by Samuel Lawrence (National Trust Photographic Library/John Bethell, copyright National Trust 1991, London); Ralph Waldo Emerson (Ralph Waldo Emerson Memorial Association and the Houghton Library, Harvard University). All have been reproduced in this volume by permission of the above-named rights holders.

The University Press of Florida is the scholarly publishing agency for the State University System of Florida, comprised of Florida A & M University, Florida Atlantic University, Florida International University, Florida State University, University of Central Florida, University of Florida, University of North Florida, University of South Florida, University of West Florida.

University Press of Florida
15 Northwest 15th Street
Gainesville, Florida 32611

For my parents,
Rabun and Elizabeth Brantley

CONTENTS

☆

ACKNOWLEDGMENTS

☆

My ongoing fascination with the triangle of philosophy, religion, and literature exemplifies my principle that the near influence is always telling. Near influences on my thinking, specifically, have determined the character of this book.

At Wake Forest University, where John A. Carter had kindled my enthusiasm for Carlyle and Emerson and where the late Judson B. Allen had helped me generate methodology, I happened to combine, during my senior year, Willard Hamrick's course in the Hebrew Prophets with Edwin G. Wilson's masterly exploration of English Romanticism. An efficacious combination of tough mind and tender heart characterizes both the Romanticism taught by Edwin Wilson and the outlook represented by the legendary teacher himself.

Although he grew up during the Great Depression, Wilson notes the bittersweet nature, and even the joys, of that time. "I've always been a rather hopeful and optimistic person," he says. "That is not to say that the Romantic poets were naive or without pain or anguish. But it is to say that there is something idealistic and something very heroic and compassionate about Romanticism." This view of Romanticism, that it emphasizes optimism without either oversimplifying intellectual problems or underestimating spiritual dilemmas, permeates my work.

My research at the University of Florida reflects the influence of the late T. Walter Herbert, who was Distinguished Service Professor of English, and of Melvyn New, former chair of the Department of English. Each shared with me his knowledge of empirical philosophy and the evangelical movement as well as his readings of eighteenth- and nineteenth-century literature.

Donald Ault, Ira Clark, Patricia Craddock, Alistair Duckworth, Anne Goodwyn Jones, Robert Ray, John Seelye, R. A. Shoaf, James Twitchell, Gregory Ulmer, and, above all, Diana Brantley solved several problems of principle and procedure. The University of Florida Division of Sponsored Research supported this project during the fall of 1986 and the summer of 1989. David Leverenz and A. Carl Bredahl, Jr., commented on portions of chapter 1.

I presented versions of this chapter to the American Academy of Religion in 1986, the Eighth Oxford Institute for Methodist Theological Studies in 1987, and "Perspectives on the Romantic Movement: An Interdisciplinary Conference" at Baylor University in 1988. Gregory Clapper, Frederick Dreyer, Giles Gunn, Richard Heitzenrater, T. Walter Herbert, Jr., Robert Langbaum, Jay Losey, Rex Matthews, and Ralph C. Wood gave various useful responses to the essay, which, as "The Common Ground of Wesley and Edwards," appeared in the *Harvard Theological Review* 83, no. 3 (July 1990): 271–303. I am grateful for permission to use that material here.

L. J. Swingle, Leonard I. Sweet, and Samuel F. Pickering, Jr., read the complete manuscript with generosity and in detail. Walda Metcalf and Teresa Jesionowski, among many other excellent staff members of the University Press of Florida, have expertly facilitated its progress through to publication.

To those graduate students in my "special topics" seminar on Anglo-American Romanticism, who entered into the spirit of the proceedings, I am especially deeply indebted. Their agreement to venture back and forth across the Atlantic supported my argument that Wesley, Edwards, Carlyle, and Emerson bridge natural and spiritual experience. These students' "willing suspension of disbelief" allowed them, if not to accept my view that this quartet of writers can plot the coordinates and set the parameters of Anglo-American Romanticism, then to indulge my "poetic faith" that it does so.

I dedicate this book to those first best influences, my parents. Their experience-validated view of the world champions my brother Bill's career in science as well as my triangulation of philosophy, religion, and literature. Their more than fifty-year commitment to southern church-related colleges amounted to a mission. Since allusions to the Bible and Shakespeare shaped the conversation in our house, literature came to have a near-religious valuation. The dedication to Rabun and Elizabeth Brantley indicates what I owe to them. Their approach to reality undergirds me yet.

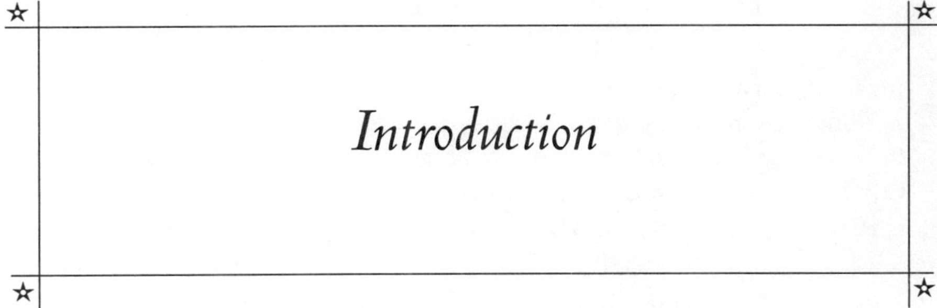

Introduction

One mark of maturity, national as well as personal, is the desire to discover a bridge from the present to the past, to seek links between what is and what was. American literature, now having come of age, having shed the "adolescent" insecurity that demanded independence from tradition, no longer needs to insist on complete separation from the literature of England. "Anglo-American literature" emerges as a valid concept. John Wesley (1703–91), founder of British Methodism, and Jonathan Edwards (1703–58), leader of the American Great Awakening, exemplify a significant link between the frequently still too narrowly conceived and usually still too rigidly separated fields of British literature and American literature. A comparison of Wesley with Edwards, a view of their combined legacy, provides an appropriately historical, substantially interdisciplinary, and even sufficiently aesthetic means of comparing Thomas Carlyle (1795–1881), Sage of Chelsea, with Ralph Waldo Emerson (1803–82), Sage of Concord. Especially characteristic of this quartet of writers is the creative tension between, and even the playful interaction of, empiricism and evangelicalism.

Although empiricism is "natural" and evangelicalism is "spiritual," the great principle of empiricism, that one must see for oneself and be in the presence of the thing one knows, applies as well to evangelical faith. Each of these two methodologies operates along a continuum that joins emotion to intellect; each joins externality to words through "ideas/ideals of sensation," that is, through perception or grace-in-perception or both. While *empiricism* refers to immediate contact with and direct impact from objects and subjects in time and place, *evangelicalism* entertains the notions that religious truth is concerned with experiential presuppositions and that experience need not be nonreligious. On the basis of the experiential common denominator between empiricism and evangelicalism, through the "both/and" logic of philosophical theology, I argue that Wesley, Edwards, Carlyle, and Emerson theologize empiricism. They ground transcendentalism in the world, balance religious myths and religious morality with scientific reverence for fact and detail, and ally empirical assumptions with "disciplined" spirit. Above all, they share the simultaneously rational and sensationalist reliance on experience as the avenue to both natural and spiritual knowledge.

Recent scholarship suggests that "any historically comprehensive treatment of the topic 'literature and philosophy,' would eventually have to treat three subjects, 'literature, philosophy, and theology,' with each subject triangulated by the other two."[1] In this work, I will attempt a historically fully unified treatment of these three subjects. Carlyle and Emerson represent a rich strain of early modern literature, especially because their heritage of Anglo-American philosophical theology is not only strong but also largely intact in their works, which derive in great measure from the empirical-evangelical influence. Whatever other heritages each reflects (and both reflect so many that the pair can seem disparate), each holds to the methodological axis of which I speak.

In an age of what Paul Ricoeur calls "the hermeneutics of suspicion,"[2] or what might be called the latter-day Marxist/Nietzschean/Freudian academic enterprise of detecting false consciousness, I find that Wesley, Edwards, Carlyle, and Emerson hold to the moment-by-moment (or at least momentary) efficacy of a consciousness more trustworthy than illusory, more true than false. Wesley and Edwards, far from just validating spiritual insights by borrowing from sense language, speak literally to experience in general, including empirical observation, scientific method, and apprehension of both God-in-nature and the unmediated Spirit. Their shared methodology, harking back to the epistemology of John Locke (1632–1704), not only links sense to reason and matter to mind but, more importantly, aligns nature with grace. The Lockean basis of their evangelical faith heralds the broadly experiential, "empirical-evangelical" vision shared by Carlyle and Emerson, who, with more awareness of worldview than of those who create worldviews and hence with no blooming "anxiety of influence,"[3] are intellectually as well as spiritually descended from a charismatic diumvirate of the Anglo-American world. Thus Wesley and Edwards form the background to a broad consideration of Anglo-American literature as represented by one British exemplar and one American exemplar of belletristic prose. Whether self-consciously (with irony), consciously, or unconsciously, Carlyle and Emerson reflect an Anglo-American philosophical theology most notably expressed by Wesley and Edwards.

ROBERT LANGBAUM, arguing that Romanticism extends well into the twentieth century, explores the proposition that Romanticism is not a straightforwardly transcendentalizing/spiritualizing reaction against Enlightenment rationality, common sense, and this-worldliness, but an evolutionary development of some fundamental epistemological concerns in Enlightenment thought.[4] Romantic writers, like their Enlightenment forebears stretching back to Locke and beyond, cultivate a powerfully skeptical strain in their thinking.[5] They worry about how we know things and how we know that we know them. They are especially inclined to address the problem by applying tests of experience, placing a primary value on empirical evidence at the same time that they half-distrust sensory experience. Although I follow the direction in Romantic studies signaled by Langbaum's *The Poetry of Experience* (1957), I try to broaden the idea of experience he makes central to such studies. The transcendentalizing/spiritualizing tendency of the Romantics is by no means inimical to the inclusively epistemological dialectic they inherited from the Religious Enlightenment of Wesley and Edwards. The philosophical theology shared by these twin pioneers of transatlantic revivalism is not only readable in its own right but also useful as the historical, heuristic, interdisciplinary context for reading Carlyle and Emerson as exemplars of Anglo-American Romanticism.

Although Romantic Modernism, or even Romantic Pragmatism, could be a more accurate label than Late Modernism for what now may be replacing deconstruction,[6] Alvin Kernan, interpreting novels by Saul Bellow, Bernard Malamud, Vladimir Nabokov, and Norman Mailer, concludes that we may be witnessing the end of "the Romantic literary system" that has persisted for almost two hundred years.[7] But even if discrete Romanticism extended only well into the nineteenth century,[8] I still describe an ample arc of it. In *Wordsworth's "Natural Methodism"* (1975), I used Wesley's theology to gloss Wordsworth's British Romanticism: Wesley's evangelical versions of practical charity, reciprocal covenant with the Holy Spirit, conversion, spiritual perfection, and the emblematic and typological "reading" of the Book of Nature influenced not only Wordsworth's themes, but also his symbology, structure, tone, irony, characterizations, and narrative patterns.[9] In *Locke, Wesley, and the Method of English Romanticism* (1984), I used Wesley's philosophical theology to gloss British Romanticism in general: Wesley absorbed and spiritualized the epistemology of Locke and then, through the complex process of cultural osmosis, passed on to Blake, Wordsworth, Coleridge, Shelley, and Keats a method for both their natural observation and their "spiritual experience."[10] Now, two hundred years after the death of Wesley, I seek both to demonstrate what ideas Wesley and Edwards hold in common (each is Lockean as well as religious) and to show how the two provide an interdisciplinary framework for interpreting the Anglo-American pairing of the Late Romantic writers Carlyle and Emerson.

Thus I will consider notable examples of mid-nineteenth-century prose against the background of similarly notable, similarly nuanced, and even "pre-Romantic" prose of the mid-eighteenth century, namely, the empirical-evangelical methodology shared by Wesley and Edwards. Although Marshall Brown attempts to revive the term *pre-Romantic* to describe the "prematurity" of the second half of the eighteenth century,[11] I am not interested in simply casting Wesley and Edwards as forerunners of Romanticism. Rather, I discern an empirical-evangelical continuum that joins Wesley and Edwards to the Romantics and vice versa. Accordingly, I seek to define the late but not belated Romanticism shared by Carlyle and Emerson as a dialectic of their desire for and trust in experience as the best means of knowing what is true, whether naturally or supernaturally. This Romanticism, a vital synthesis and complex entity indeed, rests, like the sensibility shared by Wesley and Edwards, on the fundamental yet lively principle that spiritual as well as natural experience gives rise to concepts and to words.

Thus, having already explored the influence of Wesley's philosophical theology on British Romanticism, I offer a broader, Anglo-American, case study in the sociology of ideas, as distinct from the history of ideas, with its rootedness in elite culture. The lower- and middle-class followers and readers of the middle-class poets, prose writers, and preachers in whom I am interested are not often enough thought of, by some, as trafficking in ideas at all. I seek, then, to pin down a philosophical/religious, popular, optimistic dimension of Anglo-American Romanticism.

ALTHOUGH I UNDERSTAND that Carlyle and Emerson share an Anglo-American sensibility, I take them one by one, for each, perhaps even more than either Wesley or Edwards, constitutes a subject unto himself. Criticism treating Carlyle, while rich and provocative, does not approach the number or volume of studies treating Emerson; therefore, my chapter on Emerson is longer than my chapter on Carlyle. This "disproportion" could be seen as balancing my previous work with a current emphasis on Anglo-*American* sensibility. The lack of balance, however, is finally only apparent. Since my chapter on Emerson refers to and enlarges on my chapter on Carlyle, a proper balance between these authors should emerge from an essentially cumulative, progressively amplifying procedure.

Two points of my philosophically theological triangle of Locke, Wesley, and Edwards are British, as are all five of the High Romantic poets—Blake, Wordsworth, Coleridge, Shelley, and Keats—whom I continue to treat. But I accord roughly equal space, nevertheless, to British and American cultures. Without either granting privilege to, or showing prejudice against, the British or the American manifestation of the empirical-evangelical sensibility, I seek to balance these nationally identified portions of that sensibility.

An Anglo-American family resemblance is discernible through this Anglo-American quartet of writers, for empirical-evangelical method is one of the most important indigenous roots of Anglo-American literature in the early modern world. I invite even late twentieth-century nonbelievers—in selves, male and female complementarities, presences, historical contexts, national or "binational" characters, God, nature, experiential epistemology, and the possibility, however bare, of religious knowledge—to suspend their disbeliefs for the moment, in order to grant my methodological investigation of Wesley, Edwards, Carlyle, and Emerson at least a heuristic value of "poetic faith." If Lockean elements common to the theologies of Wesley and Edwards illuminate key resemblances between the literatures of England and the United States during the early modern era, this phenomenon emerges not just because Carlyle and Emerson richly reflect an Anglo-American heritage of philosophical theology but also because that heritage itself is rich.

Wesley and Edwards, no less than Carlyle and Emerson, achieve through the dialectic of empiricism and evangelicalism the satisfying complexity, the "both/and" logic, and even the ironizing tendency of all good literature. The two national literatures can come together under a broad understanding of literature as at once *les belles lettres* and *les bonnes lettres*. Both "*les bonnes lettres,*" the old "grand, broad, and noble conception" that adds the hymns of Isaac Watts to the lyrics of Wordsworth and the fiction of Harriet Beecher Stowe to that of Melville, and "*les belles lettres,*" the "narrower, more decadent" conception of the written word, constitute the full and pertinent, though slightly stuffy, definition of literature as "everything worthy to be said, preferably the best thoughts expressed in the best manner, but above all the best thoughts."[12] Whatever reservations one may have about this pallid reference to Matthew Arnold's definition of literature as "the best that has been thought and said," this unexamined assumption of morality's difference from, and superiority to, aesthetics, and this dubious judgment concerning form versus content, one needs this twofold conception of literature to grasp the "special relationship" between British culture and American culture. Insofar as British literature and American literature demonstrate the same rich vein of *les belles lettres* and the same pure vein of *les bonnes lettres,* and insofar as the two veins are identical in content and even sometimes similar in form, the two national literatures are one. The twofold conception provides a broadly inclusive, sufficiently explanatory model for demonstrating a wide, rarely decadent, usually grand, and sometimes noble Anglo-American sensibility. When compared with the less ironic, though not less satisfactory or less complex, bonnelettristic duo of Wesley and Edwards, Carlyle and Emerson clearly constitute a duo in *les belles lettres,* but key resemblances between Wesley and Edwards parallel—and even define—key resemblances between Carlyle and Emerson.

ONE

An Anglo-American Nexus

Commonplaces stand in need of scrutiny. The special relationship between England and the United States is more than merely political, more than merely linguistic, and even more than broadly cultural, for it is at once, and perennially, intellectual and emotional. An especially useful metaphor for this relationship is the special relationship between the Englishman John Wesley and the American Jonathan Edwards. Although they never consciously cooperated with one another, they contributed to a variety of relations between their respective lands. Wesley founded Methodist movements in both England and the United States, and Edwards joined forces with the Briton George Whitefield, who undertook the arduous journey to the colonies in order to participate in the Great Awakening. Wesley and Edwards inspired popular evangelicalism in Britain and America from the 1730s, through the American Revolution, to the end of the nineteenth century. By regarding them as emblematic, I seek to delineate an especially enduring, because still resonating, Anglo-American mode of thought and feeling. The intellectual sway and fervor of Wesley and Edwards contributed to Anglo-American experience.

Whether or not the special relationship between England and the United States rests in large part, even now, on an intellectual as well as emotional frame of reference to nature and to spirit, this frame is not only the considered construct of Wesley and Edwards but also their joint legacy to the nineteenth century. Constituting an Anglo-American *genius loci,* Wesley and Edwards express and disseminate their shared definition of feeling and thought. Through their concerted roles as social forces, through an often indirect but sometimes direct and always propitious process of cultural osmosis, they make up the very model of an Anglo-American sensibility. Their religious methodologies are not, after all, so far removed from even such early twentieth-century methods as the verification principles of the British A. J. Ayer and the pragmatism of the American John Dewey. Many such "representative men"[1] (one would say "representative people") participate in the same binational entity, the same "nature-culture coevolution"[2] of Anglo-American relations.

This chapter, by examining the influence of Wesley and Edwards from the broadest possible perspective, and by addressing their common ground as one single subject, surveys an especially fertile ground of Anglo-American expression. I will consider them philosophically, rather than exclusively theologically, and approach them as methodologically alert, even where they thought themselves simply orthodox. I seek to demonstrate that they shared the same essentially Lockean insights that, as I have previously argued, informed much of British literature and theology from 1740 to 1840. I acknowledge differences between them, yet I discover their common ground, the full character of their two-way special relationship. The twin pioneers of transatlantic revivalism are brothers of both soul and mind in that both men appropriate Lockean empiricism for religious methodology. Indeed, the philosophical as well as religious epistemology of this charismatic diumvirate of the Anglo-American world exemplifies the Anglo-American imagination.

Edwards: An Orientation

Although recent scholarship on Edwards emphasizes his conservatism and his relation to Scottish Commonsense philosophy,[3] Locke was a formative influence on the Commonsense school. Edwards's indebtedness to Locke[4] is consistent with conservative principles in that Locke takes account of both empiricism and "a theocentric framework."[5] Terrence Erdt traces Edwards's language to its conservative source in Calvin and emphasizes the aesthetic dimension of that language; he also acknowledges that an understanding of Edwards's sense-language is central to an understanding of Edwards.[6] Roland Delattre argues that especially according to *The Nature of True Virtue* (1765) divine being is both present to humankind as beauty and known to humankind through emotion.[7] Similarly, though with explicit reference to Locke, I maintain an aesthetic-epistemological emphasis in my approach to Edwards's theology.

Sacvan Bercovitch regards with new respect the pioneering argument of Perry Miller that Edwards is a Lockean.[8] While I share this new respect, it is time to discover new complexities in the Lockean view of Edwards. As I confirm Wallace E. Anderson's conviction that Edwards "accepted Locke's view that it is a wholly contingent matter that each mind receives the sensory information it does,"[9] I consider the consensus that although Lockean ideas of sensation represent real qualities of bodies, real qualities in Edwards's works are often identified only with "the fixed order and relations of ideas."[10] Moreover, although Miller's argument is exclusively sense-oriented, my view of Locke's empiricism is that it is both sense- and reason-based, a view consistent with Edwards's immersion in the categories of sense perception and his desire for the consent of mind to mind.

Whatever the merits, then, of the labels *idealist, Platonist, scholastic, Calvinist,* and *mystic,* the labels *empiricist* and *sensationalist* are particularly apt for Edwards in his eighteenth-century context. The "radical theism" that Robert W. Jenson describes embraces what he sees as Edwards's most characteristic themes: God's relation to nature and history, religious experience, the presence of Christ, and the perfected human community.[11] But "radical theism" also includes the precisely philosophical, because specifically Lockean, theme of the here and now. Although Edwards rejects Newton's cosmology of the universe as a machine, he does not reject Locke's livelier, more down-to-earth world picture. Despite Edwards's life-long struggle with his age's Arminian tendency toward autonomous individuality, his radical theism preserves Locke-derived faith in individual experience.

Wesley and Edwards: An Overview

Charles Rogers, in his attempt to differentiate the pair, disclaims for Edwards any affinity with Wesley's views about providence in general and predestination in particular.[12] Wesley's comments about Edwards's *The Freedom of the Will* (1754) deplore its doctrines of irresistible grace and unconditional election.[13] Wesley's comments, however, approve of Edwards where Edwards posits the experiential context of the soul as a given of religious life: "The soul [quoted Wesley] is now connected with a material vehicle, and placed in the material world. Various objects here continually strike upon one or other of the bodily organs."[14] Albert C. Outler, on the basis of Wesley's published abridgments of five works by Edwards, suggests that Edwards was a formative influence on Wesley.[15] Without losing sight of Rogers's point of view, I concur with Outler's: although Edwards referred to Wesley just once, and disparagingly,[16] Wesley rejoiced in Edwards. Accordingly, I seek to establish the intellectual as well as emotional sense in which they should be linked.

Frederick Dreyer sees them as intellectual polar opposites.

> Edwards's thought was ultimately ontological and proceeded from the premise of necessary being. Wesley's was psychological and proceeded from the premise of self-consciousness. Wesley is satisfied with the apparent truths that ordinary mortals do in fact perceive. Edwards insists upon the necessary truths they ought to perceive.[17]

Except that I would substitute *epistemological* for *psychological,* I am in accord with Dreyer's estimate of Wesley, and Dreyer's estimate of Edwards rings true in that Edwards's ontological moods indeed recur. His early essay "On Being," for example, rests on a rationalistic base, the "platonic traditions of idealism";[18] and toward the end of his career, he clearly retreats from any ostensible harmony of empiricism and faith to a rather intransigent rationalism, a rationalism of the supernatural, if you will. Wesley does not follow this path, for while believing in the supernatural as much as anyone, Wesley holds to the senses and to sense-based reason.

In midcareer, however, Edwards comes close to having it both ways, as Wesley does throughout his life. Against the view of Edwards as exclusively ontological, I contend that his theology, like Wesley's, is often epistemological, and I accordingly emphasize that Lockean empiricism provides a philosophic reason for linking Wesley with Edwards. In "Wesley and Edwards: A Hypothesis," Appendix A of my *Locke, Wesley, and the Method of English Romanticism,* I suggest that Edwards derives his theological method from Locke's theory of knowledge. Wesley uses Locke's language to devise an analogy between the natural senses and the "spiritual sense"; he even conceives of a continuum joining scientific method and rational empiricism to natural and revealed religion. Edwards, too, in midcareer at least, envisions this analogy or continuum.

A Document

The shortest way to bring the pair into my field of vision is through Wesley's abridgment (1773) of Edwards's *A Treatise concerning Religious Affections* (1746). This last of Wesley's abridgments of five works by Edwards[19] culminates Wesley's thirty-year response to Edwards's works and hence constitutes Wesley's most mature judgment of those works. *Religious Affections* marks the central juncture of Edwards's development, at the midpoint of his career, and is thus the best representative of his mind and method.

Appearing in volume 23 of Wesley's collected works of 1771–74, *An Extract from a Treatise concerning Religious Affections* omits the entire preface of Edwards's work, the second, third, and fourth of the twelve major sections of part three, many shorter passages, and many words and phrases.[20] Published in 1762, the edition of *Religious Affections* that Wesley used is itself an abridgment by William Gordon.[21]

Although Gregory S. Clapper, in the only other full-length study of Wesley's abridgment, acknowledges that "Gordon's abridgment was about two-thirds of the original" and that "Wesley's was one-sixth," Clapper demonstrates that neither the "excisions and revisions" of Gordon nor those of Wesley "pervert the essential thrust of Edwards's work."[22] To compare Wesley's abridgment with Gordon's, then, is to compare it with *Religious Affections,* too. Wesley's abridgment is not only true to the original, but also "better," that is, less prolix.

Although Wesley often objected to works he carefully read,[23] and although his more than two hundred abridgments sometimes include matter with which he disagreed,[24] his abridgment of *Religious Affections* is so painstaking, polished, and selective that it indicates well his attraction to Edwards's sensibility. By analyzing the abridgment, I characterize Wesley's distillation of Edwards and hence Edwards's influence on Wesley. As occasion rises, I point to parallels between the abridgment and Wesley's works. Nothing Wesley ever wrote materially contradicts either the abridgment or any other version from Edwards's prime; indeed, what appears in the abridgment finds strikingly similar expression throughout Wesley's works.

The abridgment not only omits, but also alters, and some of the alterations are substantive.[25] As an Arminian who believes that "Christ died for *every Soul* of Man,"[26] Wesley excises Edwards's Calvinism and its doctrine of the elect. Where Edwards inveighs against the view that "mine own hands hath saved me," Wesley balks and quotes nothing,[27] thus suggesting that one bears partial responsibility for one's own salvation. Where Edwards says "the covenant is ordered in all things, and sure," Wesley is silent,[28] thus refusing predestinarian tincture. "Continuance in duty," writes Edwards, is "difficult to [one's very] nature," which is full of "blindness, deceit, self-flattery, self-exaltation, and self-confidence," and he adds, for good measure, that even "the saint . . . has sight of his own corruptions," but Wesley gives no quarter to this extreme belief in human frailty.[29]

Such omissions suggest an anti-Calvinist rationale for Wesley's numerous rejections of Edwards's harsh, uncharitable language. Where Edwards speaks of some religious affections as "false and counterfeit," Wesley calls them merely "mixed or degenerating,"[30] as though to soften the implication of hardened duplicity. Where Edwards argues that "persons may have a kind of religious love, and yet have no saving grace," Wesley, who often says that love and grace are so far from being thus mutually exclusive that they are in fact one and the same, keeps quiet.[31] Where Edwards insists on phrases like "great corruption," "strait and narrow way," "fears of hell," "the duty of self-denial," "deserved eternal burnings," "the infinitely hateful nature of sin," and "the infinitely inferior nature of men," Wesley will have none of it.[32] Indeed, Wesley will have very little Calvinist language of any kind, however innocuous, for though the word *saints,* with its overtones of the perseverance thereof, appears four times,[33] he usually goes to great lengths to avoid even this mild Calvinism. He replaces Edwards's "true saints," "eminent saints," "the character of the saints," and "the minds of the saints" with "Christians," "believers," "good men," "we," "those," or almost anything else he can think of.[34]

"The Eye altering alters all," declared William Blake,[35] which means not only that the organs of perception are creative, that the eye changes what it sees, but also that "the Eye altering" is changed by what it sees, that all is changed within. Similarly, though Wesley's emendatory powers transform some doctrines and improve the style of *Religious Affections,* his editorial eye is itself improved, his "doors of perception" "cleansed,"[36] by his encounter with and his obvious reverence for Edwards's methodology. Although Wesley's thought guides his editorial hand to the point of bias, the abridgment includes, as Wesley's Note to the Reader puts it, those "many remarks and admonitions" of Edwards's "which may be of great use to the children of God."[37]

Clapper, pointing out such parallels between *Religious Affections* and Wesley's works as reliance on Scripture and the theme of humble joy, concludes that

> if one were to give an irenic reading of their differences, one might say that Wesley and Edwards agreed about the sovereignty of God, but that while Edwards expressed this sovereignty through his Calvinist doctrines of predestination and the bondage of the will, Wesley expressed the same thing by emphasizing prevenient grace and the perfecting possibilities of the spirit.[38]

Since the agreement between Wesley and Edwards about the sovereignty of God did not prevent Wesley from rejecting Edwards's *language* of sovereignty at least three times in the abridgment,[39] one might quibble with part of Clapper's statement. But the statement rings true with regard to the abridgment as a whole, which, as Clapper demonstrates, is both careful to epitomize the four basic parts of Edwards's text and consistent with the basic tenets of Wesley's texts.

Finally, though, the abridgment represents more than the merely theological commonality of Wesley and Edwards. Although "edification was Wesley's ultimate criterion when evaluating the written word," Wesley, as even Clapper acknowledges, "shared Edwards's interest in science and philosophy."[40] Although Wesley's Note to the Reader complains that Edwards "heaps together so many curious, subtle, metaphysical distinctions, as are sufficient to puzzle the brain, and confound the intellects of all the plain men and women in the universe," that is, although the abridgment eschews Edwards's ontology, the abridgment is decidedly epistemological wherever Edwards is so.[41] Just as Lockean epistemology avoids regarding mind as superior to, or independent of, sense experience, so Wesley downplays diction that might be construed as rationalist.

Where Edwards speaks of "the more vigorous and sensible exercises of the inclination and will of the soul," Wesley, by writing "the more vigorous and sensible exercises of the will,"[42] omits spiritual, mentalist elements, while he retains sense-language. Where Edwards writes, "It may be enquired what are the affections of the mind," Wesley omits "of the mind."[43] Since the fourth of Edwards's twelve distinguishing signs of "Truly Gracious and Holy Affections" asserts the intellectual component in the affections—"Gracious affections do arise from the mind's being enlightened, rightly and spiritually to understand or apprehend divine things"—it may seem strange that the intellectual Wesley omitted it, until one realizes how close it is to rationalism, that is, to a reason insufficiently involved in, or insufficiently tempered by, sense experience.[44]

In line with the fact that Edwards's reasoning is not always sense-based, an entire category of passages appears to have been altered because, although philosophical or methodological enough, they are not sufficiently empirical to suit Wesley. Where Edwards complains of those who "tell you a long story of conversion" or "a fair story of illuminations and discoveries," Wesley, who likes accounts of experiential efficacy, eliminates the complaint.[45] From Edwards's phrase "doctrinal knowledge," Wesley drops "doctrinal,"[46] as though to include natural knowledge in knowledge conducive to religion. "Ministers," writes Edwards, sometimes insist too much on "distinctness and clearness of method," for the Spirit does not "proceed discernibly in the steps of a particular established scheme, one half so often as is imagined."[47] But Wesley finds no place for this passage:[48] although his "empiricism" is not unacquainted with paradox, he likes method to be clear and distinct.[49]

Thus manipulating as well as preserving the original, Wesley's editorial procedure is motivated in decisive measure by the Lockean presuppositions of his theology. Where Edwards's theology is consistent with those presuppositions, where his theology is "empirical," Wesley tends to make it more so. Witness, for example, his twofold strategy of quoting Edwards's endorsement of experiential priorities—"Without affections, one is wholly destitute of the saving influences of the Holy Spirit"—and omitting an adjacent passage in which Edwards creates some doubt about the very affectional life he advocates: "As there is no true religion, where there is nothing else but affection; so there is no true religion, where there is no affection."[50] Where Edwards speaks of "holy desire exercised in longings, hungerings, and thirstings after God," Wesley omits "longings," as though to lessen subjectivity and so to intensify the sensationalist implications of this biblical and somehow eighteenth-century phraseology.[51]

Wesley is justified in detecting empirical assumptions and empirical language in *Religious Affections,* which is reconcilable with, and even measures up to, Wesley's own Lockean tastes and expectations, his experiential bias and, above all, his doctrine of the "spiritual sense."[52] Notably, he tampers least with passages most clearly resembling his Lockean method. These passages, totaling twenty-two of the abridgment's sixty-five pages,[53] form the focus of this chapter. They constitute both a precise transformation of Lockean method and what Wesley thought was the broadest agreement between Edwards and himself. Here I consider this strain of passages both in itself and in context; I elaborate on a theological equivalent of Locke's philosophy, demonstrating the Lockean ground of both Wesley and Edwards as found in the abridgment. I enunciate a "spiritual sense" as much American as British.

Wesley's and Edwards's evangelical faiths draw in part from both the processes and the forms of late seventeenth-century empiricism, even as they laterally displace them. Wesley's editing is so thoroughly informed by Locke's *Essay concerning Human Understanding* (1690) that the abridgment emerges, without falsifying the original, as a theologizing of Locke's empiricism. To abridge is "to shorten" or even "to curtail," but the abridgment of *Religious Affections* is no mere summary, no mere abstraction, and no mere "selection of essential facts." Wesley's configuring of Edwards's "epistemology" is, in addition, a condensation that epitomizes the original without diluting it and honors the original by enhancing it. Wesley decided that *Religious Affections* is complexly but manifestly empirical, and I agree. This midpoint of Edwards's thought is indeed characterized by the same Locke-derived emphasis on experience, natural as well as spiritual, to be found in Wesley's Methodism. Wesley's abridgment, by heightening that emphasis, epitomizes the "epistemology" common to him and Edwards. Where most alike and nearest the generic level of revival imagination, they are at once methodically intellectual and in resonance with the enabling powers of empirical premises.

By the abridgment, then, I mean a bridge indeed. It is the intersection of the thought of Wesley and the thought of Edwards. The one's Arminianism and the other's Calvinism lie outside the abridgment. Wesley did not stake his theological reputation on the abridgment, nor did Edwards approve it as faithful to his thought. The abridgment contains, however, what they share, not so much the theological as the philosophical thought, the Locke-inspired emphasis on the experiential, which they then each express in their evangelical theologies and practices. So when I use the term "the abridgment" in this work, I mean the areas where the thought of Wesley and the thought of Edwards coincide.

A Reading

"Even deliberately to write against something," observes Denis Donoghue, "is to take one's bearings from it."[54] The abridgment takes its bearings from Lockean epistemology without being subsumed by it. In advocating experience as the way to knowledge, the abridgment is historically akin to and even agrees with Locke's preaching of sensation as the key to empirical knowledge. Locke, in homage to Descartes, intuits himself and deduces God:

> For nothing can be more evident to us, than our own Existence. . . . Thus from the Consideration of our Selves, . . . our Reason leads us to the Knowledge . . . That *there is an eternal, most powerful, most knowing Being.*[55]

Locke goes on to insist, however, that "the *Knowledge of the Existence* of any other thing we can have only by *Sensation*,"[56] and his epistemology of sensation is his major contribution to the ways of knowing. The abridgment, especially its twenty-two pages of Lockean method, appropriates this epistemology not only to say how one knows that natural things exist but also to indicate in what manner, and according to what similitude, one knows all spiritual things, including selves and God's own Self. Although spirit and sense would seem opposites (they can be thought of as antipodes and hence complements), the abridgment, without being either loose in applying to theology the language of sensation or glib about spiritual knowledge, attempts to locate the religious in the empirical and vice versa. Thus the abridgment suggests a way of overcoming the split between the natural and the supernatural, and indeed envisions the terms of their unification. Although the abridgment and Locke's *Essay* are not always consistent with one another, and the relation between them is one of give-and-take, they share a frame of reference and a set of methodological assumptions, a language, and an interest in the same issues.

The abridgment, first of all, falls clearly in line with Locke's stand against enthusiasm, which, *mirabile dictu,* is no more antireligious than Wesley and Edwards are fanatical. "Immediate *Revelation,*" observes Locke,

> being a much easier way for Men to establish their Opinions, and regulate their Conduct, than the tedious and not always successful Labour of strict Reasoning, it is no wonder, that some have been very apt to pretend to Revelation, and to perswade themselves, that they are under the peculiar guidance of Heaven.[57]

The abridgment similarly urges caution in speaking of, and in making claims to, immediate revelation:

> The manner of the Spirit's proceeding in them that are born of the Spirit, is very often exceeding mysterious. It is oftentimes as difficult to know the way of the Spirit in the new birth, as in the first birth: "As thou knowest not what is the way of the Spirit, or how the bones do grow in the womb of her that is with child: Even so thou knowest not the work of God, that worketh all."[58]

Thus both the *Essay* and the abridgment flatly state that the Spirit's workings hardly ever fall under the power of either human understanding or human observation.

Unlike the *Essay,* however, the abridgment proclaims the *fact* of the Spirit's proceeding and even implies, in radical homage to Locke, that the Spirit's workings sometimes significantly fall under the powers of both human understanding and human observation. Locke, on one occasion, acknowledges that God can "excite [men] to Good Actions by the immediate influence and assistance of the Holy Spirit, without any extraordinary Signs accompanying it,"[59] but Locke is primarily concerned to prevent the recurrence of mid-seventeenth-century Puritan excess.[60] His *Essay,* accordingly, though admitting the possibility of visitation, warns that people who claim it are most probably mad. The abridgment concedes that many who claim it are wrong and even that some who claim it are mad. It argues, nonetheless, that visitation is a very possible event for religious people: "How greatly," lament Wesley and Edwards, "has the doctrine of sensibly perceiving the immediate power of the Spirit of God, been ridiculed."[61] "Sensibly perceiving," although making an un-Lockean point, employs a Lockean criterion.

Almost in spite of itself, the same paragraph that warns that "no man can tell whence [the Spirit] came, or whither it went" (cf. John 3.8) uses empirical language. The paragraph, even though indirectly and by analogy, appeals to the powers of observation and perception in "we, as it were, hear the sound of it, the effect of it is discernible."[62] This language, indeed, is based on more than analogy, for "the effect of it is discernible" connotes sense perceptions as tests or validations of something prior. "We, as it were, hear the sound of it" (even with the "as it were") rings with immediacy and presence, and so stops just short of denoting the senses as preconditions for divine experience.

The abridgment often gives so much credit to Locke's experiential criteria that it entertains a thought at which Locke would be horrified, namely, the direct sensation of God's effects and presence. The following quotation, for example, places all bets on the world of sense experience: "Men will trust their God no further than they know him, and they cannot be in the exercise of faith in him one ace further than they have a sight of his fulness and faithfulness in exercise."[63] "A sight of" need not mean physical sight, but the statement implies that regarding all matters of fact and causation, including the divine, Edwards, and Wesley through him, have the courage of Locke's convictions about experiential vision.

In their evocation of Locke's trust in eyewitness accounts, moreover, Edwards and Wesley wax particularly philosophic:

> Those are very improperly called witnesses of the truth of any thing, who only declare they are of opinion, such a thing is true. Those only are proper witnesses who testify that they have seen the truth of the thing they assert.[64]

Even here, of course, ambiguities arise, for one sees not the thing, but the truth of the thing; but far from meaning only that the senses are outward analogues to inner perception, this strong statement indicates, too, the clear possibility of perceiving God and his effects directly.

Finally, in the question, "What is a tender heart, but one that is easily impressed with what ought to affect it?"[65] the abridgment evinces not only Lockean diction[66] but also, and more importantly, the entire Lockean as well as Wordsworthian premise of "wise passiveness."[67] The self in both the *Essay* and the abridgment is valued, then, insofar as it is receptive, though with a remaining ambiguity about whether "tender heart" is specifically a metaphor for receptivity to the Spirit. It mattered greatly to both the philosopher and the revivalists what is happening to us at a particular time, and what acts upon us from without.

Consider, next, their telling word *impulse. Impulse* for Locke, Wesley, and Edwards, besides meaning "something opposed to deliberate reflection, as in the phrase 'to act on impulse,'" can indicate "a movement stirred in us from without, an influence upon the individual of some force in the outer universe."[68] Here, for example, is Locke's ambiguously subjective and objective use of *impulse*. Attacking those who claim "illumination from the Spirit of God," he observes that "whatsoever odd Action they find in themselves a strong inclination to do, that *impulse* is concluded to be a call or direction from Heaven, and must be obeyed."[69] In their own mood of attacking "self-deceivers" who claim, falsely, the "discoveries and elevations" of immediate revelation, Edwards and Wesley similarly observe that "the chief grounds of the confidence of many of them are *impulses* and supposed revelations, sometimes with texts of Scripture, and sometimes without. These *impulses* they have called the witness of the Spirit."[70] Locke for his part, and Wesley and Edwards for theirs, refuse to credit the enthusiasts' objective meaning, but the *Essay* elsewhere employs the word in its objective sense:

> How often may a Man observe in himself, that whilst his Mind is intently employ'd in the contemplation of some Objects; and curiously surveyed some ideas that are there, it takes no notice of impressions of sounding Bodies, made upon the organ of Hearing, with the same alteration, that uses to be for the producing the Idea of a Sound? A sufficient *impulse* there may be on the Organ; but it not reaching the Observation of the Mind, there follows no perception.[71]

And Wesley and Edwards, insofar as they agree that even spiritual experience can be an external force that focuses on the individual soul and shapes it in the arena of human history, would concur in an objective usage of *impulse* such as one finds in a theological treatise published during Locke's lifetime: *Discourse of Angels, . . . also Something Touching Devils, Apparitions, and Impulses* (1701).[72]

Here, with a simultaneously objective and religious meaning, albeit without the word *impulse,* is the abridgment's premise that both natural and spiritual experiences write on the mind's blank tablet:

> Indeed the witness or seal of the Spirit, consists in the effect of the Spirit of God in the heart, in the implantation and exercises of grace there, and so consists in experience: And it is beyond doubt, that this seal of the Spirit is the highest kind of evidence of our adoption, that ever we obtain: But in these exercises of grace in practice, God gives witness, and sets to his seal, in the most conspicuous, eminent and evident manner.[73]

Although the senses are in this case implicitly more proof than entry, the imagery of the stamp and the seal is not far from the metaphor of mind as tabula rasa, receiving the impressions of experience. This same combination of Lockean theory and spiritual theology is to be found, say, in Charles Wesley's hymns:

> Where the indubitable seal
>   That ascertains the kingdom mine?
> The powerful stamp I long to feel,
>   The signature of love divine.[74]

Such emphasis on faith through experience, or rather on faith *as* experience, is everywhere evident in Wesley's abridgment of Edwards's treatise. The abridgment typically declares that "the Scripture represents faith as that by which men are brought into a good estate, and therefore it cannot be the same thing, as believing that they are already in one."[75] Faith is no more innate than ideas and no less dependent than ideas on the nourishment of experience: it is far from either an inherent capacity or a blind leap. The abridgment goes on to attack those "under the notion of . . . living upon Christ and not experiences."[76] Such a notion "directly thwart[s] God's wise constitution of things," for far from being mutually exclusive, Christ and experience are intimately interinvolved.

I have previously defined the epistemology of Locke as "an experiential continuum with understanding at one pole and physical sensation at the other."[77] Thus an ever-increasing though by no means innate strength of reason forms such an important part of Locke's empiricism that his empiricism should be said to include a specific appeal to this a posteriori brand of reasoning. Of all the works of Edwards's that Wesley might have chosen to abridge, *A Treatise concerning Religious Affections* shows perhaps the greatest balance between Edwards's immersion in the categories of sense perception and his desire for the consent of mind to mind. Of all five works of his that Wesley did abridge, *Religious Affections* offers the fullest range of Lockean "empiricism," namely, the same balance between sense and reason that characterizes Wesley's method.[78]

As for the abridgment's categories of sense perception, note, first, that "the influence of some extrinsic force upon [our] minds"[79] connotes the purely natural means whereby we passively receive impressions from without. Boldly, the abridgment often makes no distinction "between the influences of the Spirit of God, and the natural operations of our own minds."[80] This lack of difference is not so much to demythologize the Spirit as to honor experience. While Locke would separate the Spirit from natural operations, Wesley and Edwards do not. And while Locke would elevate natural operations by making them independent of "mere" faith, Wesley and Edwards elevate "mere" natural operations by relating them to, by mentioning them in the same breath as, the Spirit. "For any to expect the influence of the Spirit, without a diligent improvement of the appointed means, is presumption," declares the abridgment in obvious dialogue with Locke.[81] The abridgment adds: "To expect that he will operate upon their minds, without means subservient to the effect, is enthusiastical." So willingly, that is, does the Spirit condescend to work through the natural operations of our minds that spiritual and natural operations can be all but identical, or, to use the words of the abridgment, "It is frequently God's manner to make his hand visible."[82]

The abridgment laments the fact that such "sense perception" of the divine is often mistaken for enthusiasm: recall "how greatly has the doctrine of sensibly perceiving the immediate power of the Spirit of God, been ridiculed." Even where the abridgment speaks exclusively of the spiritual means whereby we receive impressions, it does so in empirical terms, or at least in terms that duplicate theologically the Lockean fascination with extrinsic power over the mind:

> And if persons tell of effects in their own minds, that seem to them not to be from the natural operations of their minds, but from the supernatural power of some other agent, should it at once be looked upon as a sure evidence of delusion, because things seem to them to be as they are?[83]

Between the abridgment and the *Essay,* in this regard, is a particularly striking connection. Here is the *Essay:*

> Thus we see the holy Men of old, who had *Revelations* from God, had something else besides that internal Light of assurance in their own Minds, to testify to them, that it was from God. They were not left to their own Perswasions alone, that those Perswasions were from God; But had outward Signs to convince them of the Author of those Revelations.[84]

And here is the abridgment:

> And so it was in most of the conversions of particular persons we have an account of in the New Testament: They were not wrought on in a silent, secret, gradual, and insensible manner; but with those manifest evidences of a supernatural power, wonderfully and suddenly causing a great change.[85]

Thus both Locke and Wesley/Edwards require rigorous standards of certification from the religiously inclined, but Wesley and Edwards, more broadly experiential than Locke himself, extend Lockean methods of inquiry to non-Lockean subject matter. By giving credence to "effects in their own minds" as well as to external signs, they include the internal in the catalogue of experience. They imply, thereby, that the senses can be thought of as analogous to, as indispensable for conceiving, the "sense" of inward evidence: while "effects *in* their own minds" draws a boundary around the mind, confining experience to it, "*effects* in their own minds" points to an action or impingement on the mind, such as would only occur through the avenue of the senses.

Wesley and Edwards, accordingly, seem aware that extrinsic power over the mind functions philosophically as well as religiously. The abridgment's expression of receptivity to external influence can be conventionally religious and explicitly biblical:

> I know of no reason why being affected with a view of God's glory, should not cause the body to faint, as well as being affected with a view of Solomon's glory. . . . My soul thirsteth for thee, my flesh longeth for thee, in a dry and thirsty land where no water is. . . . When I heard, my belly trembled, my lips quivered at the voice, and rottenness entered into my bones, and I trembled in myself.[86]

The following quotation, however, evinces not only heart-religion, but also, in equal measures, metaphysics and epistemology: "God has so disposed things as though every thing was contrived to have the greatest possible tendency to reach our hearts in the most tender part, and move our affections most sensibly."[87] This statement, as intellectual as it is emotional, rests on the assumption, the philosophical theology, that sense perception is blessedly constituted to receive every good and perfect gift.[88]

The abridgment, though, hardly depicts the mind as completely passive: Edwards's desire for the consent of mind to mind amounts, at times, to near rationalism, as though the mind were sufficient unto itself; and Wesley, though never himself so nearly mind-intoxicated, allows Edwards to express his desire. Whereas "passions" are the "more sudden" and "more violent" "actings of the will," such "affections" as "hope, love, desire, joy, sorrow, gratitude, compassion, and zeal" are "actings of the will" wherein the mind is more "in its own command."[89] The abridgment, then, though neither Cartesian in particular nor French in general, is, nonetheless and strangely, mentalist as well as Anglo-American.

The abridgment agrees even here, however, with Lockean reason as sense-based, for the affections, and not just the passions, are finally sense-related. Mind in the abridgment is between the extremes of active and passive, and truth in the abridgment is between the extremes of mind and matter.

Take, for example, the close interaction of mind and body. The issue is rampant in the age (it appears in medical treatises, and even in Descartes); Locke gives it his full attention.[90] The abridgment's lengthy argument that mind affects body and vice versa is similarly experiential, similarly other-directed, and almost nontheoretical in tone. "Such are the laws of union of soul and body," declares the abridgment, "that the mind can have no vigorous exercise, without some effect upon the body." The abridgment adds: "Yea, it is questionable, whether an embodied soul ever so much as thinks one thought, or has any exercise at all, but there is some corresponding motion in some part of the body."[91] Here, mind is tacitly superior to senses, for mental experience occurs prior to, and causes, activation of the body. Yet even here, the relation between mental experience and the body is the very evidence of mind's superiority, which, according to the abridgement as well as the *Essay*, consists in a place above, but not aloof from, the senses.

The mind, then, far from being independent of the senses, depends on them for its very identity, and its participation in the senses provides the evidence of God's acting in it. For when almost mind-intoxicated, and even when God-intoxicated, the abridgment comes no closer than it does at all other times, and no closer than does Locke, to the pure rationalism that views the mind's identity, and even its experience, as independent of the senses. Wesley and Edwards affirm, finally, a mind/body interaction in which body is often as active as, and sometimes even prior to, mind. After reiterating a certain primacy of mind—to wit, "Such seems to be our nature, that there never is any vigorous exercise of the will, without some effect upon the body, in some alteration of the motions of its fluids, especially of the animal spirits"—the abridgment includes the following significant addendum: "And on the other hand, the constitution of the body, and the motion of its fluids, may promote the exercise of the affections."[92] Here experience affects, and precedes, the mental, and insofar as "body promotes the exercise of the *affections*," by which the revivalists mean *religious* affections, the senses are not only receptors for divine truth but also building blocks of spiritual wisdom.

In Wesley's and Edwards's thought, as in Locke's, mind and world form a dialectic, if not a continuum and a harmonic whole. Reality appears to the reader of the *Essay* as a coalescence of subject and object: recall Locke's use of *impulse*. The abridgment, by teaching that mind extends to body and vice versa, implies that mind-body synthesis contacts external reality and vice versa.[93]

"Following the lead of the classical British experience-philosophy," wrote John E. Smith in his modern edition of *Religious Affections*, "Edwards placed primary emphasis upon first-person experience."[94] Smith does not explicitly apply this comment to *Religious Affections*, but the comment can help explain the treatise's emphasis on the practical and on action in matters of religion. The comment applies as well to that same emphasis in both the abridgment and other Wesley writings.

For the obvious reason that *his* experiential emphasis derives from British experience-philosophy, Wesley is careful to represent this aspect of Edwards's sensibility.

> The business of religion is from time to time compared to those exercises, wherein men are wont to have their hearts and strength greatly engaged, such as *running, wrestling,* and *warring.* . . . And as true religion is of a practical nature, and the affections are the springs of men's actions, it must consist very much in them.[95]

Or again:

> The tendency of grace in the heart to holy practice, is direct; and the connexion close and necessary. True grace is not an inactive, barren thing, for it is, in its very nature, a principle of holy action.[96]

These statements exemplify the "epistemology" of Wesley and Edwards. The first celebrates intense experience both as analogue to faith and as precondition for it. The second, besides implying an immediate connection between spiritual influx and practical charity (recall "grace *in* the heart"), contends that the connection between spiritual and natural experience is all but unmediated, that is, that spiritual experience intersects with, superimposes itself on, and, however fleetingly, becomes one with, natural experience.

The statements are broader and more inclusive than any narrowly "scientific" epistemology: "He that has knowledge only, without affection," say Wesley and Edwards, "never is engaged in the business of religion."[97] This statement can be understood in the light of another of Smith's general remarks about Edwards, namely, that he attempted "to bring the individual back to a sense of his own individuality and to the need for a broader conception of human understanding, one that does not eliminate everything but science from its concern."[98] (By "individuality," clearly, Smith means the significance of self rather than, or in addition to, its sinfulness.) Smith points out, finally, that Edwards's emphasis on first-person experience "took the form of the new *sense* or *taste* without which faith remains at the purely notional level."[99] Wesley's abridgment includes all of Edwards's statements regarding this "spiritual sense." Here I discuss several, as they accurately appear in the abridgment.

This doctrine, first of all, is Bible-based: "The Scripture is ignorant of any faith in Christ or the operation of God," say Wesley and Edwards, "that is not grounded in a spiritual sight of Christ."[100] They add proof texts. "True faith in Christ," they write, "is never exercised any further than persons 'behold as in a glass, the glory of the Lord,' and have 'the knowledge of the glory of God in the face of Jesus Christ.'"[101] The abridgment's opening passage, concerning the persecuted Christians to whom Paul wrote, constitutes a biblically oriented announcement of the "spiritual sense":

> There was nothing visible that could induce them thus to suffer, and could carry them through such trials. But though there was nothing that the world saw, or that they themselves saw with their bodily eyes, that thus supported them, *yet* they had a supernatural principle of love to something unseen; they loved Jesus Christ, whom they *saw spiritually.*[102]

One thinks, in this connection, of John 20.29 ("Blessed are they that have not seen, and yet have believed"). Note that, even where indicating what lies beyond the grasp of sense and even where mainly quoting the Bible, the abridgment's doctrine of the "spiritual sense" employs sensate language for a distinctively historical reason. Although neither Wesley nor Edwards could avoid the Lockean hegemony, both of them exploit it. They read certain proof texts in the context of the empiricist climate, as though to enhance both the climate and the texts. Both of them reflect a sense bias in their most biblical understanding of spiritual experience, for even in that understanding, they interpret such experience in alignment with an earthly methodology: they appeal to sense experience, if only as analogue.

Their other depictions of the "spiritual sense" are more philosophical than biblical, and as much philosophical as theological. The doctrine, to the extent that it covers immediate revelation, or the Spirit's operations in the present, carries authentically Lockean implications of the senses as tests, and even as manifesters and harbingers. For purposes of consideration in this light, this tough-minded passage is worth requoting: "Men will trust their God no further than they know him, and they cannot be in the exercise of faith in him one ace further than they have a sight of his fulness and faithfulness in exercise."[103] "A sight of" intimates a not so much analogical or metaphorical as literal dimension of the "spiritual sense," for in the absence of such labels as *spiritual,* the connotation is of physical sight, as though the knowledge of God were direct or metaphysical.

In the following statement of the "spiritual sense," moreover, the abridgment shows itself fully epistemological:

> In those gracious affections which are wrought through the saving influences of the Spirit of God, there is a new inward perception or sensation, entirely different in its nature, from any thing that ever their minds were the subjects of, before they were sanctified. If grace be, in the sense above described, an entirely new kind of principle; then the exercises of it are also entirely a new kind of exercise. And if there be in the soul a new sort of exercises which it knew nothing of before, and which no improvement, composition, or management of what it was before conscious of, could produce, or any thing like it; then it follows that there is, as it were, a new spiritual sense in the mind, or an entirely new kind of perception or spiritual sensation, which is in its whole nature different from any former kinds of sensation.[104]

True, this statement tends toward the analogical, and in its insistence that God works a *new* sense into the mind-soul, it does not sound Lockean or empirical. But this "spiritual sense," though wholly unlike the physical senses, is almost consciously Lockean in its explicit adherence to tabula rasa and hence to the pivotal powers of experience in general. In speaking of the minds of newborn people, that is, converts, as the *subjects* of inward perception or sensation, Wesley and Edwards imply the rationalist point that mind is always ultimate, always prior to senselike spiritual experience. Clearly, they seek the consent of mind to mind even as their language of sense perception waxes most Lockean. "Subjects *of*," however, is ambiguous. The phrase implies that minds are subjected or subordinated to spiritual sensation, which in this case, though inward, is other than, added to or prior to, mind. In spiritual experience, then, and not just in natural experience, the priority lies not in mind alone, nor even exclusively in senselike avenues to something rich and strange, but in the interchange highlighting now one, and now the other.

Although Locke implies that immediate revelation is unlikely or even impossible, because all thought comes from sense perception rather than from the extrasensory, he argues, nonetheless, that biblical revelation is true because it showed itself in action. Wesley and Edwards, in their doctrine of the "spiritual sense," apply this argument to their brief for immediate revelation, which, if confirmed after the fact by the criteria of natural experience, is true. Wesley and Edwards, of course, hold that supernatural intakings and reshapings of the mind constitute ultimate reality, but they use Locke to defend such visitations against charges of enthusiasm. In the passage just quoted, for example, the inward perception does not exist before the natural time, and does not inhere apart from the natural place, of particular spiritual influx. This notion is Lockean insofar as it assumes that grace, like everything else, is dependent on experience. Tough-mindedly experience-oriented rather than exclusively analogistic, the passage iterates the senselike perception of God's things as "a new sort of exercises which [the soul] knew nothing of before."

Thus Wesley and Edwards do not so much follow what Locke thinks as in their own way practice how he thinks and even how he speaks. Although they need not be labeled Lockean (their vision was their own), they do not hesitate to use Locke's distinguished epistemology. The piety of Wesley and Edwards is "natural":[105] not only do they believe in the God of nature, and not only do they think that sense experience can point to, if not include, God, but they also base their supernatural religion on experience. Not only do they assume that what happens in one's inward life is significant in the same way as what happens in one's sense experience but they also link, as their journals indicate, their sanctifications to the passage of time. They assume, in short, that what happens in one's inward life may interact with, and grow out of, what happens in one's sense experience. For them, experience both constitutes matter and mind, considered separately and together, and binds the senses to the soul.

A passage toward the end of the abridgment is perhaps most telling in suggesting this philosophical theology. It duplicates Edwards's attempt to describe faith through the language of both rational empiricism and scientific method. It not only elaborates, but also distills, the doctrine of the "spiritual sense," that is, "that sense of Divine things, which governs [our] heart and hands."[106]

> Not only does the most important part of Christian experience lie in spiritual practice, but nothing is so properly called by the name of experimental religion: For that experience which is in these exercises of grace, that prove effectual at the very point of trial, is the proper experiment of the truth of our

> godliness, wherein its victorious power is found by experience. This is properly Christian experience, wherein we have opportunity to see, by actual experience and trial, whether we have a heart to do the will of God, and to forsake other things for Christ, or no.[107]

By our experience, that is, we see God's prior reshapings of our hearts; but the passage indicates, too, that the range of spiritual experience can be identical with the range of natural experience. Indeed, the diction is so fully experientialist as to include an insistently scientific tenor: *by actual experience and trial, see, experiment, prove, practice,* and, not least (uncharacteristically for Wesley) the redundant uses of *experience*—all denote the particular empirical method whereby such religious problems as the knowledge of revelation appear to be raised by and solved by one's sense-oriented as well as mental life. Wesley is more empirical than even the Edwards of *Religious Affections.* But the Edwards of *Religious Affections,* as Wesley recognizes, employs the language of actual experience and trial, and both Wesley and Edwards hold that subjectivity corresponds with and, when God-suffused, commands objective truth.

This experiential assumption informs, and may even determine, one of their most characteristic doctrines, namely, assurance. Wesley's version of it derives not just from the Moravians' emphasis on Romans 8.15—"For ye have not received the Spirit of bondage again to fear; but ye have received the Spirit of adoption, whereby we cry, Abba, Father"—but also from Locke's emphasis on "Assurance" as the label for "the highest degree of Probability" in the realm of empirical belief.[108] Wesley, therefore, has his philosophic reason for amply representing Edwards's doctrine of assurance, which, as a thoroughly experiential interpretation of the Bible, is itself a doctrine of the age of Locke. Edwards and Wesley both write:

> God, in the plainest manner, revealed and testified his special favour to Noah; Abraham; Isaac; Jacob, Moses, David, and others. Job often speaks with the greatest *assurance.* David, throughout the book of Psalms, almost every where speaks in the most positive manner of God as his God. Hezekiah appeals to God, as one that knew, "he had walked before him in truth and with a perfect heart;" (2 Kings xx.3;) the Apostle Paul, through all his epistles, speaks in an *assured* strain, ever speaking positively of his special

> relation to Christ, and his interest in, and expectation of, the future reward.[109]

In sum, then, Wesley and Edwards do not subscribe to the notion of tabula rasa when they believe that we are born with a heavy burden of sin, but their equally characteristic emphasis on conversion admits of Lockean sanction. Conversion ascribes so much importance to what might happen, not only at inner moments but also in one's experience in the world, that whatever precedes such experiential sea-change is by comparison mere tabula rasa. Edwards, a Calvinist, does not assume as much responsibility as Wesley, an Arminian, does for the working out of one's own salvation. But Edwards's doctrine of "testing the spirits" gives even him, in the words of Smith, "some basis for judging the state of his own soul."[110] Although Edwards and Wesley through him warn against making "too much of [our] own doings, to the diminution of the glory of free grace," they finally ask, "Which way is it inconsistent with the freeness of God's grace, that holy practice should be a sign of God's grace?"[111] The nearest analogue to this emphasis on experience as test and not as conduit is the doctrine of good works, but the emphasis makes so much of our "own doings" that it emerges as implicitly Lockean, and the doctrine of the "spiritual sense" is where Edwards's similarity to both Locke and Wesley seems most pertinent.

I submit, now, by way of rounding off my Wesleyan-Lockean perspective on *Religious Affections,* Wesley's most Lockean statement of the "spiritual sense." The statement, from *An Earnest Appeal to Men of Reason and Religion* (1743), includes an explicit subscription to the fundamental, though only potentially theological, tenet of tabula rasa:

> Before it is possible for you to form a true judgment of the things of God, it is absolutely necessary that you have a *clear apprehension* of them, and that your ideas thereof be all *fixed, distinct,* and *determinate.* And seeing our ideas are not all innate, but must originally come from our senses, it is certainly necessary that you have senses capable of discerning objects of this kind: Not those only which are called natural senses, which in this respect profit nothing, as being altogether incapable of discerning objects of a spiritual kind; but spiritual senses, exercised to discern spiritual good and evil. It is necessary that you have *the hearing ear,* and *the seeing eye,* emphatically so called; that you have a new class of senses opened in your soul, not

> depending on organs of flesh and blood, to be "the evidence of things not seen" [cf. Heb. 11:1], as your bodily senses are of visible things; to be the avenues to the invisible world, to discern spiritual objects, and to furnish you with ideas of what the outward "eye hath not seen, neither the ear heard" [cf. I Cor 2:9].[112]

This statement, formulated a scant three years before *Religious Affections* first appeared, accords with Edwards's "spiritual sense," which, whether in its analogistic dimension or in its implication that even the natural senses are visionary, proceeds, too, from Lockean assumptions. Like Wesley's *Appeals to Men of Reason and Religion* (1743–45), *Remarks upon Mr. Locke's Essay on Human Understanding* (1781), and *On Living without God* (1790),[113] Edwards's *Treatise concerning Religious Affections* teaches four points: (1) we receive an inrush of spirit and then "see" abstractions manifested in our sensible experience; (2) we walk avenues to the invisible; (3) we receive the divine from the visible; and (4) we discover the divine in the visible. Where Locke coalesces sense experience with mind, Wesley and Edwards coalesce nature with spirit. To state the conclusion another way, the "spiritual sense" of Wesley and Edwards joins rational empiricism to both theistic natural religion and immediate revelation.

A Comparison

In *Locke, Wesley, and the Method of English Romanticism,* I argue, among other things, that Wesley's abridgment (1730) of *The Procedure, Extent, and Limits of Human Understanding* (1728) by Peter Browne (d. 1735), Bishop of Cork and Ross, is a key to Wesley's thought: the abridgment demonstrates the Lockean affinity between Browne and Wesley. Wesley's access to Locke—through Browne—parallels, and serves to gloss, Wesley's access to Locke through Edwards. Since both the abridgment of *Religious Affections* and the abridgment of *The Procedure* theologize Locke's *Essay* even more thoroughly than do the originals, a brief comparison of the two abridgments can serve to reinforce my view of the Lockean agreement between Wesley and Edwards.

First, as highlighted by the abridgment of *The Procedure,* here is Browne's doctrine of analogy:

> Metaphor is mostly in Words, and is a Figure of Speech; Analogy a Similis Ratio or Proportion of Things, and an excellent and necessary Method or Means of Reason and Knowledge. Metaphor uses Ideas of Sensation to express Immaterial and heavenly Objects, to which they can bear no real Resemblance or Proportion [e.g., "I am the Good Shepherd"]; Analogy substitutes the Operations of our Soul, and notions mostly formed out of them, to represent Divine Things to which they bear a Real tho' Unknown Correspondency and Proportion [e.g., "God is love"]. In short, Metaphor has no real Foundation in the Nature of the Things compared; Analogy is founded in the Very Nature of the Things on both Sides of the Comparison.[114]

This doctrine, as I have indicated, derives from Locke's emphasis on analogy as "the only help we have in inferring unseen causes." Locke's view that a "wary reasoning from Analogy leads us often into the discovery of Truths . . . which would otherwise lie concealed" (1) emphasizes the transcendent otherness of the Creator, (2) intimates, nonetheless, the accessibility of divine truth, (3) implies that just as there is unity among things above and just as there is unity among things below, so there is correspondence, if not continuity, between the natural and the spiritual worlds, (4) devalues metaphor because of the arbitrary nature of its comparisons (here, Locke is the true son of Puritans who preferred simile to metaphor), (5) proposes analogy as a nonfigurative, philosophically correct means of expressing this correspondence of things, and (6) recommends analogy as our "great Rule of Probability" in theological inquiry.[115] Although thinking by an analogy of opposition that emphasizes the distance between this world and another was attacked both by skeptics such as David Hume and by such orthodox thinkers as Samuel Johnson,[116] Locke's analogy was one of proportionality. His analogy, indeed, was so far from being outmoded that it was adapted by such as Browne and Wesley, who made it the prolegomenon to all future epistemologies of faith.

No more than Locke, of course, does either Browne or Wesley wax glib about the relation between God and the world, for like Locke, both Browne and Wesley limited what could be predicated of God. But while Aquinas predicated much through "the assumption of the neo-Platonist scale of Being,"[117] Browne and Wesley predicated much through the Locke-related instrument of sense-language. With the possible exception of the attempt by the later Edwards to conceive of spirit through a congruence of abstractions and logical harmony, it is not feasible to talk about spirit except by analogy to the senses. Christ's method of parables is nothing more nor less than such analogy, as are the medieval fourfold method of exegesis and the analogies of Luther. But the version of analogy in Browne and Wesley is especially empirical in its view of the senses as providing evidence, if not as providing a source, of spiritual knowledge. Just as in Lockean terms sense perception of a human being is the only means of knowing him or her, so in terms of Browne and Wesley the feeling of love is such a good access to the nature of God that it amounts to a "spiritual sense" of him. The feeling of love, with its implication of sexual union, is at once so deep and so relational that it out-senses the senses.

Thus the abridgment of *The Procedure* delineates the analogistic dimension of the spiritual sense, but analogy in the abridgment of *The Procedure* as a whole does not so much indicate the difference between humanity and God as occupy the continuum joining nature to revelation, and such analogy of proportionality is matched by the abridgment of *Religious Affections*. Characteristically, for example, Wesley and Edwards employ that analogy's very form:

> As the affections not only belong to the human nature, but are a great part of it; so holy affections do not only belong to true religion, but are a very great part of it. . . . And as in worldly things, worldly affections are the springs of men's actions; so in religious matters, the spring of their actions is religious affections.[118]

Or again:

> As the taste of honey is diverse from the ideas men get of honey by only looking on and feeling it, so the new sense of spiritual and Divine things is entirely diverse from any thing that is perceived in them, by natural men.[119]

Here, somewhat surprisingly, the abridgment implies that, like the sense of taste, the spiritual sense renders a truth that is deep precisely because it is imageless: compare Demogorgon's "the deep truth is imageless" from Shelley's *Prometheus Unbound*. These samples of the abridgment, moreover, are so analogistic, so detached from the world, that they evince distrust of the senses. But the distrust is directed more to the sense-image world of metaphor, with its distance from the spiritual world, than toward the sense-related instrument of analogy, which describes interiority or spiritual experience according to the model of perception. Taste, after all, is a sense like seeing and hearing, albeit with an image so deep as not to resemble the images of sight and sound.

The abridgment, necessarily or not, retains senselike criteria as the only means available to Lockean temperaments with a need to express the methods of the soul. The term *affections,* significantly, belongs to the language of sense impression and sense perception. Far from abandoning such language, Wesley and Edwards use a strange, vaguely oxymoronic, but nonetheless efficacious version of it, namely, *religious* or *holy affections,* to express a precise analogy between, if not the interpenetrations of, the spirit realm and the world of natural experience.

This doctrine, then, proportional rather than oppositional, helps Wesley and Edwards as Browne's doctrine helps him, namely, to believe that what is both felt and thought approaches, without dispelling the mystery of, what has been and is being revealed. Without quite valuing the familiar for its own sake, the doctrine of Wesley and Edwards honors the familiar as an especially faithful counterpart to what would otherwise lie entirely outside the range of human expression. The senses convince the intellect of what they have to tell. What is felt and thought, in turn, proves spiritually veridical, that is, theologically equivalent to philosophical seeing and philosophical believing.

Thus, on the relative certainty of natural knowledge, the spiritual sense of Wesley and Edwards establishes the probable truth of a theistic (distinct from Deistic or pantheistic) natural religion, and even of revelation. The twin pioneers of transatlantic revivalism search for an inclusive, intellectually current way of describing how the mind knows God, and how anyone can verify another's faith. They find that way in Lockean doctrine.

An Epitome

Although close reading, especially of Wesley's abridgment of Edwards's *Religious Affections,* recommends itself as "the fascination of what's difficult,"[120] I am concerned, here, to facilitate what is difficult, without losing the fascination of, say, philosophical theology as semiotics. I want to abstract, without diluting, the complex empiricism of Wesley and Edwards.

When teaching that mind is where divine experience takes place, the abridgment puts grace prior to the senses, which become mere physical analogues to inward spiritual experience. Insofar as the experience of Wesley and Edwards is an "experience" of God as otherworldly, a consent of being to being beyond self and senses, the abridgment demonstrates additional non-Lockean ends.

Its validation of those ends, however, its proof that spiritual experience has occurred, appeals to the senses and so amounts to a sufficiently Lockean means. Spiritual inrush, though merely analogous to sense perception, appears in a strong Lockean light, for Locke's view that impressions striking the senses are worthy guides to knowledge informs, and indeed enables, the trust of Wesley and Edwards in influxes "flooding [the] soul with glory divine."[121]

An especially intriguing trait of this philosophical theology is its implication that the senses are indispensable for an experience of the divine. The senses are secondary when they are tests for inwardness and analogies to communicate supernatural reality to a Lockean world. But the senses are primary when they are attendants on, and preconditions for, faith, that is, when natural experience not only sets the terms of, but also either becomes or combines with, spiritual experience. At "a quarter to nine" on the evening of May 24, 1738, in Aldersgate Street, London, Wesley's heart was "strangely warmed" (shades, or foreshadowing, of Blake's talking with Isaiah in the Strand).[122] This famous conversion, this spiritual watershed of English cultural life, has as much to do with time, place, and the specific circumstances of Wesley's sense experience as with his state of mind. Such a nearly empirical recipe for grace is a particular means of the abridgment, which, above all, holds to the senses.

Since Locke's tenet that one's very language depends on the senses was a given of the intellectual climate,[123] all expressions of the divine were necessarily Lockean, that is, sensuous, including the most analogistic and, for that matter, most rationalistic expressions. But the paradox of the God-centered yet sincere self is the crux in the abridgment, the sense-language of which, in accord with the abridgment's understanding of the senses themselves, is now analogue to, and now validation, manifestation, and harbinger of, spiritual experience. Whether a literal or a figurative reading of Locke, whether an uneasy attempt to incorporate senses into near-rationalism or a balance between sense perception and the consent of mind to mind, the abridgment is saturated with Lockean language.

Even its consciousness of God not only submits to what Wordsworth, after Locke, calls "the language of the sense,"[124] but also arrives through that language. The very title, virtually the same as the original's, implies the Locke-derived oxymoron "spiritual sense," for *Religious Affections* ambiguously straddles the line between faith and experience.

Natural experience and spiritual experience, then, are not stark oppositions for Wesley and Edwards, whose spiritual experience, like their natural experience, is Lockean, that is, of both the mind and the senses. Just as Lockean epistemology conceives of a link between sense and reason, matter and mind, so the philosophical theologies of Wesley and Edwards, their appropriations of Locke for religious methodology, conceive of a bridge that transports us from nature to grace, returns us from grace to nature, and joins nature and grace, justifying the reality of both. This spiritual sense is even more flexible and even more up-to-date than Lockean epistemology, for it out-Lockes Locke, or carries him to his logical conclusion. It applies to the religious arena that secular trust in experience that helped the early modern mind to position itself in the natural world.

The spiritual sense of Wesley and Edwards rests, specifically, on a view of experience more inclusive, and a respect for experiential criteria greater, than Locke's. While Lockean experience is primarily natural and Lockean theology is almost entirely apart from nature, they both stress the participation of God in creation, and so enlist spirit in the catalogue of experience. The spiritual sense of Wesley and Edwards, indeed, for its part in the eighteenth century's burgeoning discipline of philosophical theology, is imaginative. For by its imaging of heavenly joy on earth, if not by its hope of earthly joy in heaven, it draws on the model of sense perception to detect, and express, a radically immanent Christianity. And by so modernizing Christianity, Wesley and Edwards lay the intellectual as well as emotional groundwork for religious expression not simply in the Anglo-American Enlightenment, but in the Anglo-American world of the nineteenth century as well.

Ramifications

Wesley's abridgment of Edwards's *Religious Affections,* without fudging differences or papering them over, denotes links among comparative philosophy, philosophical theology, conversion, and the leap of faith. Similarly, the abridgment links mind to mind. Just as the reader crosses the abridgment to Wesley, so the reader and Wesley cross it to Edwards. Thus a well-traveled transatlantic bridge facilitates both the intellectual overtones of evangelical zeal and the interdisciplinary character of evangelical intellect. Since the abridgment not only balances empirical and evangelical idioms but also disperses empirical and evangelical idiolects, it connotes an especially full "sense" in which the Anglo-American world is one. The Lockean ground common to the theologies of Wesley and Edwards extends, for example, to their revivals, which, even during the Revolution, preserved an intellectual as well as emotional link between England and America.

The methodological influence of Wesley, first, is not in doubt.[125] His English itinerants were "clearly in command" of American Methodism until 1777, "when their British nationality seemed to make it imperative . . . that they should leave."[126] Even then, however, the American Methodist Conference declared its loyalty to "the whole Methodist Discipline." This discipline, partly Lockean, was fully methodological wherever it was subscribed to. Frank Baker, alluding to Wesley's correspondence with the Reverend Samuel Davies of Hanover County, Virginia, quotes Davies in a way that suggests the "spiritual sense" as transatlantic bridge. The Wesley brothers, wrote Davies in the 1750s, "appear very benevolent, devout, and zealous men, that are labouring with all their might to awaken the secure world to a *sense* of religion."[127] Baker adds that Wesley's admiration of Edwards "underlines his continued commitment to the religious life of America."

Wesley's abridgments, of course, popularized what they digested, and they disseminated, in the United States as well as England, empiricism as well as evangelicalism. Wesley's determination to make challenging books available in brief and handy yet attractive and durable form means, among other things, that he was a Mortimer J. Adler, for his abridgments, in particular, amount to a *synopticon* of many "great books of the Western world." *A Christian Library: Consisting of Extracts from and Abridgments of the choicest Pieces of Practical Divinity, which have been publish'd in the English Tongue* (1749–55) is a logical product of his prolific editorial pen, but his scientific encyclopedia for the common reader, *A Survey of the Wisdom of God in the Creation: or A Compen-*

dium of Natural Philosophy (1763), is also typical of him. These collections of abridgments were read as companion sets, as an interdisciplinary vade mecum, for more than one hundred years.[128] The abridgment of *Religious Affections* was published three years after a reprint of *A Compendium of Natural Philosophy,* and takes its final place in the second edition of *A Christian Library,* which removed views contradicting Wesley's own.[129] It includes the range and sums up the content of both collections, and it indicates the full nature of Wesley's influence, and for that matter his joint influence with Edwards.

Besides balm for the soul, Wesley dispensed nostrums for health, hygiene, and prosperity: his *Primitive Physick: or, An Easy and Natural Method of Curing Most Diseases* (1747) was, from 1750 to 1850, among the dozen or so most widely read books of the English-speaking world.[130] Besides thus bettering the lot of his followers on both sides of the Atlantic, he did much to educate them along interdisciplinary lines. "Reading Christians," declared Wesley, "will be knowing Christians."[131] The statement suggests a twofold ambition: first, to make the rising middle class of the Anglo-American world literate and, second, to educate that class about science as well as theology. By ensuring the "spiritual sense" of transatlantic culture, he ensured, as well, a continuing unity of it.

Because Edwards's congregation ejected him, his influence would seem less than extensive, but Sacvan Bercovitch, Philip Greven, and Peter Shaw extend Alan Heimert's argument for Edwards's centrality to the Revolution.[132] Because of *Religious Affections,* especially in light of Jay Fliegelman's recent work on Locke's influence in America from 1750 to 1800, Edwards's Lockean influence on his mass movement is no more in doubt than Wesley's is on his.[133] Because of *Religious Affections,* to say nothing of other Lockean works by Edwards, Locke and Edwards operated jointly as well as separately, spiritually and philosophically as well as politically, and, in view of the continuing popularity of *Religious Affections,* late as well as early in the century.[134]

Fliegelman's emphasis on *Some Thoughts concerning Education* (1693) establishes an important sense in which, by the eighteenth century's second half, Lockean hegemony extended to America. The educational doctrine of nurture over nature is to be found, for example, even in Edwards's *The Freedom of the Will,* which argues that, though man does not determine the will, he nonetheless does as he will. Lockean pedagogy, however, follows from Lockean philosophy, and had Fliegelman emphasized *An Essay concerning Human Understanding,* he would have been able, if one may assume his familiarity with *Religious Affections,* to connect Locke not only with Edwards's general awareness of nurture over nature, but also with his particular fortification of the "spiritual sense" with the natural senses.

Nineteenth-century revivalism, in keeping with its twin sources in Wesley and Edwards, was interdisciplinary as well as transatlantic. While emphasizing such social effects as moral reform, antislavery, and temperance, Richard Carwardine observes such intellectual effects as the following: Charles G. Finney, leader of the Second Great Awakening, was received at Yale "with universal and entire cordiality"; British Methodists "gave American Methodism social status by strengthening its literary and educational character"; the American James Caughey, in his 1844 campaign in Sheffield, England, converted Albert Bradwell, whose education emphasized not only Locke, but also Hobbes and Hume; and in 1851, Finney went to England and converted John Moore, who, besides becoming a Methodist preacher, developed "a penchant for metaphysics and philosophy."[135]

The efforts of Finney and Caughey, like the influence of Edwards on Wesley, illustrated America's influence on England, but Wesley, like Locke, had exercised almost as much influence on America as he did on England. Just as his edition of *Religious Affections* had amounted to a British shaping of, and a British contribution to, the American (as well as Lockean) method of Edwards, and just as American Methodist discipline, even as late as the Revolution, had remained fully British in both origin and continuing authority, so the Atlantic cross-pollinations of the nineteenth century were just as likely to be from England to America as the other way round. David Hempton, keeping an eye on intellectual history, points out that the Locke- as well as Wesley-inspired political thought of nineteenth-century British Methodism so fully blossomed in the rich soil of its immediate historical context, namely, England's Chartist Movement, that the seed took root in at least the Arminian ground of American revivalism.[136]

Much of the nineteenth century, if not the twentieth (I write this after the American presidential campaign of 1988, with its evangelical preacher-candidates from both sides of the political spectrum), belonged to the evangelicals. Even when their numbers were small, they represented an especially significant Anglo-American trend, not least because their "social contract" originated in the decidedly "Lockean" (as well as simply Christian) "Societies" that flourished among Methodists on both sides of the Atlantic during the eighteenth century.[137] The Methodist Episcopal Church in America grew from a membership of less than ten thousand in 1780 to more than five hundred thousand by 1830.[138] A similar pattern obtained in England. Although Methodists made up only about 5 percent of the adult British population in 1840, they were "the largest and most influential element in a much larger constituency."[139] By 1851, there were more than two million Sunday-School scholars in England alone, six hundred thousand of whom were Methodists, and they represented 76 percent of working-class children between the ages of five and fifteen.[140]

Inasmuch as Methodism grew into a great world church and the Great Awakening of the 1730s and the 1740s grew into the Second Great Awakening of the 1820s and the 1830s, and inasmuch as the revivalism of both the eighteenth and the nineteenth centuries was both transatlantic and emotional-intellectual, Wesley and Edwards were indeed twin shapers of a widespread, recurrent mode of thought and feeling, a mode in which sense perception of natural things formed the model for "sense perception" of the divine. Just as Wesley's methodology grounded his transatlantic revival, so the Lockean ground common to Wesley and Edwards grounded transatlantic revivalism in general. Just as the spiritual sense of Wesley and Edwards proceeded from natural as well as spiritual things, through ideas/ideals of sensation, to words of grace as well as nature, so this sense grounded Anglo-American culture in alternately objective and subjective worlds and even in a simultaneously objective and subjective world. Thus the Lockean and the evangelical understandings of experience came together in the Anglo-American middle class. The Anglo-American character of which I speak, though not confined to the middle class, which tends upward, is primarily of that class, and it arose from an empirical as well as evangelical emphasis of the eighteenth century. Epistemology and ontology, however esoteric, filter down to those who live within a worldview, distinct from those who create it (witness the analogy of "Freudians" who do not read Sigmund Freud).

For the remainder of this book, I look for the mature expression of this Anglo-American character in the vital synthesis and complex entity of nineteenth-century British and American letters, for the abridgment, as I have approached it, provides access to Carlyle and Emerson. Having pointed to the dual role of the abridgment as description of and blueprint for Anglo-American experience, and continuing to regard the combined sensibilities of Wesley and Edwards as the emblem of a binational character, I conclude the present chapter by associating the abridgment with *les belles lettres*. Having read the abridgment closely, examining its cadences with an ear for nuance, I already regard it as literature. This skillful redaction responds to critical method as readily as the poems of Wordsworth, and so emerges as an ingenious instance of *les bonnes lettres*. By providing for the incongruous modes of empirical philosophy and evangelical faith a single accommodating location for both their interplay and their interaction, the abridgment engages the theory of literature as paradox. Since some famous lines of Wordsworth have formed one of the categories by which I have sought, as fully as possible and from many different perspectives, to interpret the abridgment, I have already drawn on *les belles lettres*. "He washed himself clean," like all other prolepses, is "a figure by which a thing is represented as already done, though in reality it is to follow as a consequence of the action which is described," and as though the abridgment adumbrates Wordsworth, I have made proleptic reference to Romanticism. The next step, a logical one, is to complete the connection between the abridgment and American as well as British Romantic literature.

Difficult as it will be for me to resist requoting the abridgment, I will refrain from doing so, but I will everywhere adduce its thought, for I offer not simply a full, but emphatically a fully ramifying, interpretation of it. Wesley's abridgment of Edwards's *Religious Affections,* by addressing the paradox of mundane and otherworldly points of view in both England and the United States, intimates perhaps the most inclusive sense in which British literature and American literature merge. As compendium and chief repository of Wesleyan-Edwardsean "epistemology," it forms a substantial subject in itself; as perhaps the most resonant common document of Methodism and the Great Awakening, it epitomizes and indexes, that is, quintessentially embodies, a "spiritual sense" to be found in transatlantic revivalism and hence, significantly, in the Anglo-American world; and as a background to and context for a particularly important binational amalgam of *les belles lettres,* it raises the distinct possibility that just as spiritually transposed empiricism bridges empiricism per se and early modern apologetics, so imagination bridges natural observation and early modern "poetic faith."

TWO

The Empirical / Evangelical Dialectic of Thomas Carlyle

Carlyle did not so much "set individual experience . . . against the eternal and limitless perspectives of Time and Space"[1] as include those perspectives within individual experience. From 1827 through 1843, he focused on reconciling the transcendent with the immanent. His actual-ideal sense of the real derives from the empirical-evangelical and hence broadly experiential sensibility of his time and place and, for that matter, of eighteenth- as well as nineteenth-century England and America.

Eloise M. Behnken argues that "[Carlyle's] skepticism, his honesty, and his insistence that values must be corroborated by individual experience" define him as "modern."[2] George P. Landow finds that, like Arnold and Ruskin, Carlyle is "the master of prophetic experience."[3] I find that his concern with experience is not only pre-Modern, that is, tending toward complete skepticism, but also post–eighteenth century, that is, dynamically poised between skeptical questioning and prophetic possibility. His philosophical sensibility relates to his faith according to the gloss provided by the philosophical theology of Wesley and Edwards, whose methodology parallels, even where it does not underlie, Carlyle's experiential orientation toward science as well as religion. Thus, his experiential sensibility is descended from the empirical/evangelical dialectic.

Although Carlyle was much influenced by Goethe, his radical skepticism comes not so much from Goethe's Wilhelm Meister, who passes through sterile self-questioning to understanding and action, as from British empiricism, albeit by way of Cartesian methodology.[4] When Carlyle rejected the church as a career, though not Christianity as an influence, he threw himself into scientific/empirical studies, and Michael Timko stresses Carlyle's familiarity with Newton and Hume.[5] Carlyle reacted against the church as much from his native empirical perspective as from any foreign perspective, German or other.

His evangelical origins, of course, are largely Calvinist, and he could hardly have had a purer access to Calvinism than the Burgher Secession of Scottish Calvinism in which he grew up.[6] Charles Frederick Harrold argues that Carlyle seeks in "German thought and elsewhere" an "acceptable intellectual restatement" of such Calvinistic emphases as "fatalism, a transcendent God, the elect, and irrationalism."[7] Thus, in Harrold's memorable phrase, Carlyle is "a Calvinist without the theology." Even when most "German" or most ideally, transcendentally philosophical, Carlyle remains "Calvinist." He never loses what Ian Campbell calls "the broad outlines of the duty-dominated Calvinist world-picture of his youth."[8] In this context, incidentally, David J. DeLaura's argument that Carlyle, along with Arnold, is an essentially religious conservative who "gradually assembled a 'reconceived' Biblical religion" echoes with even more resonance than before.[9]

Behnken, however, argues that the worldview Carlyle "gradually builds and refines" has "much more in common with the death-of-God theology of the 1960s and 1970s than with the Calvinism he is often said to have inherited."[10] I agree with her perhaps unintentional implication that Calvinism is by no means the only way of understanding Carlyle's religious affinities. Though no churchgoer, for example, he harbors admiration for Edward Irving, whose theological enthusiasm harks back to Wesley's.[11] Broadly evangelical, too, are the affiliations between Carlyle's ideas and both Thomas Scott's view of prophecy and the social gospel of the Arminian evangelical R. B. Seeley.[12] Especially Arminian are both Carlyle's lifelong generosity toward the selected objects of his charity and his clear belief that the responsibility for human salvation lies "on men's shoulders, not on God's."[13] Although Behnken sees Carlyle's emphasis on individual responsibility as only "modern," it is also Arminian.

Just as one needs Arminianism as well as Calvinism to understand fully the evangelical dimension of Carlyle's religious sensibility, then, so one needs empiricism as well as evangelicalism to understand fully his experiential sensibility. The great German idealists—Schiller, Richter, Fichte, Kant, and Novalis—whom he read as a young man, may have "provided him with both a source of inspiration and a mode of expression."[14] Such "transcendental principles" as the categorical imperative, "time and space as appearances," and "nature as the symbol of the divine" seem to have formed "the nucleus of Carlyle's faith as late as 1879."[15] But Campbell argues that Carlyle's early translations from the Germans drew on "his knowledge of Germans who wrote creatively (Goethe, Schiller) and philosophically (Kant), as well as on those who combined these functions (Richter, Novalis) to produce work which Carlyle frankly did not understand but which he did manage to incorporate into his own original ideas."[16] His original ideas have more to do with his various English-language origins, empiricism and evangelicalism among them, than with German sources. Ruth apRoberts argues that he borrows from German method to become the pioneer of comparative religion in England, and that he finds the "Key to all Mythologies" in Eastern religion.[17] (Note foreshadowings of the fruitless search by Casaubon in George Eliot's *Middlemarch* and, for that matter, the fruitful search by Mircea Eliade.)[18] One need not wander from English-language contexts, however, for by grounding understanding of German methodology in the religious as well as "scientific" method that derives from Wesley and Edwards, Carlyle grounds transcendentalism.

Carlyle from 1827 to 1831

Experience forms an especially inclusive category of Carlyle's early thought. According to *On History* (1830), for example, "Experience" becomes "Philosophy" when "intelligibly recorded."[19] "History," similarly, is "Philosophy teaching by Experience," or "the essence of innumerable Biographies" (53). Carlyle's formative essays, those written before 1831 when *Sartor Resartus* established his reputation, acknowledge that experiential epistemology is problematic: *On History* warns that since "the inward condition of Life" is "the same in no two ages," and since "one Biography, nay our own Biography, study and recapitulate it as we may, remains in . . . many points unintelligible" (53), historical knowledge is all but unattainable. Indeed, historical events are themselves elusive, for "it is, in no case, the real historical Transaction, but only some more or less plausible scheme and theory of the Transaction, or the harmonised result of many such schemes, each varying from the other and all varying from truth, that we can ever hope to behold" (55). Thus observation itself falsifies, or at best alters, its objects: "Nay, were our faculty of insight into passing things never so complete, there is still a fatal discrepancy between our manner of observing these, and their manner of occurring. The most gifted man can observe, still more can record, only the *series* of his own impressions: his observation, therefore, to say nothing of its other imperfections, must be *successive,* while the things done were often *simultaneous*" (55). "Laws themselves, political constitutions," are finally "not our Life"; in *On History,* he declares that laws and political constitutions "are but the bare walls of the house; all whose essential furniture, the inventions and traditions, and daily habits that regulate and support our existence, are the work not of Dracos and Hampdens, but of Phoenician mariners, of Italian masons and Saxon metallurgists, of philosophers, alchymists, prophets, and all the long-forgotten train of artists and artisans; who from the first have been jointly teaching us how to think and how to act, how to rule over spiritual and over physical Nature" (53–54). Carlyle the historian is interested not so much in "the rudder of Government," "the spigot of Taxation," courts, camps, soldiers, and ministers as in "the mighty Tide of Thought and Action," "still rolling on its wondrous course, in gloom and brightness, . . . its thousand remote valleys, a whole world of Existence" (58); thus he assumes that knowledge is attainable through an experience so broad as not only to constitute, but also to precede, culture.

Experience is from the outset of his career prior to even so fundamental a semiotic as language. In *Goethe* (1827), for example, he writes, "Goethe's culture as a writer is perhaps less remarkable than his culture as a man" (39). Rather than learning from "Art and Literature," Goethe, and by implication Carlyle, learn from "action and passion, in the rugged school of Experience" (39). Compare this with the following passage from *Past and Present* (1843): "The cloudy-browed, thick-soled, opaque Practicality, with no logical utterance, in silence mainly, with here and there a low grunt or growl, has in him what transcends all logic-utterance: a Congruence with the Unuttered. The Speakable, which lies atop, as a superficial film, or outer skin, is his or not his: but the Doable, which reaches down to the World's centre, you find him there!"[20] A. Abbott Ikeler argues that Carlyle views experience as nonverbal, but where Ikeler finds in Carlyle's work a "dichotomy between aesthetic and moral, literary and practical,"[21] I find a dialectic, for Carlyle views experience not only as prior to but also as inclusive of language.

In *Voltaire* (1829), Carlyle elaborates his view of experience, evincing an early confidence in the epistemological efficacy of sense-based reason. Vulnerable from the perspective of empirical schematics, Voltaire's rationalism makes objects lie around him not in "pictorial" or "scientific grouping," but in "commodious rows, where each may be seen and come at, like goods in a well-kept warehouse" (50). The "best gifts" of Voltaire's mind—"order," "perspicuous Arrangement," "intellectual vision," "intensity," "clear quick vision," "instinctive decision," "logical coherence," intelligibility, and transparency—are the "peculiarly French qualities" that he "manifests" in a "more than French degree" (48). But insofar as his mind-set "sees only to a short depth" (49), it amounts by implication to mentalism, that is, to an excessive independence from the senses and hence to what Carlyle thinks of as the peculiar problem of being French. (A whole book might be written on the Francophobia of eighteenth- and nineteenth-century British writers.) Voltaire's writings, at any rate, oversimplify reality in that, rather than resembling the "deep natural symmetry" in "a forest oak," the meticulously observed cartoons of Raphael, or, especially significantly from the British point of view, "the plan . . . of our so barbarous *Hamlet*," they resemble, instead, "the simple artificial symmetry of a parlour chandelier," "a geometrical diagram by Fermat," or "a polished, square-built Tuileries" (50). Thus Voltaire, though in general "humane" and "mildly affectionate," lacks "feeling" (50). He never sufficiently escapes the mind to "see into the life of things."[22]

To "see into the life of things," as Wordsworth writes, serves not coincidentally to epitomize the procedure of Carlyle's empirical-evangelical imagination, which, like Wordsworth's, rules over spiritual as well as over physical nature. Voltaire, though in his empirical moods "king" of this lower world, is never "god" of it (46). Although he has "many common talents" in "unparalleled combination," presumably including powers of perception, he lacks "any finer or higher one" (49), e.g., spiritual discernment. "Susceptibility of mind" and even "assiduous perseverance" are his, but not that "sort of meditation" which reveals "Truth" (47). "A purely business Method" he practices well, but not that sort of "poetic Method" which is "the fruit of deep feeling" (49–50). In the word

"Method," especially since *Voltaire* employs phrases like "*spirit* of Method" (49; my italics), one is tempted to find a pun on *Methodism,* that inclusively English, far from French, fruit of deep feeling. Thus, besides reading Voltaire with no little Francophobia, Carlyle reads him with fully English eyes, for he faults this particular *philosophe* for his lack of both sharp sense and holistic spiritual vision.

What is observable, what falls within the purview of experience, is so mysterious to the young Carlyle that it falls, too, within the purview of religion as well as science. *On History,* while understanding events along carefully empirical lines, is never enamored of empiricism: "The Historian . . . examines some special aspect of History; and from this or that combination of circumstances, political, moral, or economical, and the issues it has led to, infers that such and such properties belong to human society, and that the like circumstances will produce the like issue; which inference, if other trials confirm it, must be held true and practically valuable" (57). The essay adds that the historian "is wrong only, and an artisan, when he fancies that these properties, discovered or discoverable, exhaust the matter; and sees not, at every step, that it is inexhaustible" (57). In accordance with the view that "all Action . . . is based on Passion and Mystery," Carlyle imbues the ideal historian with a salutary reverence, viz., "As thanksgivings were once wont to be offered 'for unrecognised mercies,' [so the historian should] look with reverence into the dark untenanted places of the Past. . . . Narrative is *linear,* Action is *solid.* Alas for our 'chains,' or 'chainlets,' of 'causes and effects,' which we so assiduously track through certain handbreadths of years and square miles, when the whole is a broad, deep Immensity, and each atom is 'chained' and complected with all!" (54–55).

Such a historical study requires not mere "onlookers," but a "Seer," with spiritual as well as natural senses (56). "In reverent Faith," the historian must "pause over the mysterious vestiges of Him, whose path is the great deep of Time, whom History indeed reveals, but only all History, and in Eternity, will clearly reveal" (56). With veiled reference to Methodism, Carlyle calls "wonderful" the sort of spiritual experience that other historians would brand mere "enthusiasm" or "superstition" (57). "Our whole spiritual life," he believes, "is built" on "History" (56), "a real Prophetic Manuscript," or account of spiritual experience in natural time and place (51).

Although *Signs of the Times* (1829) includes more ideas than any of Carlyle's other early essays, it has not received its share of attention.[23] It formulates experience decisively. As for natural experience, he declares that "all our systems and theories are but so many froth-eddies or sand-banks, which from time to time [Nature] casts up, and washes away" (75). This is an especially memorable expression of Carlyle's developing view that nature precedes, produces, and supersedes mind—that is, that ideas, to put the matter in Lockean terms, are sense-dependent.

"Instruction," for its part, turns out to be writing by experience on the tabula rasa, or the "communing of Wisdom with Ignorance" (65). "Intellect" is not just "Logic, or the mere power of arranging and communicating" but, more intriguingly, "the power man has of knowing and believing" (77), that is, of creatively interacting with objects. Scientific education advances, accordingly, in harmony with the model of classical empiricism. Just as Newton "discovers the system of the world from the falling of an apple" (66), so the mind's willingness to submit to external impressions produces spectacular results, e.g., "We remove mountains, and make seas our smooth highway" (64), or, "Nothing can resist us; we war with rude Nature; and, by our resistless engines, come off always victorious, and loaded with spoils" (64).

> What wonderful accessions have thus been made, and are still making, to the physical power of mankind; how much better fed, clothed, lodged and, in all outward respects, accommodated men now are, or might be, by a given quantity of labour, is a grateful reflection which forces itself on every one. (64)

This empiricism, despite the humble methodology in "by a given quantity of labour," forms the basis of Carlyle's Victorian optimism. *Signs of the Times* optimistically claims that "doubtless this age . . . is advancing": "[The age's] very unrest, its ceaseless activity, its discontent contains matter of promise. Knowledge, education are opening the eyes of the humblest; are increasing the number of thinking minds without limit. This is as it should be; for not in turning back, not in resisting, but only in resolutely struggling forward, does our life consist" (83).

Set alongside such exuberant philosophical experientialism, however, is an equally exuberant evangelical experientialism. While scorning Ireland's "Penny-a-week Purgatory Society" and denouncing the "Bible-society" as a "religious machine" (64–65), *Signs of the Times* is not anti-evangelical. It is evangelical with a vengeance. Hear, for example, this rhapsody on a freedom more Arminian than political: "Freedom, without which indeed all spiritual life is impossible, depends on infinitely more complex influences than either the extension or the curtailment of the 'democratic interest'. . . . It is towards a higher freedom than mere freedom from oppression by his fellow-mortal, that man dimly aims. Of this higher, heavenly freedom, which is 'man's reasonable service,' all his noble institutions, his faithful endeavours and loftiest attainments, are but the body" (75, 84). *Signs of the Times,* indeed, features a more religious than utopian, more millennial than apocalyptic version of Wesley's doctrine of spiritual perfection: "To reform a world, to reform a nation, no wise man will undertake," since "all but foolish men know, that the only solid, though a far slower reformation, is what each begins and perfects on *himself*" (85).

An evangelical emphasis on the here and now specifically informs some of the essay's most characteristic idioms. Implying nostalgia for the amelioristic bustle of evangelical practical charity, Carlyle laments that "the distance between the rich and the poor" has altered "old relations" (65). Something of the same nostalgia, incidentally, is to be found in Wordsworth's "The Old Cumberland Beggar" (1797). The immediately spiritual inheres in Carlyle's announcement that "vaticination," or prophecy, is not a matter simply of foretelling the future but, more intriguingly, of spiritually living in the present (61).

"Our grand business undoubtedly is," he proclaims, "not to *see* what lies dimly at a distance, but to *do* what lies clearly at hand" (61). His elaboration of this point is not only both vivid and well sustained but also, if secular in content, overwhelmingly evangelical in diction and general atmosphere:

> [The radical millenarians] prophesy from the Bible, and the Utilitarians from Bentham. The one announces that the last of the seals is to be opened, positively, in the year 1860; and the other assures us that "the greatest-happiness principle" is to make a heaven of earth, in a still shorter time. . . . Meantime, we too admit that the present is an important time; as all present time necessarily is. The poorest Day that passes over us is the conflux of two Eternities; it is made up of currents that issue from the remotest Past, and

> flow onwards into the remotest Future. We were wise indeed, could we discern truly the signs of our own time; and by knowledge of its wants and advantages, wisely adjust our own position in it. . . . Perhaps . . . something of [the perplexity of the scene whereon we stand] will disappear, some of its distinctive characters and deeper tendencies more clearly reveal themselves. (63–64)

Even more characteristically, though, *Signs of the Times* mixes secular content with evangelical content. Some passages imply an unbridgeable gulf between the empirical and the spiritual: e.g., "The truth is, men have lost their belief in the Invisible, and believe, and hope, and work only in the Visible; or, to speak it in other words: This is not a Religious age" (77). The essay uses the language of sense-based reason, however, to investigate, and even to understand, the "inward world" of the spirit as well as "the outward" world of the senses (77).

"Nature," writes Carlyle, "continues" to lend its "instinctive, unbounded force" to humanity (73), and although this idea is pantheistic, it strikingly parallels the doctrine of immediate revelation, the Holy Spirit's operation in the present. Both art and science accordingly inspire the idea of grace: "They were not planted or grafted, nor even greatly multiplied or improved by the culture or manuring of institutions," but have been "from first to last" the "free gift of Nature; an unsolicited, unexpected gift" (73). Anything "grounded on little more than a metaphor," Carlyle suggests, is groundless (78), and this antimetaphorical bias points to his preference for analogy: implicit in his belief that poetry should preserve "an *eye* for the Invisible" (80; my italics) is a "spiritual sense" parallel to, if not coterminous with, the natural senses. The senses, then, remain a guide to the otherworldly, for the invisible is not more remote for being analogous to the visible.

Indeed, "the invisible world" is never "wanting" insofar as it "dwells in man's soul, and this last is still *here*" (83; my italics). Though not *of* the world, the soul is *in* it, and world and soul have in common at least the quality of mystery: "When we can drain the Ocean into mill-ponds, and bottle-up the Force of Gravity, to be sold by retail, in gas-jars" (that is, never), then, and only then, can we "hope to comprehend the infinitudes of man's soul" under "formulas of Profit and Loss" (75). Even *sense* perception can be suffused with *spiritual* light, such that the senses implicitly attend, or prepare for, faith. "Religion," *Signs of the Times* concludes, is "a thousand-voiced psalm from the heart of Man to his invisible Father," who is "revealed" in "every revelation" of "Goodness, Beauty, Truth" (79).

As for "the Christian religion," in particular, it "must ever be regarded as the crowning glory, *or rather the life and soul,* of our whole modern culture" (73; my italics). It, like nature, underlies culture. Where Carlyle adds that Christianity was "spread abroad" by "simple, altogether natural and individual efforts" (74), he implies that evangelical Christianity overlaps, or is partially commensurate, with nature. "Deep, paralysed subjection to physical objects," he observes, "comes not from Nature," not from objects themselves, "but from our own unwise mode of *viewing*" them (83). The fault lies not in the natural world, but in ourselves, that we should feel trapped by it.

The essay's blend of nature with spirit, at any rate, specifically builds on Locke's *Essay.* Although from Locke's time "downwards," "our whole Metaphysics" has been "physical" (68), *Signs of the Times* calls for a "spiritual philosophy" that reveals not simply "the grand secrets of Necessity and Freewill, of the Mind's vital or non-vital dependence on Matter" but, even more experientially, "our mysterious relations to Time and Space, to God, to the Universe" (68). The "scientific work" in Locke's *Essay* is still "a curious indication" of the spirit of "these times," that is, the Late Romantic Period (68). But what "these times" need, in addition to Locke's "genetic history of what we see *in* the mind" (Carlyle's italics), is "a philosophy *of* the mind" (my italics), namely, a comprehensive understanding of the relation of mind to matter, spirit to nature (68).

One might even say in this connection that Carlyle calls for the relation of empiricism to evangelicalism. He implies that prophets should retain "the use, not only of their understandings, but of their bodily senses" (61). He states unequivocally that they should cultivate both "thought and feeling," both "head and heart," and both "internal perfection" and "external combinations and arrangements" (67). Where *Signs of the Times* concludes that "the thinking minds of all nations call for change," that even philosophers recognize the need for conversion, and where it predicts that such change will not just be "observable" but even be so manifest as to be "spectacular" (84), Carlyle draws on the evangelical point that conversion is, or should be, commensurate with intellectual processes and should follow from them.

Perhaps the most thoroughly Lockean dimension of the essay's "empirical" evangelicalism is its appropriation of the tabula rasa, which underlies dependence on experience. "He, who has been born," declares Carlyle, "has been a First Man," and has "lying before his young eyes, and as yet unhardened into scientific shapes, a world as plastic, infinite, divine, as lay before the eyes of Adam himself" (83). Although eschewing the exclusively scientific, this statement implies the coexistence of religion with material or sensible form, the inhering of religion in the objective world on which subjectivity depends from birth. Religious knowledge, no less than natural, depends on experience, for spiritual truth may be revealed with unique effect on the individual in the here and now: "*One* man that has a higher Wisdom, a hitherto unknown spiritual Truth in him, is stronger not than ten men that have it not, or than ten thousand, but than *all* men that have it not" (78).

Carlyle laments the fact that we typically see nothing by "direct vision," but only by "reflection," and in "anatomical dismemberment" (78–79). Thus he implies that seeing by direct vision, whether through the natural senses or through the "spiritual sense," points out to us how to experience both fully and intensely what we have not grasped before. Religion "must have a Natural History" (79), not in Hume's sense of being explained or explained away by nature, but in the evangelical sense that the supernatural and the natural coinhere. Because religion is thus experiential, or because empiricism and evangelicalism coexisted in the nineteenth century as well as in the eighteenth, Carlyle concludes that "a new and brighter *spiritual* era is slowly *evolving* itself for all men" (84; my italics).

In the context of such "empirical" evangelicalism, we should understand that the denunciation of science in *Signs of the Times* is only apparently total. In a curious anticipation of Darwin, Carlyle regrets that "veneration for the physically Strongest" has spread from science to literature (65). He believes that industrial technology has made not only science, but also religion, too mechanical: "Not the external and physical alone is now managed by machinery, but the internal and spiritual also" (81). The extreme empiricism of Reid, Hume, and Hartley, and especially of Hartley's "vibrations and vibratiuncles," is ultimately responsible for the excessively "material and mechanical" aspects of nineteenth-century science, for "the deep meaning of the Laws of Mechanism lies heavy on us, and in the closet, in the marketplace, in the temple, by the social hearth, encumbers the whole movements of our mind, and over our noblest faculties is spreading a nightmare sleep" (82). It is important to note, though, that his turning away from such science is very much in keeping with the moderate, Lockean empiricism of the eighteenth century, especially with the eighteenth-century combination of empiricism and evangelicalism. While reserving a role for the science of mechanics, Carlyle emphasizes in addition, "a science of Dynamics," which "treats of, and practically addresses, the primary, unmodified forces and energies of man, the mysterious springs of Love, and Fear, and Wonder, of Enthusiasm, Poetry, Religion, all which have a truly vital and *infinite* character" (72). He might even have Wesley in mind, among others, where he adds that "Moralists—Poets or Priests, . . . without neglecting the Mechanical province, deal chiefly with the Dynamical; applying themselves chiefly to regulate, increase and purify the inward primary powers of man" (72).

What Carlyle calls the mechanical and dynamical constitutes an interdependency consistent with my view that the empirical and the evangelical can be one. Here, at some length, is perhaps the most inclusive methodological statement of *Signs of the Times:*

> To define the limits of these two departments of man's activity, which work one into another, and by means of one another, so intricately and inseparably, were by its nature an impossible attempt. Their relative importance, even to the wisest mind, will vary in different times, according to the special wants and dispositions of those times. Meanwhile, it seems clear enough that only in the right coordination of the two, and the vigorous forwarding of *both,* does our true line of action lie. Undue cultivation of the inward or Dynamical province leads to idle, visionary, impractical courses, and, especially in rude eras, to Superstition and Fanaticism, with their long train of baleful and well-known evils. Undue cultivation of the outward, again, though less immediately prejudicial, and even for the time productive of many palpable benefits, must, in the long-run, by destroying Moral Force, prove not less certainly, and perhaps still more hopelessly, pernicious. (76)

This dynamic interrelation of the inward and the outward is perhaps as far as anything can be from rationalism.

Indeed, *Signs of the Times* waxes explicitly antirationalistic, for Carlyle denounces the kind of "intellectual dapperling of these times," who "boasts chiefly of his irresistible perspicacity, his 'dwelling in the daylight of truth,' and so forth; which, on examination, turns out to be a dwelling in the *rush*-light of 'closet-logic,' and a deep unconsciousness that there is any other light to dwell in or any other objects to survey with it" (78). He has in mind the French mathematicians. The calculus, the differential, and the integral of Lagrange and Laplace add up to only a "cunningly-constituted arithmetical mill" (68). He thinks that, as a result, "the whole French Institute" is so foolish as to see nothing in the saying "God geometrises!" but "a sentimental rodomontade" (68). Carlyle embraces the saying, for "God geometrises!" assumes that the mathematics of geometry is a language not of solipsism or of mental order alone but of both God and nature. (Scholars, of course, recognize the importance of mathematics to Carlyle, but his mathematics is thought to be a language of mental order alone or at best of God and *mind:* Carlisle Moore argues that Carlyle's philosophy synthesizes "the best" of mathematics with "the best" of German transcendentalism.)[24] Carlyle's Francophobia, like many of his other attitudes, derives from his native empirically imaginative and even empirically evangelical perspective.

Carlyle from 1831 to 1850

Of *Sartor Resartus* (1831), Carlyle wrote to his brother John: it "glances from heaven to earth and back again."[25] In line with this emphasis on "heaven," *Sartor Resartus* includes much praise for the purely transcendental, for Teufelsdröckh's "Philosophy of Clothes" teaches that "reality is only embodied within infinite and spiritual perspectives" and that "finite circumstances are accidental and ultimately irrelevant."[26] Teufelsdröckh's words can be explicitly antiempirical: "The WHERE and WHEN, so mysteriously inseparable from all our thoughts, are but superficial terrestrial adhesions to thought; . . . the Seer may discern them where they mount up out of the celestial EVERYWHERE and FOREVER" (92).

The "editor" of Teufelsdröckh's "works," however, is by turns whimsical, satirical, and ironic, and he takes Teufelsdröckh's transcendentalism with a grain of salt. He calls it "gaseous-chaotic" and "aqueous-chaotic" and suggests that its apparent "Elysian brightness" comes down to mere "Pandemonian lava" and even that its "beatific Asphodel meadows" are only "the yellow-burning marl of a Hell-on-Earth" (105, 111). (Here, of course, Carlyle refers to *Paradise Lost.*) The "editor" accords admiration to Teufelsdröckh only insofar as his "transcendentalism" is theistic, that is, grounded:

> Our Professor's method is not, in any case, that of common school Logic, where the truths all stand in a row, each holding by the skirts of the other; but at best that of practical Reason, proceeding by large Intuition over whole systematic groups and kingdoms; whereby, we might say, a noble complexity, almost like that of Nature, reigns in his Philosophy, or spiritual Picture of Nature: a mighty maze, yet, as faith whispers, not without a plan. (89–90)

Writing of the "genuinely original . . . form and content" of *Sartor Resartus,* Campbell argues that it "combines biography, autobiography, essay, and political commentary with a layered structure and avoidance of final meaning which makes it seem well in advance of its time."[27] Its "layered structure" and its "avoidance of final meaning," however, do not preclude consideration of the gist of the work, namely, the final four chapters of book 1, as *part* of its time, that is, as indicative of the subtle complexity of Carlyle's empirical-evangelical worldview.[28]

Although the antiempirical hovers near Teufelsdröckh's uneasiness with the Humean notion that "use-and-want everywhere lead [men] by the nose"—"Thus let but a Rising of the Sun, let but a Creation of the World happen *twice,* and it ceases to be marvellous, to be noteworthy, or noticeable" (91)—the at least quasi-empirical inheres in the implicit perceptual categories and hence the at least Berkeleyan manner with which Teufelsdröckh expresses his transcendentalism: "Matter exists only spiritually, and to represent some Idea, and *body* it forth" (93). The decidedly empirical inheres in the radically skeptical attitude by which the "editor" systematically questions received tenets:

> Which of your Philosophical Systems is other than a dream-theorem . . . ? This Dreaming, this Somnambulism is what we on Earth call Life; wherein the most indeed undoubtingly wander, as if they knew right hand from left; yet they only are wise who know that they know nothing. . . . Our Professor,

> like other Mystics, whether delirious or inspired, gives our Editor enough to do. (105–6)

The empiricism of *Sartor Resartus* is explicitly consistent, indeed, with the broad strokes and untroubled robustness of Locke's philosophy, and this is nowhere more evident than in the "editor's" underlying assumption of tabula rasa, his experiential emphasis. He admires Teufelsdröckh because his "demonstration lay much in [his] individuality; as if it were not Argument that had taught him, but Experience" (90). The "editor" agrees with "Hofrath Heuschrecke," the "biographer" of Teufelsdröckh:

> However it may be with Metaphysics, and other abstract Science originating in the Head [observes "Heuschrecke"], . . . no Life-Philosophy . . . can attain its significance till the Character itself is known and seen; till the Author's View of the World . . . and how he actively and passively came by such a view, are clear: in short till a Biography of him has been philosophico-poetically written, and philosophico-poetically read. (108–9)

Such a radically skeptical attitude, of course, belongs as much to Descartes as to Locke, and Teufelsdröckh can sound quite Cartesian: "Who am I; what is this ME? . . . *Cogito, ergo sum*" (90). His cogito, however, is sense-based, and therefore rational rather than rationalistic: "Alas, poor Cogitator, this takes us but a little way. Sure enough, I am; and lately was not: but Whence? How? Whereto? The answer lies around, written in all colours and motions, uttered in all tones of jubilee and wail, in thousand-figured, thousand-voiced, harmonious Nature" (90). Thus his cogito is Lockean enough. Although the external world can seem to Teufelsdröckh only a projection of the self—"Nature . . . [is] but the reflex of our inward Force" (92)—that world is importantly present to him, nonetheless. He understands the self as product of sense-experience more than as purely transcendental cogito.

Like Locke, finally, Teufelsdröckh offers an explicitly empirical critique of language. (While Berkeley and Hume sustain no language theory, the entire third book of Locke's *Essay* is one.) Language, unlike the here and now, tends toward the inaccessible, the abstract, and, in Teufelsdröckh's view, this is unfortunate, for "High Air-castles are cunningly built of Words, the words well bedded also in good Logic-mortar; wherein, however, no Knowledge will come to lodge" (91). Thus unreliable as a means of contact between the mind and externality, words are not to be unduly revered: "Be not the slave of Words" (91).

In line with book 3 of Locke's *Essay,* too, is Teufelsdröckh's view of language as an at least possible means of such contact. Teufelsdröckh points out that even such an abstraction as "*Attention*" is, etymologically speaking, "a Stretching-to," and this concreteness of words, he thinks, approaches sense experience (107). Language preserves expression not "solid-grown and colourless," but "fluid and florid," that is, aglow with "the flush of vigorous self-growth" (107). While Teufelsdröckh admits that his language is "sometimes not without an apoplectic tendency" (107), he searches for the vital expression that, according to Locke, grows only, and more or less immediately, out of experience. Teufelsdröckh's language method lets him risk explosive speech.

The continuum in *Sartor Resartus* that joins science to religion is the most inclusive, if not the most straightforward, strain of the book. Alongside Teufelsdröckh's "metaphysico-theological Disquisition" are his "detached Thoughts on the Steam-engine" (110). Near this juxtaposition, in turn, as though to suggest further the experiential bridge from science to religion, is his emphasis on "the continued possibility of Prophecy" (104), the hope of revelation in the here and now. "Science," exclaims Teufelsdröckh, never proceeds "in the small chink-lighted, or even oil-lighted, underground workshop of Logic alone" (103). Such would be rationalism, a head "screwed off, and set in a basin to keep it alive" (103). Thus embracing empirical method, Teufelsdröckh also acknowledges that even the scientist must cultivate the spiritual sense:

> The man who cannot wonder, who does not habitually wonder (and worship), were he President of innumerable Royal Societies, and carried the whole Mecanique Celeste and Hegel's Philosophy, and the epitome of all Laboratories and Observatories with their results, in his single head,—is but a Pair of Spectacles behind which there is no Eye. Let those who have Eyes look through him, then he may be useful. (104)

Teufelsdröckh declares, indeed, that "all objects are windows through which the philosophic eye looks into infinitude itself" (106), a declaration reminiscent of both the philosophic form and the religious content of the evangelical "spiritual sense."

His reference, of course, can be to sense-as-analogue, as in "The thing Visible, . . . what is it but a Garment, a Garment of the higher, celestial Invisible?" (102). But ultimate reality can also be directly perceived by the senses: "Matter" is both "manifestation of Spirit" and "Spirit" (102). Although he does not "see" "the Unslumbering," he "suspects" Him in those "rare half-waking moments" when the "God-written Apocalypse" of nature yields "articulate meaning" to "cunning eye and ear" (91). *Sartor Resartus,* then, "glances from heaven to earth and back again" not so much to reject the world of sense as to include that world in the dialectic of spiritual with natural experience.

The French Revolution (1737), perhaps the most tough-minded of Carlyle's works, fits at the empirical extreme of his empirical-evangelical continuum. Although one may fault the work for its dependence on memories rather than on genuinely primary sources,[29] it shows, among other virtues, narrative skill, careful structure, and a keen sense of irony.[30] Mark Cumming, emphasizing its originality of form, argues that Carlyle's "epic of the Revolution" is precisely "a revolutionary epic."[31] The epic's close attention to historical minutiae is especially worthy of note.[32] Carlyle's willingness to be keenly observant of passing events without any irritable reaching after their meaning derives most clearly from the early modern historiography of David Hume, who, of all empiricists, was least receptive to transcendentalism of any kind.

The epic implies, for example, that history lies quite beyond the individual's power to control or understand it:

> The oak grows silently, in the forest, a thousand years. . . . Nay, when our oak flowered, or put on its leaves (its glad Events), what shout of proclamation could there be? Hardly from the most observant a word of recognition. These things *befell* not, they were slowly *done;* not in an hour, but through the flight of days: what was to be said of it? This hour seemed altogether as the last was, as the next would be. (115)

Events occur inexorably, and seemingly without purpose. Although Carlyle pays lip service to the idea of free action—"The All of Things is an infinite conjugation of the verb *To do*" (133)—and although this particular idea is both philosophically existential and theologically Arminian, the emphasis in *The French Revolution* is on the passive victim of whatever befalls. Even Louis XVI, as much as any beggar, deserves pity:

For Kings and for Beggars, for the justly doomed and the unjustly, it is a hard thing to die. Pity them all: thy utmost pity, with all aids and appliances and throne-and-scaffold contrasts, how far short is it of the thing pitied! (143)

Collective human behavior can influence the course of history:

Hast thou considered how each man's heart is so tremulously responsive to the hearts of all men; hast thou noted how omnipotent is the very sound of many men? How their shriek of indignation palsies the strong soul; their howl of contumely withers with unfelt pangs? (125)

But such behavior derives from mob psychology more than from rational concentration: "Great is the combined voice of men; the utterance of their *instincts,* which are truer than their thoughts" (125). The one force that seems to operate with consequence, ominously, is mindless, aimless violence: the Bastille is "beleagured, in this its last hour, . . . by mere Chaos come again!" (122). Such "order" as there is smacks of predestination, for the Calvinistically theological hovers near the following:

Or, apart from all Transcendentalism, is it not a plain truth of sense, which the duller mind can even consider as a truism, that human things wholly are in continual movement, and action and reaction; working continually forward, phasis after phasis, by unutterable laws, towards prescribed issues? . . . The seed that is sown, it will spring! . . . The Beginning holds in it the End. (133)

But this "order" is finally neither theological nor supernatural. Such extreme empiricism, with no tincture of any theology but the harshest, no more fully represents Carlyle's point of view than "Mad Song" represents Blake's. Even in *The French Revolution,* one finds the tender-minded, for John D. Rosenberg argues that Carlyle's historical writings amount to "a moving plea for community," and, insisting that *The French Revolution,* in particular, is Carlyle's best work, Rosenberg even conceives of it as a successor to the Bible.[33] Reality in the work, though on the same plane as the self and hence far from otherworldly, is at least outside the self and thus empirical. But the narrow point of view in *The French Revolution* is the more memorable, the more sharply focused, for being narrow.

Chartism (1840), attracting the sustained attention of Landow alone,[34] is epistemologically prescriptive. History should turn away from "the obscure fighting of kites and crows," that is, the wars of kings, and concentrate, instead, on how "the Thought and Practice of men" perfected ways to fell forests, drain bogs, make fields arable, build towns, and write laws (203). Economics should eschew the virulent form of rationalism, namely, utilitarian statistics: "Tables," writes Carlyle, "are like cobwebs, like the sieve of the Danaides; beautifully reticulated, orderly to look upon, but which will hold no conclusion" (157). He adds that "there are innumerable circumstances; and one circumstance left out may be the vital one on which all turned. . . . With what serene conclusiveness a member of some Useful-knowledge Society stops your mouth with a figure of arithmetic!" (157). Politics, "filled with an idea of a theory," discovers only "*half*-truth" (164).

In "political economy," however, a humble spirit of inquiry, a submission to the most basic data-gathering, informs Carlyle's willingness to address its smallest questions:

> The average rate of day's wages is not correctly ascertained for any portion of this country; not only not for half-centuries, it is not even ascertained anywhere for decades or years: far from instituting comparisons with the past, the present itself is unknown to us. And then, given the average of wages, what is the constancy of employment; what is the difficulty of finding employment; the fluctuation from season to season, from year to year? Is it constant, calculable wages; or fluctuating, incalculable, more or less of the nature of gambling? (159)

He does not underestimate the difficulty of these less than hopeful questions: "The researches have yielded us little, almost nothing" (156). But his skepticism, that is, his dynamic process of knowing (as opposed to any static state of unbelief), is "not without hope" of meeting "some assent from many candid men" if he can just "get uttered" his "general notion" of the "condition-of-England" (156). He displays faith that in the social sciences, as in intellectual inquiry generally, things exist that correspond to our ideas of them:

> On the whole, O reader, thou wilt find everywhere that things which had had an existence among men have first of all had to have a truth and worth in them, and were not semblances but realities. Nothing not a reality ever yet got men to pay bed and board to it for long. (196)

Thus *Chartism* resumes the accustomed breadth of Carlyle's experiential bias and, in its variety of stated goals for the social sciences, grows epistemologically ambitious.

The experientialism of *Chartism,* indeed, is classically empirical in cast. Although Carlyle denounces the Industrial Revolution as "a hideous World-Steamengine" (178) and traces this "blind No-God of Necessity and Mechanism" to "Hume Scepticisms" as well as "French Philosophisms" and "Diderot Atheisms" (183), he preserves respect for Locke. Harking back by implication to *Some Thoughts concerning Education,* Carlyle issues an early Victorian call for universal public education: "To impart the gift of thinking to those who cannot think, and yet who could in that case think: this, one would imagine, was the first function a government had set about discharging" (222). This statement clearly assumes the principle of tabula rasa on which Locke founds the early modern philosophy of education. The experiential Lockean belief in knowledge through induction, moreover, underlies Carlyle's fundamental conviction that "each man expands his own hand-breadth of observation to the limits of the general whole; more or less, each man must take what he himself has seen and ascertained for a sample of all that is seeable and ascertainable" (158).

Such empiricism, making a virtue of the necessity of individual point of view, can produce "millennium." As Carlyle puts it in an especially arresting juxtaposition, "When Arkwright shall have become mythic like Arachne, we shall still spin in peaceable profit by him; and the Sword-dance, with all its sorrowful shufflings, Waterloo waltzes, Moscow gallopades, how forgotten that will be!" (213). Alongside *Chartism*'s reverence for empiricism, accordingly, lies its respect for religion. What disturbs Carlyle most about the French Revolution, after all, is its overthrow of religion: "That one whole generation of thinkers should be without a religion to believe, or even to contradict; that Christianity, in thinking France, should as it were fade away so long into a remote extraneous tradition, was one of the saddest facts connected with the future of that country" (192–93).

Chartism favors, first, a politically transposed Calvinism. One may hear overtones of the elect, for example, in Carlyle's contrast of Saxon men who cleared the soil of Britain, with "crowds of miserable Irish" who "darken all our towns" (171). More than a whiff of predestination emanates from his comments on the influence of Robert Clive in India:

> Not fit for book-keeping alone, the man was found fit for conquering Nawaubs, founding kingdoms, Indian empires! . . . Accidental all these things and persons look, unexpected every one of them to man. Yet inevitable every one of them; foreseen, not unexpected, by Supreme Power; prepared, appointed from afar. Advancing always through all centuries, in the middle of the eighteenth, they *arrived.* (213)

At least as strong as Carlyle's belief in human rights is his "Calvinist" emphasis on human frailty: "What are the rights of man? All men are justified in demanding and searching for their rights; moreover, justified or not, they will do it: by Chartisms, Radicalisms, French Revolutions, or whatever methods they have. Rights surely are right: on the other hand, this other saying is most true, 'Use every man according to his *rights,* and who shall escape whipping?' These two things, we say, are both true; and both are essential to make up the whole truth" (184). "Surely of all 'rights of man,'" Carlyle expostulates, "this right of the ignorant man to be guided by the wiser, to be, gently or forcibly, held in the true course by him, is the indisputablest" (189). This antidemocratic spirit, if not this might-makes-right, protofascist authoritarianism, boasts a theological rationale: "No man is justified in resisting by word or deed the Authority he lives under, for a light cause, be such Authority what it may. Obedience, little as many may consider that side of the matter, is the primary duty of man. . . . Recognised or not recognised, a man *has* his superiors, a regular hierarchy above him; extending up, degree above degree, to Heaven itself and God the Maker, who made His world not for anarchy but for rule and order" (218).[35]

Alongside such "Calvinism," though, Carlyle consciously, or unconsciously, lays (after the manner of John Wesley) a distinctly un-Calvinistic "theology." (Paradigms war in Carlyle.) In his longing for a "strong man" to come out of Parliament (154) may be a vestige of election, but in his passionate conviction that something must be *done,* in his animadversions against laissez-faire economics, he implies a democratic, "Arminian" view of individual latitude and potentiality. "It is sadder than tears," he writes, "the laugh Humanity is forced to, at *Laissez-faire* applied to poor peasants, in a world like our Europe of the year 1839!" (174). "A government of the under classes by the upper on a principle of *Let-alone,*" he writes further, "is no longer possible in England in these days" (187). What *is* needed for every "practical man . . . in Parliament and out of it" is to gird up for "actual doing" (220). The following subscription to free will, in which Carlyle uses the first person to represent all practical people of whatever class, is specifically theological: "I have the miraculous breath of Life in me, breathed into my nostrils by Almighty God. I have affections, thoughts, a god-given *capability* to be and do. . . . My soul, breathed into me by God, my *Me* and what capability is there; that is mine, and I will resist the stealing of it. . . . Society, it is understood, does not in any age prevent a man from being what he *can* be. A sooty African *can* become a Toussaint L'Ouverture" (194–95).

Such an Arminian cast is everywhere to be found in the preaching of evangelical practical charity in *Chartism,* its assumption that social progress can occur among people energized as well as dignified by their spiritual nature. Carlyle's hatred of workhouses, his crusade against gin, his confident expectation that the poor will save money, his campaign against idleness, his perfectionist faith in the efficacy of education, and, not least, his occasional kind words even for the Irish[36]—all are reminiscent of Wesley's charitable projects, and all these emphases, like Wesley's projects, arise from a religious justification of the common person:

> All men, we must repeat, were made by God, and have immortal souls in them. The Sanspotato is of the selfsame stuff as the superfinest Lord Lieutenant. Not an individual Sanspotato human scarecrow but had a Life given him out of Heaven, with Eternities depending on it; for once and no second time. With Immensities in him, over him and round him; with feelings which a Shakespeare's speech would not utter; with desires illimitable as the Autocrat's of all the Russias! (169)

Carlyle's concept of Arminian freedom, moreover, combines with his reminiscence of the doctrine of assurance: "Every mortal can do something: this let him faithfully do, and leave with assured heart the issue to a Higher Power!" (170). When speaking of remedies for Ireland, finally, he draws on the Arminian concept of conversion: "The cure, if it is to be a cure, must be in the heart: not in his condition only but in himself must the Patient be all changed" (170).

Thus containing a dose of Arminian doctrine as well as empiricism, *Chartism* suggests that the material and the spiritual are not finally opposites. When "spiritual life has departed," "material life . . . cannot long remain behind" (183). Where Carlyle teaches that "the heart always . . . sees, before the head *can* see" (179), and where he defines faith as a "*sense* for the true and false" (183), he implies that physical sight is mere analogy for the mysterious vision of another world, that is, that the here and now serves transcendental ends. "Events," he remarks, are "written lessons, glaring in huge hieroglyphic picture-writing, that all may read and know them" (187). His transcendental expression, and his language of observation, however, sometimes merge in a synthesis: "And yet so long as an Ideal (any soul of Truth) does, in never so confused a manner, exist and work within the Actual, it is a tolerable business" (196). Or: "He who believes no *thing,* who believes only the shows of things, is not in relation with Nature and fact at all" (209). "Ideas," Carlyle knows, "produce revolutions," but he adds that "not spiritual ideas only, but even mechanical" ones do (213). A blend of the empirical and the religious, then, and even of the empirical and the evangelical, makes for the millenarian social consciousness of *Chartism.*

Of all the essays making up *On Heroes, Hero-Worship, and the Heroic in History* (1841), *The Hero as Man of Letters* is most pertinent here. It is closest to the spirit of Carlyle's immediate historical context. While he admired much of the literature of his day,[37] he found little other promise of heroes in Victorian Britain. *On Heroes, Hero-Worship, and the Heroic in History* addresses itself primarily to the nature of greatness in the far past, but *The Hero as Man of Letters,* like *Chartism,* is characterized, first, by a combination of, a balance between, or simply an irresolution concerning, Calvinism and Arminianism. The sovereignty of God, on the one hand, removes responsibility for salvation quite from the individual: "For the saving of the *world* I will trust confidently to the Maker of the world" (255). With trust in individual initiative, on the other hand, Carlyle "will look a little to my own saving, which I am much more competent to!" (255).

The essay contributes, moreover—and here is my emphasis—to Carlyle's experiments in philosophical theology. Kinetic not deadening, and reminiscent of Locke more than Descartes, "Scepticism" is "not an end but a beginning," that is, not "the decay of old ways of believing" but "the preparation afar off for new and wider ways" (251). Indeed, skepticism is akin to, and a prerequisite for, faith. The following, significantly, is as reminiscent of the eighteenth-century evangelicalism of Wesley and

Edwards as, say, of the tough-minded seventeenth-century faith of Sir Thomas Browne:

> Doubt, truly, is not itself a crime. Certainly we do not rush out, clutch-up the first thing we find, and straightway believe that! All manner of doubt, inquiry, . . . dwells in every reasonable mind. It is the mystic working of the mind, on the object it is *getting* to know and believe. (253)

Thus the faith arrived at is "empirical," of the here and now. "The world," exclaims Carlyle, "is alive, instinct with Godhead, beautiful and awful, even as in the beginning of days" (254). He rejoices, accordingly, that "here and there one does now find a man who knows, as of old, that this world is a Truth" (254). Such language evokes not so much pantheism as theism, a world in which God acts.

Out of Carlyle's "empirical" faith grow both his definition of the "man of letters" and his very understanding of the nature of writing. The "act of writing," he observes, relates "all times and all places with this our actual Here and Now" (241). As he puts it in another place, "Literature" is a "'continuous revelation'" (the phrase is Fichte's) "of the Godlike in the Terrestrial and Common" (243). "Men of Letters," accordingly, "are a perpetual Priesthood, from age to age, teaching all men that a God is still present in their life" (237). This, perhaps, is the most fully suggestive statement in *The Hero as Man of Letters,* if not in all of his works, for the statement's this-worldliness, though not explicitly Lockean, epitomizes in the context of the essay as a whole the experiential common ground of empirical philosophy and evangelical faith.

A faith defined in the language of perception and the here and now finds a final ringing affirmation in *Past and Present* (1843). The following passage makes heart-religion almost empirical: "For the faith in an Invisible, Unnameable Godlike, present everywhere in all that we see and work and suffer, is the essence of all faith whatsoever; and that once denied, or still worse, asserted with lips only, and out of bound prayer-books only, what other things remain believable?" (279). This affirmation rings true to the spirit of classical Methodism, with its all but empirical experientialism. Such Methodism, indeed, explains Carlyle's stricture against the attenuated Methodism of the nineteenth century, which sacrificed its heritage of empirical sensibility to an oddly solipsistic because too-subjectively-transcendental stance: "Methodism with its eye forever turned on its own navel; asking itself with torturing anxiety of Hope and Fear, 'Am I right? am I wrong? Shall I be saved? shall I not be damned?—what is this at bottom, but a new phasis of *Egoism,* stretched out into the Infinite; not always the heavenlier for its infinitude!" (274–75).

Because of what John D. Rosenberg sees as its creeping Calvinism, he calls *Past and Present* Carlyle's "*last* great work" (my italics).[38] In it, indeed, Carlyle begins to lose his way, to change from "a moving plea for community" to "a frightened call for authority." Arminian evangelicalism emphasizes community over authority, and *Past and Present* remains Arminian insofar as it retains its "moving plea": the book closest to it, after all, is R. B. Seeley's work of evangelical criticism, *The Perils of the Nation; An Appeal to the Legislature, the Clergy, and the Higher and Middle Classes* (1843).[39] But the frightened call for authority and the fire-and-brimstone diction that characterize Calvinist evangelicalism also characterize *Past and Present,* which warns that because of "these last two centuries of Atheistic Government," we "are now, very ominously, shuddering, reeling, and let us hope trying to recoil, on the cliff's edge" (278) of a subjective abyss.

The Calvinism thus implicit in *Past and Present* is full-blown, alas, in *Latter-Day Pamphlets* (1850). The Calvinism of Carlyle's youth, somewhat reemergent not only in *Past and Present* but also in *The Hero as Man of Letters* and *Chartism,* now reasserts itself the more virulently for having lain dormant. In *Latter-Day Pamphlets,* classical Methodism yields to a far more than merely "Edwardsean" fire and brimstone, a Calvinism of the very harshest sort.

Pamphlet 6, for example, can no longer address the traditionally Arminian theme of freedom without an upstart Calvinist hint of no-freedom: "The free man is he who is *loyal* to the Laws of the Universe" (310). Pamphlet 2, with more-than-Edwardsean harshness, attacks the Wesleyan "method of love" in prison reform (288). Note especially the quite un-Wesleyan, even Swiftean, flavor of apoplectic imprecation in Carlyle's description of inmates as "miserable distorted block-heads, the generality; ape-faces, imp-faces, angry dog-faces, heavy sullen ox-faces; degraded underfoot perverse creatures, sons of *in*docility, greedy mutinous darkness, and in one word, of STUPIDITY, which is the mother of such" (288). This is the "mother" of all "Calvinistic" denunciations.

More than a hint of predestination, or divine ordination, is in the rationale of Pamphlet 6 for slavery as a natural, almost desirable institution:

> Slave or free is settled in Heaven for a man; acts of parliament attempting to settle it on earth for him, sometimes make sad work of it. . . .
>
> My friends, I grieve to remind you, but it is eternally the fact: When Heaven has made a slave, no parliament of men nor power that exists on Earth can render free. . . . Him the Supreme Powers marked in the making of him, *slave;* appointed him, at his and our peril, not to command but to obey, in this world. (308–9)

This obviously specious argument on behalf of slavery is a shockingly nonironic descendant of the irony with which Blake, in *Visions of the Daughters of Albion* (1793), undercuts Bromion's speeches.

More than a hint, finally, of electionist bias, not to mention un-Lockean anticontractualism, colors the same pamphlet's antidemocratic ravings. Denouncing the "dead pedantries, unveracities, indolent somnolent impotences, and accumulated dung-mountains" of Downing Street (307), Carlyle concludes that "either some new Downing Street and Incipiency of a real Hero-Kingship again, or else Chartist Parliament, with Apotheosis of Attorneyism, and Anarchy very undeniable to all the world: one or else the other, it seems to me, we shall soon have" (307). Such heavily authoritarian, if not protofascist, language finds antecedents, to be sure, as early as *Signs of the Times,* for even the young Carlyle, while denouncing government when it acts as a "parish-constable," wants it to be, somehow, "a father" (71). But once such language sets in with a vengeance, the Carlyle in whom I am interested is no more.

Campbell, it is true, tries to put the best face on Carlyle's later career:

> Trapped between a warm personality (he gave, generously, to various objects of charity) and an urgently, overwhelmingly pressing view of order, Carlyle found himself in his private life and, increasingly, in his public writing torn between a vision of a freer humanity (in his early works) and a vision of collapsing anarchy in society (in all his later ones). . . . Faced with the reality of human suffering, he always responded with human warmth; only in the privacy of his study did abstract ideas work him into righteous frenzy, and his style made that mood the memorable one. . . . We have passed beyond

> the need to venerate him as sage, of Chelsea or of Ecclefecchan. Rather we see him as an emblem of the complexity, contradiction, and sometimes absurdity of the era.[40]

But one is left with Samuel Butler's conclusion that "Carlyle led us into the wilderness, and left us there."[41] The harsh quality of the later career indeed derives from Calvinist doctrine, for after the death of Carlyle's Burgher-Secessionist father in January 1832, Carlyle felt increasingly "fully justified in promoting, unapologetically, the ascetic, authoritarian, gloomy, pragmatic prejudices of his Puritan ancestry."[42] "Those transcendental and Puritan precepts to which Carlyle owed a dual allegiance," Ikeler adds, "represented, in almost every way, antithetical views of life." Ikeler believes that Carlyle's career had been at odds with itself from the beginning. I cannot fully agree, for transcendental and Puritan precepts are not always in conflict, but this belief is sufficiently applicable to the later career to cause a variety of critics to stop with *Past and Present*.[43]

Up through *Past and Present,* Carlyle's transcendentalism is not antithetical to either Wesleyan evangelicalism or, for that matter, the empiricism to be found in Wesleyan and Edwardsean evangelicalism. Perhaps the most inclusive model of reality in all of Carlyle is the image of the blacksmith in *Sartor Resartus*. The smithy fire represents empirical science in its Victorian, geological form: the fire was "kindled at the Sun; is fed by air that circulates from before Noah's Deluge" (106). The smith himself, who "preaches forth the mystery of Force; nay preaches forth (exoterically enough) one little textlet from the Gospel of Freedom, the Gospel of Man's Force" (106), lends a more than experientially reliable, because "Arminian," authority to the evolutionary principle, and thus, in the context of Carlyle in his prime, the smith lends to that principle the status of empirical-evangelical truth.

Anglo-American Ground

Just as Carlyle's origins were in the English-speaking world, so his impact was on that world. *Signs of the Times* not only anticipated but also deeply influenced Ruskin's *Unto This Last* and Arnold's *Culture and Anarchy,* but Emerson responded early to Carlyle, and because of Emerson's immediate admiration for *Sartor Resartus,* Boston published the work in book form before England did.[44] By the 1840s, Carlyle's essays "were widely available on both sides of the Atlantic."[45]

In *Chartism,* Carlyle seizes the opportunity to include America with England as the audience for whom his message is intended. He harks back to A.D. 449, when Hengist and Horsa founded an Anglo-Saxon society that anticipated "Wellingtons, Washingtons, . . . William Pitts and Davie Crocketts" (202). *Chartism*'s praise for America, indeed, is explicit: "Thou little Mayflower hadst in thee a veritable Promethean spark; the life-spark of the largest Nation on our Earth,—so we may already name the Transatlantic Saxon Nation" (208–9). The treatise ends with the hope that the poor of England will find new life in America's "boundless Plains and Prairies unbroken with the Plough" (231).

In "the land of Malebranche, Pascal, Descartes, and Fenelon," writes Carlyle in *Signs of the Times,* "is now no such thing as a Science of Mind" (67). He adds that although Germany has made some effort in "psychological science," the true "Philosophy of Mind" prevailed only in England, until it "languished and finally died out" with "Professor Stewart" (67). In *Chartism,* Carlyle uses "the Germanic" simply to offer a perspective on England; note especially his long eighth chapter, on "The Eras of England." His Anglo-Saxon bias is evident even in *Sartor Resartus,* where "the Diligence and feeble thinking Faculty of our English Editor" endeavors to evolve "printed Creation out of a German printed and written Chaos" (112). The "editor" predicts that Teufelsdröckh's "Philosophy of Clothes," that is, his as much empirical-evangelical as German-idealist methodology, "will stand clear to the wondering eyes of England, nay thence, through America" (110).

Intra-Romantic Connections

Carlyle's Anglo-American sensibility indicates the nature of his Romanticism. Timko emphasizes the differences between Romanticism and Carlyle, who regarded Romantic writers as inferior to Shakespeare.[46] Basil Willey, however, points out that Carlyle is "the Romantic who lived on,"[47] and now I wish to fill out a portrait of him as Romantic.

His Romanticism remains in the English-language and empirical-evangelical world, for the empirical-evangelical roots of other British, if not some American, Romantic writers nourish Carlyle, too. Although his "opposition to the over-valuation of the rational" forms part of his Romanticism, it is too much to conclude that another part of it is his "mistrust" of eighteenth-century science.[48] By specifically appealing to that science, he achieves a proper valuation of the rational, namely, his recognition of its foundation in the senses. His Romanticism, moreover, achieves a proper valuation of science in relation to religion.

Carlyle saw himself, first, as living in a period that had begun in 1789. Since that year, as he pointed out in *Chartism,* "there is now half a century complete; and a French Revolution not yet complete!" (*Chartism,* 181). The French Revolution was perhaps the most formative event of British as well as Continental Romanticism, and by fearing the excesses of the Revolution, Carlyle showed his fear of Romanticism, too. (In this respect, he was no different from Wordsworth or Coleridge.) Specifically quoting Montesquieu—"Happy the people whose annals are tiresome"—Carlyle adds this twist: "Happy the people whose annals are vacant" (*The French Revolution,* 115). He deeply regrets the passing of much that the Revolution has destroyed:

> One reverend thing after another ceases to meet reverence: in visible material combustion, chateau after chateau mounts up; in spiritual invisible combustion, one authority after another. With noise and glare, or noiselessly and unnoted, a whole Old System of things is vanishing piecemeal: the morrow thou shalt look, and it is not. (*The French Revolution,* 136)

He warns, finally, that "these Chartisms, Radicalisms, Reform Bill, Tithe Bill . . . are *our* French Revolution" (*Chartism,* 181).

Like his precursors in British Romanticism, however, Carlyle seems torn or poised between such apocalyptic fears and his strong hope that the Revolution would bring millennial, rather than further violent, results. He announces that "the French Revolution is seen, or begins everywhere to be seen, 'as the crowning phenomenon of our Modern Time;' 'the inevitable stern end of much; the fearful, but also wonderful, indispensable and sternly beneficent beginning of much' " (*Chartism,* 182). He remains aware that "hope ushers in a Revolution" (*The French Revolution,* 117). His hope, like that of such other later Romantics as Shelley and Byron, is never quite dashed. "The French Revolution itself had something higher in it than cheap bread and a Habeas-corpus act," for "here too was an Idea; a Dynamic, not a Mechanic force. It was a struggle, though a blind and at last an insane one, for the infinite, divine, nature of Right, of Freedom, of Country" (*Signs of the Times,* 74–75).

The French Revolution, like the English one, "originated in religion" (*Signs of the Times,* 74). Carlyle believes in a "divine spirit" that "arose in the mystic deeps of man's soul; and was spread abroad by the preaching of the word, by simple, altogether natural and individual efforts; and flew, like hallowed fire, from heart to heart, till all were purified and illuminated by it" (*Signs of the Times,* 74). This spiritual source of revolution glosses, though retroactively, Wordsworth's "Lines Written in Early Spring" (1798): "Love, now a universal birth, / From heart to heart is stealing." This thesis, affirmed when the halcyon early days of the French Revolution were a fresh memory to the poet, undoubtedly helped to preserve in the Romantic Carlyle the fresh memory of a French-inspired seedbed of British Romanticism. The Romantic Carlyle, however, is no more French than Blake, Wordsworth, Coleridge, Shelley, and Keats are, and, like them, he is rooted in such English-language and religious/philosophical sources of Romanticism as, *mutatis mutandis,* the philosophical theology shared by Wesley and Edwards.

With regard to the empirical dimension of that philosophical theology and its relation to Carlyle's Romanticism, literature, for him, is consistent with robust empiricism as much as, say, with the purely noumenal. "Poetry," though properly "held to be mysterious and inscrutable," is "no longer without its scientific exposition" (*Signs of the Times,* 79). The entire literary enterprise, including the interaction of work and reader, is alternately, or even at once, natural and spiritual. Carlyle, believing that poetic language should be judged according to its natural-spiritual or fully experiential level of sincerity, finds Byron wanting in this particular criterion of Romanticism. Carlyle clearly believes that Byron is different, in this respect, from other British High Romantics and from himself. With the possible exception of "the latter parts" of *Don Juan,* he declares, Byron's poetry is "not true" (see *Burns* [1828], 44).

Byron, he adds, "refreshes us, not with the divine fountain, but too often with vulgar strong waters, stimulating indeed to the taste, but soon ending in dislike, or even nausea. Are his Harolds and Giaours, we would ask, real men; we mean, poetically conceivable and consistent men? Do not these characters, does not the character of their author, which more or less shines through them all, rather appear a thing put on for the occasion; no natural or possible mode of being, but something intended to look much grander than nature? Surely, all these stormful agonies, this volcanic heroism, superhuman contempt and moody desperation, with so much scowling, and teeth-gnashing, and other sulphurous humour, is more like the brawling of a player in some paltry tragedy, which is to last three hours, than the bearing of a man in the business of life, which is to last threescore and ten years" (*Burns,* 44–45). By sincerity, surely, Carlyle means the genuineness of all good experience. "To every poet, to every writer," he observes, "we might say: Be true, if you would be believed" (*Burns,* 44), and he adds, "Let a man but speak forth with genuine earnestness the thought, the emotion, the actual condition of his own heart; and other men, so strangely are we all knit together by the tie of sympathy, must and will give heed to him."

The goal of every talent, Carlyle thinks, should be "to *read its own consciousness without mistakes*" (*Burns,* 45; my italics). Since this embrace of sincerity assumes that even the most spiritual aspect of consciousness is built up from, and informed by, sense experience, there is no hint of solipsism here. "As face answers to face," declares Carlyle, "so does the heart of man to man" (*Burns,* 44); thus, his sense-based consciousness guarantees the possibility of intersubjectivity. His Romanticism, like the philosophical theology shared by Wesley and Edwards, is pragmatic as well as expressive, kerygmatic as well as testimonial.

As for the pertinence of evangelicalism to Carlyle's Romanticism, *Signs of the Times* presents a Blakean-evangelical call to spiritual renewal. Compare "the mind-forged manacles I hear," from Blake's "London" (1794), with Carlyle's "Nay, after all, our spiritual maladies are but of Opinion; we are but fettered by chains of our own forging, and which ourselves also can render asunder" (*Signs of the Times,* 83). Compare the "spiritual-sense"-like cleansing of the doors of Blakean perception ("If the doors of perception were cleansed every thing would appear to man as it is, infinite" (*The Marriage of Heaven and Hell* [1790–93], plate 14) with Carlyle's own spiritual diagnosis, worth repeating: "this deep, paralyzed subjection to physical objects comes not from Nature, but from our own unwise mode of *viewing* Nature" (*Signs of the Times,* 83; Carlyle's italics). Just as Shelley, finally, shows ambivalence about the transcendental quest (recall "pinnacled *dim* in the intense *inane*" [*Prometheus Un-*

bound; my italics]), so Teufelsdröckh's "editor" sees Teufelsdröckh as struggling "towards these *dim* infinitely-expanded regions, close-bordering on the impalpable *Inane*" (*Sartor Resartus,* 108; my italics). Like Shelley, then, Carlyle is not so much antitranscendental as theistical, and thus Carlyle's Romanticism is consistent with the "transcendentalism" of not only British, if not Anglo-American, Romantic modalities but also empirical/evangelical modalities.

Chris R. Vanden Bosshe, in *Carlyle and the Search for Authority* (1991), emphasizes that Carlyle "was the contemporary of Shelley and Keats," and thus Vanden Bosshe is in accord with the view of Carlyle as a Romantic.[49] He shows, in particular, that Carlyle "belonged to the generation of Romantic artists who attempted to make art a religion, a discourse with a visionary and transcendental status." Vanden Bosshe discerns much destructive tension in Carlyle's Romantic stance. His "Romantic transcendentalism" and the "literary formalism that evolved from it," he argues, are "at odds with the Romantic desire to intervene in the political world," for transcendentalism and formalism remove "art and the artist from the historical processes of social formation," and "by raising the artist *above* society, this view of art brought into question the artist's ability to act *in* society." According to Vanden Bosshe, then, Carlyle could not maintain the delicate balance between Romantic transcendentalism and Romantic interventionism. He leaned too much to one side, and eventually transformed his "aesthetic transcendentalism" into a "political authoritarianism" that he regarded as "the sole means of counteracting the destruction of values and social cohesion by the emerging industrial order." Thus never solving the "dilemma of literature," Carlyle was to "anticipate later critics in discovering that the Romantic religion of art, far from recovering the transcendental and escaping individualism, merely intensified interiority." Vanden Bosshe concludes that this problem "led Carlyle, in the latter part of his career, to seek the recovery of authority in the hero as king."

I welcome Vanden Bosshe's recognition that the "visionary and transcendental status" of Carlyle's discourse makes his Romanticism as much religious as philosophical. Vanden Bosshe's view of the early part of Carlyle's career—his argument that Carlyle is both within and above culture—parallels my own view that the complexity of Carlyle's best work can be understood along lines of the creative tension between, the playful interaction of, his worldliness and his otherworldliness.

Carlyle, however, is not just within and above culture. He is within and beneath it, for he is within, as well as outside, nature. The empirical-evangelical perspective on Carlyle's Romanticism supplements Vanden Bosshe's perspective. Is there too much "either/or" logic in Vanden Bosshe's otherwise helpful analysis? Carlyle's Romanticism, after all, includes the "spiritual sense." Since an "empirical-evangelical" Romantic is, by definition, *in* the world even though not *of* it, there may be more dialectic than aporia in the Carlylean categories of artist "*above* society" and artist "*in* society." The "both/and" logic of "empirical-evangelical" Romanticism relieves the urgency of the question that Vanden Bosshe finds at the heart of Carlyle's midcareer.

By Carlyle's time, Vanden Bosshe argues, "empiricism and individual reason had replaced the discourses of tradition and transcendental revelation." My view is different. The arc from Wesley and Edwards to Carlyle, that is, from the Religious Enlightenment of the Anglo-American world to a particularly influential worldview of English-language Late Romanticism, does not finally separate "empiricism and individual reason" from "the discourse of tradition and transcendental revelation." The Anglo-American Romanticism of Carlyle, by joining empiricism to heart-religion, "answers" its own questions through an essentially cumulative, progressively amplifying procedure that entails further questions, further answers. His Romanticism, most precisely described as Anglo-American in that its "spiritual sense" rivals the methodological efficacy of Wesleyan-Edwardsean philosophical theology, is most fully defined as the coexistence of his "empirical" as well as evangelical ideality with his "evangelical" as well as empirical tough-mindedness.

THREE

The Empirical / Evangelical Dialectic of Ralph Waldo Emerson

Although there is no more obvious a truism of Emerson studies than that he is a "Transcendentalist,"[1] he is far from rejecting "a scientific attitude toward Nature,"[2] since he reserves an honored place for science in his thought and shows little Platonic *contemptus mundi*.[3] His scientific approach to nature leads to, and even strengthens, his idealism, which is as much in the world as otherworldly and as much religious as philosophical. Members of his Transcendental Club are generally "repelled by John Locke's view that the mind is a passive receiver of sense impressions," preferring "Coleridge's alternative view of the mind as creative in perception,"[4] but Emerson is both a transcendentalist and an empiricist. Coleridge, for that matter, is not entirely un-Lockean,[5] nor Locke entirely deterministic.[6] I isolate for immediate scrutiny, as well as for later exploration, not only a wide range, but also a mixture, of Emerson's themes from the philosophic to the prophetic. I focus on his belletristic prose, his "only formal achievement" (Bloom writes), reluctantly omitting, for now, his poetry (which Bloom refers to as that "double handful of strong poems").[7] Thus I situate Emerson on the empirical ground of evangelical faith. "Certain ideas," he declares in *Fate* (1852), "are in the air,"[8] and both empiricism and evangelicalism, though they emanate from the eighteenth century, contribute to his works.

From certain pertinent scholarship and his journals, I forge the empirical-evangelical perspective that I use to examine his *Nature* (1836). Without necessarily agreeing with Bloom that the journals are Emerson's most "authentic" works[9] and without sharing David Van Leer's suspicion of them as sources of empirical evidence (he does grant the journals "epistemic status"), I participate in Van Leer's awe of them as "the great *roman-fleuve* of American Romanticism."[10] Van Leer, confining his study of Emerson's epistemology to just four essays,[11] remarks that "by reading so meticulously a small number of texts, I [myself] surely illustrate what one critic" of scholarly thick description "has called the 'failure of tact,'" and Van Leer realizes that "what friendly readers may find indefatigable [in his study] will strike others as merely relentless."[12] I, too, risk "tactlessness," but *Nature,* after all, is the longest, most representative essay by Emerson, and as such, it deserves a full analysis. Written in the mid-1830s, at the formative moment of his career and the height of his powers, it shows how his outlook was indeed empirically evangelical.

Although I omit such fashionable works as *Circles, Montaigne,* and *The Lord's Supper,*[13] I shall place my close reading of *Nature* within the context of Emerson's life of writing, specifically his production from the late 1830s through the early 1850s of the seven most frequently anthologized essays. *The American Scholar* (1837), *The Divinity School Address* (1838), *Self-Reliance* (1841), *The Over-Soul* (1841), *The Poet* (1844), *Experience* (1844), and *Fate* all call for a full analysis in empirical-evangelical terms, but I use these essays, here, to indicate the applicability of what I say about *Nature* to Emerson's Anglo-American ground and his intra-Romantic relationships.

A Bibliographical Orientation

In his explicitly philosophical criticism of Emerson, Van Leer notably succeeds in his goal of "read[ing] Kant into the record of American idealism."[14] He gives due prominence to Emerson's assessment of Kant:

> The first thing we have to say respecting what are called *new views* here in New England, at the present time, is, that they are not new, but the very oldest thoughts cast into the mould of these new times. . . . What is popularly called Transcendentalism among us, is Idealism; Idealism as it appears in 1842. . . . It is well known to most of my audience, that the Idealism of the present day acquired the name of Transcendental, from the use of that term by Immanuel Kant, of Konisberg [*sic*], who replied to the skeptical philosophy of Locke, which insisted that there was nothing in the intellect

> which was not previously in the experience of the senses, by showing that there was a very important class of ideas, of imperative forms, which did not come by experience, but through which experience was acquired; that these were intuitions of the mind itself; and he denominated them *Transcendental* forms. The extraordinary profoundness and precision of that man's thinking have given vogue to his nomenclature, in Europe and America, to that extent, that whatever belongs to the class of intuitive thought, is popularly called at the present day *Transcendental*.[15]

Van Leer pursues the implications of this passage as far as they will go toward arguing that Emerson is a Kantian. Van Leer sums up Kant, and by implication Emerson, this way: "Kant saw his idealism as half of a necessary dualism: the true transcendental idealist was also an empirical realist."[16] Like Kant, indeed, Emerson is both a transcendental idealist and an empirical realist, but his empirical realism is closer to Locke's than to Kant's, for although Emerson reserves considerable room for "intuitions" and "imperative forms," he gives much space, too, to the skepticism that naturally attends one's subscription to the tabula rasa. Everyone knows that Hume woke Kant from his dogmatic slumbers, but Emerson goes over Hume's head, and harks back to Locke, in order to explain Kant. Thus Emerson suggests that the founder of British empiricism is the ultimate empirical precursor of Kant's philosophy, for Emerson interprets that philosophy as itself an assimilation of Locke, and he even seems to think that Kant made deliberate use of Locke's broad, as distinct from Hume's narrow, skepticism. Emerson's assessment of Kant, in short, nicely complicates Emerson's own developing understanding of Lockean methodology.

Not only like Berkeley, with his transcendental realism and empirical idealism, but also like Locke, in Locke's more religious moods, Emerson reflects the capacious, and even the susceptibly "transcendental," empiricism of England. Although the Anglo-American response to Descartes was "much more direct" than the response to Kant,[17] and although Hume was more aware of Descartes and Malebranche than of Berkeley, Hans Aarsleff and Norman Fiering overrate the French influence where they argue, as Van Leer paraphrases them, that "the traditional distinction between French rationalism and English empiricism creates a false dichotomy."[18] One need not go so far afield as either French rationalism or German idealism to find transcendental elements for British empiricism, for as Wesley, Edwards, and Carlyle, if not Berkeley and Locke, make clear, transcendental elements are already within British empiricism. (The sources for Emerson's knowledge of Kant, incidentally, are the secondhand accounts in William Drummond, Dugald Stewart, Samuel Taylor Coleridge, and, not least, Thomas Carlyle, as well as in Victor Cousin and Mme de Stael.)[19]

John Michael argues that "Emerson's engagement with skepticism and his search for confirmation of his vision of the world are far more severe and far less conclusive than has been admitted."[20] Michael goes against such a reading as that of Evan Carton, who argues in the post-Cartesian context of Kant and Hegel that Emerson's works enact "the romantic longing to articulate spirit in language."[21] Michael, recognizing that "Emerson's realism is far more commonsensical than Kant's and far more earthly than Hegel's," emphasizes the "peculiar cast" that Scottish realism in general and Hume's philosophy in particular give to Emerson's "engagement with ideas."[22] Just as, according to Michael, Hume "links the identity of the self to the other's recognition," so, in Michael's view, "identity for Emerson" is "first and foremost a social creation."[23] Michael explores Emerson's "often painful awareness of his audience's presence." It is odd, in view of Michael's emphasis on self-identity, that he offers no extended reading of *Self-Reliance,* but it is salutary, from my point of view, that he examines the British influence on Emerson's philosophy. By adding to that influence the British as well as American influence on Emerson's theology, I seek both to supplement Michael's work and to balance his overemphasis on "the issue of skepticism" as the "central problem," rather than the "enabling strategy," of Emerson's methodology.[24] Michael's Emerson is too much "our contemporary" and too little "the Victorian moralist or the romantic."

Michael acknowledges that Emerson draws from Lockean philosophy for his general notion of identity:

> In the Lockean philosophical tradition the figure of the body represents that part of our identity accessible to others. In Emerson there is often a metaphorization of the relation between self and other that assimilates it to the corpus of his work. Emerson aspires to and worries about the embodiment of himself in his text.[25]

This notion is illustrated, for example, in what Emerson says of Montaigne, that "the sincerity and marrow of the man reaches to his sentences. . . . Cut these words, and they would bleed; they are vascular and alive."[26] No one to my knowledge, however, has compared Emerson to Locke in the way that Michael compares him to Hume and to Montaigne, or that Van Leer compares him to Kant. If it is true that Emerson is more commonsensical than Kant, it is true, too, that he is more commonsensical than Hume, and it takes nothing from his sophistication to say that he is commonsensical in the way that Locke is. Although Cameron Thompson has emphasized differences between Locke and Emerson,[27] the recent publication of the journals[28] affords the opportunity to examine new evidence. In doing so, I attempt to keep in mind Stephen E. Whicher's sage and witty advice, which recognizes a complexity in "modern philosophy" that Emerson would undoubtedly have acknowledged:

> Take a quantity of Kant; add unequal parts of Goethe, Schiller, Herder, Jacobi, Schleiermacher, Fichte, Schelling, Oken, and a pinch of Hegel; stir in, as Emerson did, a generous amount of Swedenborg; strain through Mme de Stael, Sampson Reed, Oegger, Coleridge, Carlyle, Wordsworth, Cousin, Jouffroy, Constant; spill half and season with Plato—and you have something resembling the indescribable brew called modern philosophy whose aroma Emerson began to detect in his corner of the world in the 1820s.[29]

Michael adds that "the dominant flavor of the 'indescribable brew' is extracted from the fruits of Scottish realism that grew from Hume's fertile skepticism,"[30] but while I applaud Michael's all-too-unusual emphasis on Emerson's English-speaking roots, I include in the "dominant flavor" the sufficiently skeptical as well as fully realist philosophy of Locke, to say nothing, for the moment, of the realist and "skeptical" theology of Wesley and Edwards.

Explicitly theological criticism of Emerson is well illustrated by Bloom's well-known insight that Emerson "founded the central American religion, which is Protestant without being Christian."[31] What Perry Miller deplores, that Emerson's optimism is attenuated Puritanism or "Edwardseanism without original sin,"[32] does not bother Bloom. Bloom insists that "sin, error, time, history, a God external to the self, the visiting of the crimes of the fathers upon the sons . . . were precisely of no interest whatsoever to Ralph Waldo Emerson."[33]

On the basis of scholarship that relates Emerson to Unitarianism, however, one must answer "yes and no," if not a simple "no," to both Bloom and Miller. Lawrence Buell and David Robinson demonstrate the considerable residuum of precise Unitarian theology in Emerson's thought.[34] According to Robinson, in particular, one's historical understanding of Emerson "must begin with the pietism of the early Unitarian movement,"[35] and Robinson argues, too, that the "problem" in Emerson's thought is not so much "tragic" as "theological" in nature.[36] Although Emerson was committed to the idea of Unitarian "self-culture, which he saw as the evolving of the soul toward an ultimate perfection," he realized that he was "calling for the pursuit of an unattainable end": "Without a concept of the better, self-culture was impossible; but with such a vision, it could never be completed."[37] One's historical understanding, though, should not end with Emerson's Unitarian pietism, any more than with his philosophical roots. It should include, as well, his other-than-Unitarian theological roots.

Leonard Neufeldt's reading of Emerson as a "prophet" is reinforced by the specificity of Sacvan Bercovitch's argument that "the long foreground of Emerson the prophet" is not so much Unitarianism as "the legacy of the colonial Puritan fathers."[38] I would only add: and, for that matter, the legacy of the Anglo-American evangelical fathers and mothers in concert with Anglo-American empiricism.

On November 21, 1834, Emerson wrote in his journal: "When we have lost our God of tradition and ceased from our God of rhetoric then may God fire the heart with his presence."[39] This entry exemplifies his doctrine of what Robinson calls "the God within": Emerson argued, in 1831, that because "God is with us and in us," we should "hold [our] own nature in reverential awe."[40] But "the God within" is not so much either entirely original or largely Unitarian as it is largely consistent with the reliance of Wesley and Edwards on immediate revelation. Wesley's last words, after all, were: "The best of all is, God is with us"; and he would not have objected to the addition: "and in us." Such an addition would be consistent with the doctrine of God's indwelling Spirit. Although Emerson ceased from the second God, that is, "our God of rhetoric," or what Bloom identifies as "the political clerics and the clerical politicians,"[41] he never gave up his search for the first God, "our God of tradition," the God of the Bible. Although Barbara Packer and Karen

Kalinevitch argue that the Higher Criticism of the Bible drew Emerson away from supernaturalism and although Robinson argues that Emerson's resulting antisupernaturalism received special encouragement from the Unitarian community, I argue, to the contrary, that Emerson often found supernaturalism even in the Bible.[42] I argue, in particular, that the third God of Emerson's prayer, the God who "fire[s] the heart with his presence," and in whom Emerson most fully believes, is specifically the Holy Spirit.

Although Emerson is no controversialist, and although his relation to the Calvinist/Arminian controversy is complex, his thought leans to the Arminian side. Robinson, despite his emphasis on Unitarianism, speaks especially clearly of the Arminianism in Emerson's evangelical background:

> In reaction against the Great Awakening of the 1740s, a liberal party emerged in the Puritan churches and attempted to accommodate the prevailing orthodoxy to the pressures of change. The liberals, Arminian in their theology, found certain aspects of Puritan Calvinism repugnant, especially the doctrine of God's determining omnipotence and its conflict with a belief in the freedom of the human will. The Calvinist stress on human depravity combined in a frightful way with the image of an absolute God whose will had determined that depravity and whose purity demanded that it be punished.[43]

"The Emerson family," Phyllis Cole demonstrates, was "uniformly pro-Awakening," not only "in the era of Edwards and Whitefield" but also for long afterwards,[44] and what she does not argue, but what is clear from what she quotes, is that the family was largely pro-Arminian. Emerson's grandfather, the Reverend William Emerson (1743–76) of Concord, Massachusetts, favored such Arminian language as the following (albeit from his sermon "On the Death of [the Calvinist] Mr. W[hitefiel]d" [1770]): "Now my hearers, ye who have been so happy as to experience the sensible presence of the blessed God, know that 'tis high Joy on Earth, that is the most lively Emblem of Heaven. . . . God is the center of the Soul's Happiness."[45]

Robinson remarks that "Emerson's Calvinist Aunt Mary Moody Emerson stood as a constant reminder to him of what the drift of modern liberalism stood to lose."[46] But in what Cole quotes of Mary Moody

Emerson's thousand-page, fifty-three-year-long spiritual journal or "Almanack," I find Arminianism. Although, in her words, she "premise[s] [God's] electing love" and "was taught & received the full terrors of Calvinism," she was "yet never terrified."[47] Instead, she "sympathized with the joys of the vulgar—I trod on air—I danced to the music of my own imajanation."[48] Emerson's debt to Mary Moody Emerson is especially clear from a journal entry of 1837, in which he pays tribute to her for being "a saving counterforce" (Cole's phrase) against Harvard's "levitical education" (Emerson's phrase):

> I cannot bear the young men whose theological education is exclusively owed to Cambridge and to public institutions without feeling how much happier was my star which rained on me influences of ancestral religion. The depth of the religious sentiment which I knew in my Aunt Mary imbuing all her genius & derived to her from such hoarded family traditions, from so many godly lives & godly deaths of sainted kindred at Concord, Malden, and York, was itself a culture, an education. . . . In my childhood Aunt Mary herself wrote the prayers which first my brother William & when he went to college I read aloud morning & evening at the family devotions, & they still sound in my ears with their prophetic & apocalyptic ejaculations. Religion was her occupation, and when years after, I came to write sermons for my own church I could not find any examples or treasuries of piety so high-toned, so profound, or promising such rich influences as my remembrances of her conversations and letters.[49]

It would be hard to overemphasize the importance of this passage as justification for the view that Emerson's evangelical roots are at least as important as his Unitarian roots.

What Cole says of the relation between Emerson's evangelical and his Unitarian backgrounds is not quite true, that "Harvard early declared itself against Awakening religion."[50] As Daniel Walker Howe has shown, even Harvard Unitarians "were more than participants in the Second Great Awakening; they were among its pioneers."[51] In the light of Howe's study, what Robinson sees as the two-sided coin of Emerson's Unitarian self-culture is the same as the Calvinist/Arminian tension in his evangelical culture; Emerson, "a believer in unity who still recognized duality," was also

> a believer in perfection who saw his own imperfections with painful clarity. While much of his early preaching stressed the possibilities of moral and spiritual progress, his journal entries in the same period recorded many messages of frank and unflattering self-analysis, or of despair at what he felt was personal failure—a failure always heightened by his counterpointing faith in human progress through the culture of the soul.[52]

Calvinism, accordingly, occurs in Sermon 45; although Emerson "labeled as an 'extravagance' Samuel Hopkins's [Calvinist] theory of a 'disinterested love of God,' a love so strong that it could content the soul 'to perish forever' for God's glory and the benefit of the universe," Emerson was nonetheless attracted to Hopkins's idea of "utter self-abnegation as the ultimate moral act" (Robinson's paraphrase): "There is something so generous and sublime in [the theory's] absurdity," writes Emerson, "that good men will forgive it."[53]

As William G. McLoughlin has shown, Calvinism gradually declined during the Second Great Awakening, due in no small measure to efforts by the Unitarians.[54] Although Joseph Stevens Buckminster and Andrews Norton in biblical scholarship and W. E. Channing and Henry Ware, Jr., in moral philosophy "did not reject the fact of evil or of limitation, or overlook the grimmer aspects of life," they argued, nonetheless, that "life was best seen as a trial, or probation, in which certain intrinsic powers of human nature were given the chance to develop and thrive."[55] Arminians on the theology faculty at Harvard countered the Calvinists at Andover Seminary, and by 1823, "it was depressingly clear to the Calvinist leader Lyman Beecher that much of Boston and eastern Massachusetts had been lost."[56] In 1825, in "The Faith Once Delivered to the Saints," Henry Ware, Jr., Emerson's predecessor in the pulpit of the Second Church, attacked Beecher's sermon of that same title (1823), arguing, in particular, that the individual "neither virtuous nor vicious, neither holy nor sinful" develops "reason and conscience" "to exalt and purify his spiritual nature" and that life is "a moral or spiritual proving ground" that "counters election" (cf. the possibility that Keats's doctrine of the Vale of Soul-Making is anti-Calvinist).[57]

Emerson's Sermon 14 (1828) argues that "the recent progress of religion had consisted in overcoming the Calvinist denigrations of human potential."[58] This argument echoes the as much Arminian-evangelical as Unitarian and indeed the Arminian-evangelical *because* Unitarian "Unitarian Christianity" (1819) of W. E. Channing.

> Calvinism tends to discourage the timid, to give excuses to the bad, to feed the vanity of the fanatical, and to offer shelter to the bad feelings of the malignant. By shocking, as it does, the fundamental principles of morality, and by exhibiting a severe and partial Deity, it tends strongly to pervert the moral faculty, to form a gloomy, forbidding, and servile religion, and to lead men to substitute censoriousness, bitterness, and persecution, for a tender and impartial charity.[59]

Philip Gura argues that Emerson's indebtedness to Unitarianism was in the realm not of doctrine but of exegetical principles,[60] but I would point to the continuation in Emerson's sermons of doctrines as much Unitarian as Arminian-evangelical, namely, postbiblical prophecy, "the God within," millennial expectation, and, clearly not least, the "spiritual sense."[61] Robinson observes that the "moral sense" of Emerson and the Unitarians demands such "pious dedication, fervent belief, and continual self-sacrifice" that it rivals "anything devised by the Puritans."[62] This, I suggest, is because their "moral sense" derives not just from the Scottish moralism of Francis Hutcheson (1694–1746) and the Scottish Commonsense philosophy of Thomas Reid (1710–96) and Dugald Stewart (1753–1828) but especially from the "spiritual sense" of British as well as American Puritan-evangelicals.

Criticism of Emerson includes little that can be called philosophically theological criticism. Michael complains that Robinson "mutes the violence of the rupture between Emerson and the Unitarians" and worries that, in Robinson's view, the "continuities" between Emerson and the Unitarians "explain away Emerson's rebellion."[63] Even Michael, however, acknowledges that those continuities "define" Emerson's rebellion. Robinson's summary of Emerson's theology, despite its only implicit recognition of the evangelical overtones in Unitarian faith, deserves full quotation here; it is consistent with my view of Emerson's theology as philosophical.

> The importance of Emerson's connection with the tradition of liberal theology represented by New England Unitarianism is . . . essential to a just

> portrait of his career. Because he was nurtured in a tradition which affirmed human potential, he could reject confining and damaging barriers, but could stand on firm ground to do so. He could rebel without being a rebel, for his revolutionary gestures were affirmative ones, and were not without precedent.[64]

My philosophically theological approach to Emerson's works allows for such a summary, for although his rebellion against theology was partially philosophical, his rebellion does not finally preclude philosophical theology, that is, empirical-evangelical methodology.

A Biographical Overview

Emerson's now fully available journals reveal, among other things, his thorough familiarity with Locke's philosophy. Required reading at Harvard, for example, was *An Essay concerning Human Understanding,* a text in the curriculum for his sophomore year (1818–19).[65] With obvious intent to maintain his ownership of the *Essay,* he recorded, on June 10, 1821, his loaning of volume 2 to "Hill."[66] Still under the influence of the Harvard curriculum in February 1829, he borrowed an unspecified volume by Locke from a library.[67] So knowledgeable was he of Lockean procedure that from the beginning of his journals he adopted Locke's system of indexing.[68]

On April 4, 1820, Emerson observed that in the turn-of-eighteenth-century split between "the Ancients" and "the Moderns," Locke belonged with "the Moderns."[69] Emerson does not mean, of course, that Locke is finally like such another "Modern" as Descartes, for a journal entry of 1821 quotes, approvingly, Locke's antirationalist, antideductionist, and hence fully characteristic remark that "Human Reason never yet from unquestionable principles or clear deductions made out an entire body of the law of nature."[70] Van Leer observes that "in the rationalist preoccupation with the clear and distinct idea of mathematical certainty," the philosophy of idealism took on "the uncertain, finally skeptical, tone that characterizes modernity"; for "Descartes redefined idealism, previously the doctrine of a supernatural world of permanence, in terms of subjectivity"; and "philosophical inquiry," therefore, "shifted from ontology to epistemology, the being outside to the ideas within."[71] Indeed, if Descartes did not pass on to Locke and Emerson an at least residual aspiration to mathematical certainty, he bequeathed to them "the ideas within," epistemology, subjectivity, and skeptical modernity, but Locke and Emerson did not finally share Descartes's deep suspicion of sense experience.[72]

Emerson, knowing full well that reason tempers Locke's sensationalist epistemology, specifically regards empiricism not as rationalist but as decidedly rational or reasonable. Although Emerson's "College Theme Book" for 1822 includes, significantly, the "ancient maxim of philosophy" that "there is nothing in the understanding which was not previously in the sense," the theme book goes on to observe that "the great improvement of *modern* philosophy" is expressed by the addition of the phrase "except the understanding itself."[73] The credit for this "improvement," Emerson adds, belongs to both Leibniz and Locke.[74]

"Newtons, Bacons, & Lockes," wrote Emerson in 1824, are not "bred," but made, for they "owe their development" to a particular kind of environment, that is, not to "shops & stables," but to "universities."[75] Thus Emerson not only recognizes but also seems in agreement with Locke's embrace of the tabula rasa, his distinguishing emphasis on nurture over nature. On August 18, 1828, in an entry especially predictive of the best of Emerson's journal insights, he indicated that in both origin and continuing flavor his own experientialist bias was strongly Lockean:

> Keep a thing by you seven years, and you shall find use for it. You will never have waste knowledge. I like the sentence of Locke: "that young men in their warm blood are often forward to think they have in vain learned to fence if they never show their skill in a duel."[76]

What one has learned, Emerson and Locke imply, will pay unexpected dividends.

The Emerson of the early 1830s thought that such a mind as Locke's outweighs many nations. On September 4, 1830, Emerson wrote that

> there are some kingdoms of Europe whose whole population for ages does not possess an equal interest with some single minds. The history of John Locke or of Isaac Newton is a far more important part of the stock of knowledge we carry out of the world, than the whole history of Poland or Hungary.[77]

(Cf. Carlyle's *On Heroes, Hero-Worship, and the Heroic in History.*) On November 30 of that year, Emerson wrote cryptically, but clearly enough, that "one mind may hold Europe in Counterpoise: Locke & Poland."[78]

As for the influence of Locke, his philosophy only just began its international sway toward the end of the eighteenth century. As Emerson wrote on November 15, 1836, "The book & its direct influence on my mind, are one fact, but a more important fact is the verdict of humanity upon it, a thing not suddenly settled, &, in the case of great works, not for an age. Not until the French Revolution, is the character of Locke's Essay on the Human Understanding finally determined."[79] (Cf. Carlyle's *The French Revolution.*) Here, then, is an empirical, and even English, reason for Emerson's experiential identification with the French-Revolutionary spirit of the early 1790s. "If there is any period one would desire to be born in," he writes in *The American Scholar,* "is it not the age of Revolution; when the old and the new stand side by side, and admit of being compared; when the energies of all men are searched by fear and by hope; when the historic glories of the old, can be compensated by the rich possibilities of the new era?"[80]

In his *History of the United States* (1834–75), George Bancroft observed that "the huge world has at last come round to Roger Williams, George Fox, William Penn; & time-honored John Locke receives kicks"; and on October 2, 1837, Emerson responded with pleasure to this statement by Bancroft.[81] But when, on November 11, 1841, Emerson wrote that "Locke thinks for thousands just as much as Clay or Cushing at Washington vote for thousands,"[82] he not only made a statement about the representative nature of every thinker but also associated Locke's characteristic activity with representative democracy in general and the United States in particular.

In 1849, Emerson lamented that in leaving out the unconscious mind, Locke had left out much: "Dreams make dreadful revelations & leave Locke and Hegel little to tell you."[83] Thus Emerson may be said to have engaged in pre-Freudian exploration of the unconscious. As he observed on January 15, 1835, "Proud may the bard be among his fellow men, but when he sits waiting his inspiration he is a child, humble, reverent, watching for the thoughts as they flow to him from their unknown source."[84] On November 28, 1836, he wrote of Edward Taylor that Taylor's "unconscious instinct" is his "nucleus or point of view, & this defies science &

eludes it."[85] Consider, in this connection, Carlyle's own exploration of the unconscious in *Characteristics* (1831):

> The fever of Scepticism must needs burn itself out, and burn out thereby the Impurities that caused it; then again will there be clearness, health. The principle of life, which now struggles painfully, in the outer, thin and barren domain of the Conscious or the Mechanical, may then withdraw into its inner sanctuaries, its abysses of mystery and miracle; withdraw deeper than ever into that domain of the Unconscious, by nature infinite and inexhaustible; and creatively work there. From that mystic region, and from that alone, all wonders, all Poesies, and Religions, and Social Systems have proceeded: the like wonders, and greater and higher, lie slumbering there; and, brooded on by the spirit of the waters, will evolve themselves, and rise like exhalations from the Deep.[86]

One thinks of Tennyson's "The Kraken" (1830) as a perhaps ironic, but nonetheless striking, parallel to such explorations, for the kraken lies "battening upon huge sea worms in his sleep, / Until the latter fire shall heat the deep" (cf. Revelation 16.3–9 and 13.1), and then, "once by man and angels to be seen, / In roaring he shall rise and on the surface die."

On October 27, 1827, Emerson wrote that "in experience, the narrowness of intelligent citizens irresistibly suggests the material hypothesis of mental acts, as of 'channels often worn' of Locke, or, of the ruts of wheels. How many good people who can never understand a joke, or a trope, but remain staunch literalists after having been joked & poetised & musicized & rhetorized for eighty years."[87] Here, Emerson objects to Locke because he seems, if not humorless, then drearily "behaviorist." Emerson is anything but antiludic.

In 1853, Emerson associated the literal-mindedness of what Blake called "Single vision & Newtons sleep" with Locke's vision: "No idealist is or was in England; Locke and Paley rule,—men without horizon, without second sight."[88] Again in 1853, Emerson identified Locke's very nationality as a possible condition of his unfortunate fixedness, his inability to maintain what Blake called "double vision" or the combination of "outward" and "inward Eye":

> The English mind now is superstitious before facts, facts. They make a great ado about a truth. The oldest musstiest formularies we expect from them,

> and find; no deep apercu, no all binding theory, no glimpse of distant relations, & the *quoddam vinculum* [i.e., certain chain]. There is poor-smell, & learned trifling, & Locke instead of Berkeley.[89]

(Cf. the "Mechanical" in Carlyle's *Signs of the Times.*) By 1854, accordingly, Emerson decided that he preferred Bacon to Locke,[90] and, in 1856, in *Literature,* he discounted Locke once more.[91]

Even for the Emerson of the 1850s, though, Locke's greatness associates itself with, even as it rivals, the greatness of England, for on April 23, 1852, Emerson wrote that "there is not a country or a town in England, but has yielded its contingent of worthy men, in old or in new times, to the country & the race," and "Chaucer Spenser Hooker Taylor Dryden & Locke" closely follow "Shakespeare Newton Milton Bacon" in order of importance.[92] Emerson's praise of Bacon's mix of ideal and actual during the 1850s sounds like Emerson's earlier, recurring, implicit, and explicit praise of Locke, for although Locke is "the influx of decomposition" ("Bacon and the Platonists" are the influx of "growth"), even "the influx of decomposition" is necessary: "Bacon held of both; of ideas in his genius, as of English trade, in his politics."[93] One may conclude that in Emerson's usual description of Locke, Locke himself "held of" both "decomposition" and "growth," that is, both actual and ideal, for during the 1850s, as well as before, Emerson always completely understands, always grasps the importance of, and even often embraces certain key Lockean tenets.

Emerson's evangelical cast of thought, for its part in the journals, is evident, first, in the experiential nature of his identification with Jonathan Edwards. According to Perry Miller, Edwards regarded the world as "dynamic" and was "filled with the presence of God, quickened with divine life, pervaded with joy and ecstasy."[94] Although Miller thus overlooks Edwards's Calvinism and makes him too much of an early transcendentalist, he understands Edwards's Arminian/experiential and hence sufficiently pre-Emersonian mode. Emerson praises Edwards's "able & skillful statements" as early as October 5, 1823.[95] By "able & skillful statements," Emerson clearly means Edwards's characteristic heart-religion; this is consistent with Miller's emphasis and with the first chapter of this book.

In 1824, Emerson placed Edwards among "the great men of our second [apostolic] age."[96] In 1828, in Sermon 26, Emerson described the religious affections as the distinguishing element of the religious character. "Religion," the sermon argues, requires that "you give your affections to God" in a continuous act of pietistic devotion.[97] The "intense religious experience" that came to Emerson in 1830–31 is surely more than casually comparable to the "sweet inward burning" that Edwards had "delighted in describing."[98]

On January 22, 1834, Emerson wrote that "Luther & Napoleon are better treatises on the Will than Edwards's," for "men have more heart than mind."[99] Emerson objected, in other words, to Edwards's rationalistic view of the will, which, after all, deemphasized the experiential faith otherwise emphasized in Edwards's tenets. Even here, however, Emerson implicitly distinguishes between the generality of "men" and men like himself. *He* would presumably cultivate mind as much as heart, and Edwards's balance of heart and mind, therefore, would appeal more to Emerson than the one-sided, if mighty-hearted, will of either Napoleon or Luther.

Young man Emerson, in 1824, listed Edwards among the Puritans who can be said to have "settled N. America."[100] Thus theology and philosophical theology have their civilizing influences. More importantly for my triangle of philosophy, religion, and literature, however, is that the same young Emerson rated Edwards higher *as a writer* than, strange to say, Benjamin Franklin.[101] The styles of Franklin and Edwards are so very different as hardly to bear any comparison at all. Edwards's, to say the least, is far less readable. One can readily imagine the effect of Wesley's editorial pen on the following passage from Edwards's *Religious Affections:*

> But certainly our obligation to love and honor any being, is in some proportion to his loveliness and honorableness, or to his worthiness to be loved and honored by us; which is the same thing. We are surely under greater obligation to love a more lovely being, than a less lovely; and if a being be infinitely lovely or worthy to be loved by us, then our obligations to love him, are infinitely great: and therefore, whatever is contrary to this love, has in it infinite iniquity, deformity, and unworthiness. But on the other hand, with respect to our holiness or love to God, there is not an infinite worthiness in that. The sin of the creature against God, is ill-deserving and hateful in

> proportion to the distance there is between God and the creature: the greatness of the object, and the meanness and inferiority of the subject, aggravates it. But 'tis the reverse with respect to the worthiness of the respect of the creature to God; 'tis worthless, and not worthy, in proportion to the meanness of the subject. So much the greater the distance between God and the creature, so much the less is the creature's respect worthy of God's notice or regard. The great degree of superiority, increases the obligation on the inferior to regard the superior; and so makes the want of regard more hateful: but the great degree of inferiority diminishes the worth of the regard of the inferior; because the more he is inferior, the less is he worthy of notice, the less he is, the less is what he can offer worth; for he can offer no more than himself, in offering his best respect; and therefore as he is little, and little worth, so is his respect little worth. And the more a person has of true grace and spiritual light, the more it will appear thus to him; the more will he appear to himself infinitely deformed by reason of sin, and the less will the goodness that is in his grace, or good experience, appear in proportion to it. For indeed it is nothing to it: it is less than a drop in the ocean: for finite bears no proportion at all to that which is infinite. But the more a person has of spiritual light, the more do things appear to him, in this respect, as they are indeed. Hence it most demonstrably appears, that true grace is of that nature, that the more a person has of it, with remaining corruption, the less does his goodness and holiness appear, in proportion to his deformity; and not only to his past deformity, but to his present deformity, in the sin that now appears in his heart, and in the abominable defects of his highest and best affections and brightest experiences.[102]

Wesley, in fact, omitted the passage, but the passage, to put it mildly, is a diverting instance of Edwards's prolixity. For Emerson to have admired Edwards's writing, his admiration of Edwards's thought must have been great indeed.

An other-than-Edwardsean example of the link between theology and literature shows, again, Emerson's experiential identification with evangelical thought. On December 28, 1830, Emerson praised the Reverend Edward Thompson Taylor (1793–1871), pastor of Seaman's Bethel in Anne Street, Boston, by calling him "that living Methodist[,] the *Poet* of the Church."[103] Thus in Emerson's thinking, another evangelical personage is associated with high literary standards. Despite the fact that Taylor is Arminian while Edwards is Calvinist, the fact that both are *eloquent* evangelicals is enough for Emerson.

Emerson's sermons exemplify the transition from *les bonnes lettres* to *les belles lettres*. Leonard Neufeldt shows that Emerson realized the full literary dimension of his homiletical tradition,[104] and even after October 1832, when he resigned his pulpit at Boston's Second Church (the church of Increase and Cotton Mather), he continued to preach. Robinson shows that until the moment of Emerson's resignation, his ministry at the Second Church was a positive experience: "Emerson found in his pastorate an opportunity for expression that was vital to his development."[105] "That he eventually left his ministry," Robinson continues, "is in some respects a measure of how much he was able to grow there." From 1835 to 1837, Emerson preached regularly in the Unitarian church in East Lexington (later called the Follen Church).[106] In a letter to his brother William, Emerson explained that in preaching "I aspire always to the production of present effect thinking . . . . For a strong present effect is a permanent impression."[107] After hearing him preach often, Emerson's brother-in-law William Kent, of Concord, New Hampshire, described Emerson as a "man of force & popular address."[108]

Far from being "a preacher with a *narrow* literary appeal" (my italics), Emerson, like Wesley, was "an effective orator for a large class of people."[109] It might even be said that, also like Wesley, who was literarily the rival of Franklin, Emerson was an effective *evangelical* preacher.[110] Henry Ware, Jr., called the Second Church by the Wesleyan name of "Society."[111] As for *what* Emerson preached, it was not the less "evangelical" for being broadly literary and intellectual, for Unitarian sermons in general, as Robinson points out, were literary, learned, rational, and emotional, and they included both "appeals to the affections" and "artful use" of such rhetorical devices as illustration, and such poetic devices as metaphor.[112]

The evangelical cast of Emerson's journals is evident, too, in his experiential identification with John Wesley, or, at least, with what Wesley stood for. As Wesley himself would have done, for example, Emerson objected to emotional excess and excessive narrowness among nineteenth-century Methodists. On March 1, 1827, Emerson recorded a report from North Carolina of "monstrous absurdities of Methodist enthusiasm there, how they barked like dogs on all fours and '*treed Jesus*.'"[113] On September

17, 1840, he compared undue sentimentality to a "maudlin Methodist or Moravian."[114] On October 6, 1850, he resisted the common tendency to think that the "idea of God ends in a paltry Methodist meetinghouse."[115] Emerson is listed (along with William H. Pope and Amos Goodwin) in the Harvard commencement program for 1821 as a participant in "A Conference 'On the Character of John Knox, William Penn, and John Wesley.'"[116] Whatever Emerson might have said on this occasion, which ran the gamut from Scots Calvinism to the much more open-ended experience-theology of both the classical Quaker and the chief Methodist-Arminian, Emerson wrote on April 26, 1834, almost at variance with his own recurrent opposition to fanatical enthusiasm among the Methodists, that "a religion of forms is not for me: I honor the Methodists who find like St. John all Christianity in one word, Love."[117] The Arminian tenor of this statement links it with Wesleyan, as opposed to Calvinist, Methodism.

Emerson resembles Wesley, moreover, in the territorial boldness of his preaching, which continued not only as preaching per se but also in the form of lectures at lyceums throughout New England.[118] Just as "the world" was Wesley's "parish,"[119] so New England was Emerson's, for although neither his lecturing nor his preaching was exactly extramural, an air of itinerancy, and hence the field-preaching spirit of Wesley himself, hovered near the high "romance" of Emerson's wide-wandering proclamations. By "romance," I allude to William Hazlitt's account of the as much evangelical as Unitarian, if not evangelical *because* Unitarian, preaching of Coleridge:

> A poet and a philosopher getting up into a Unitarian pulpit to preach the Gospel, was a *romance* [my italics] in these degenerate days, a sort of revival of the primitive spirit of Christianity, which was not to be resisted.
>
> It was in January, 1798, that I rose one morning before day-light, to walk ten miles in the mud, and went to hear this celebrated person preach. . . . [I]t seemed to me, who was then young, as if the sounds had echoed from the bottom of the human heart.[120]

Emerson's journals, finally, are not only by turns but also at once empirically philosophical and evangelically theological. He acknowledges, to be sure, that his is a more religious than philosophical temperament, for in 1824, in a mood to explore what to do in life, he observed that he was not a "Reasoning Machine" like "Locke & Clarke & David Hume," and that he could not write either "an Essay of Hume" or, for that matter, a "Butler's Analogy."[121] Somewhat against the grain of his religious temperament, however, he admitted in the same year that since "Locke may . . . be true," "every system of religion yet offered to man" may be "wholly false."[122] Thus Emerson knows the difference between faith and philosophy and recognizes the threat of Locke's philosophy to faith of any kind, but rather than reject either his own personal faith or Locke's particular philosophy, he seeks to bring them together, for the same entry announces his devotion both to "those inexplicably curious cords that fasten us to matter" and to "the analysis of those high relations which unite us to God." He wants his "grasp" on both "heaven & earth" to be "tenacious," and he finds his model for such grasp in the mix of empiricism and evangelicalism, for as though religious method belongs to sense-based reason he speaks of spiritual experience as a "strong impulse" acting upon us from without (cf. the objective usage of *impulse* by both Wesley/Edwards and Locke).

The journals of Emerson find exemplars of empirico-religious method among evangelicals other than Wesley and Edwards. On November 3, 1830, he defined Methodist enthusiasts, along with Quaker and Swedenborgian enthusiasts, not as fanatics but as "they who have [legitimately] attained . . . to the *perception* of God" (my italics).[123] This formulation is perhaps as far from fanaticism as it is possible for religious formulations to get, for these enthusiasts' perceptions, presumably, lay no claim to private or exclusive spiritual communion but, by the nature of all perceptions, remain potentially verifiable by the natural as well as the spiritual perceptions of others. He adds that the one thing lacking to make the enthusiasts "*wise* devout men, Newtons, Fenelons, Channings" is the training of "all their *intellectual* powers" (Emerson's italics).

On May 27, 1840, when the Reverend Edward Thompson Taylor, perhaps at Emerson's invitation, spoke to the Transcendental Club, Emerson described him as a philosophical theologian, that is, as an experiential thinker at once decidedly of this world and otherworldly. A "Mover" and a "Power" and a man of taste, learning, emanation, eloquence, "prodigious nature," efficiency, and "earnest impassioned action," Taylor, above all, is one whose "deeps of love and wisdom" culminate in "the *beauty* of his nature" (Emerson's italics).[124] "This hardfeatured, scarred, & wrinkled Methodist[,] whose face is a system of cordage[,] becomes whilst he talks a gentle[,] a lovely creature."[125] Emerson concludes that "I felt in a higher degree the same happiness I have formerly owed to that man's public discourses, the exhilaration and cheer of so much love poured out through so much imagination." Taylor was "philosophy speculating on his own breath."

On September 4, 1842, Emerson compared Bronson Alcott's "natural clearness of spiritual sight" with the spiritual sense of "my Methodist Tarbox," a laborer with whom Emerson had worked in the fields during the summer of 1825.[126] Tarbox had helped Emerson to "understand prayer."[127] In midsummer 1848, Emerson paid specific tribute to Tarbox's combination of natural religion and spiritual vision: "I still return, or did last night, to the eulogy of those natural priests who . . . have yielded us some token of having read the laws of heaven—beginning as usual with my poor churl Tarbox at Newton. . . . [He] is the outcropping of the granite which is the core of the world."[128] Emerson adds that "I seem to meet no more such." If 1848 was the *terminus ad quem* of such people, if few embodiments of the empirically evangelical outlook lasted thereafter, Emerson himself kept faith with that model of reality, even beyond the empirical-evangelical, more Late Romantic than Victorian, height (1827–43) of Thomas Carlyle's career.

Nature

According to one early reviewer, "*Nature* is not a Christian book but one influenced by a range of idealistic philosophies, ancient and very modern, Transcendentalism being merely the latest name for an old way of thinking."[129] Among the "modern" idealistic philosophies that influence it, that of Berkeley, according to Gay Wilson Allen, is decisive.[130] Idealistic philosophy, indeed, may be so central to *Nature* that, as Joel Porte has argued, a flat denial of matter's worth, and hence of the worth of sense experience, is its central theme.[131] Buell, while hardly finding *Nature* an orthodox book, emphasizes its continuities with Unitarianism,[132] but those who take a religious approach to Emerson do not generally pay much attention to it: Neufeldt, though exploring a vaguely biblical sense of prophecy in Emerson, argues that *Nature* is not the centerpiece of his career.[133] *Nature,* I argue, not only arrays idealistic philosophies alongside material ones but also draws sympathetically on the Christian-moral interpretation of life: I will highlight the pure empiricism of *Nature*'s materialist perspective and draw out the specifically evangelical quality of its Christian-moral view. More than exclusively idealistic, if not sometimes almost Christian, *Nature* employs empirical/evangelical strategies within its actual-ideal language, and thus it puts forward a unique set of insights on which Emerson bases the ingenious but cohesive variations of his subsequent career.

Jonathan Bishop, though regarding *Nature* as "our primal book," treats it only in parts; Bloom, referring to its "inadequate chapters," discusses it little; Whicher, despite comprehensive sympathy for Emerson, regards *Nature* as stiff, overelaborate, and irrelevant; and Warner Berthoff, correctly I think, "find[s] the awkwardness simply that of a novice author that in no way reflects on his intellectual project."[134] The empirical/evangelical approach to *Nature* reaffirms its centrality in the Emerson canon.

Barbara Packer, while examining *Nature* thoroughly, sees its "confusion of voices" as a problem to be explained,[135] but an attempt to eliminate the division of signs to achieve "harmony" may well preclude the possibility of knowledge or expression.[136] I see not so much a collapse of opposition between *Nature*'s empiricism and its evangelicalism as a proliferation of meaning that results from the juxtaposition of the two and the exploration of their interaction. It is "impossible," as Michael observes, "to subsume so eccentric a text as *Nature* completely into the paradigm of any preexisting system, and [Gay Wilson] Allen rightly uses Berkeley's name . . . more to approximate the peculiar brand of ideal theory Emerson presents in his book than to refer to any metaphysical scheme discoverable outside it."[137] Without losing sight of the eccentricity of *Nature,* however, I subsume much of the book into an empirical-evangelical paradigm that allows for the *fröhliche Wissenschaft* of multiple perspectives. This formative work of Emerson's thought and practice, while eschewing harmonization pure and simple, seeks the strange harmonization of empirical philosophy with evangelical faith.

Several of the modern as well as ancient philosophies highlighted by *Nature* are thoroughly idealistic. Emerson alludes to Plato's allegory of the cave: "Nature is a great shadow pointing always to the sun behind us"

(851). If there is no *contemptus mundi* in chapter 6, there is an almost antiempirical stance: "[Idealism] beholds the whole circle of persons and things, of actions and events, of country and religion, not as painfully accumulated, atom after atom, act after act, in an aged creeping Past, but as one vast picture, which God paints on the instant eternity, for the contemplation of the soul" (851). Emerson concludes that "the soul holds itself off from a too trivial and microscopic study of the universal tablet" (851); "it respects the end too much, to immerse itself in the means," for "it is a watcher more than a doer, and it is a doer, only that it may the better watch" (851). The decidedly Cartesian cast of *Nature*'s idealism entertains so little doubt of the cogito as to doubt the senses: "Idealism acquaints us with the total depravity between the evidence of our own being, and the evidence of the world's being. The one is perfect; the other, incapable of any assurance" (852). Emerson's reason, like Kant's, is specifically "the intuitive power of the mind":[138] "Man is conscious of a universal soul within or behind his individual life, wherein, as in a firmament, the natures of Justice, Truth, Love, Freedom, arise and shine. This universal soul, he calls Reason: it is not mine or thine or his, but we are its; we are its property and men" (834–35).

The most suggestive guide to the philosophic influences that Emerson accepts, however, is his memorable formulation: "Broad noon shall be my England of the senses and the understanding" (830). This formulation more than merely recalls Locke's reliance on sense-based reason. Locke's *Essay concerning Human Understanding* focuses on the senses, is quintessentially British, and preaches that much, if not all, knowledge is to be acquired through the sort of waking consciousness suggested by "broad noon." "'What we know,'" quotes Emerson, "'is a point to what we do not know'" (840). Although Bishop Joseph Butler and Sir Isaac Newton said this,[139] Descartes first pointed out that we search for what we cannot doubt, not in order to rest content, but to build up doctrine anew. What Emerson admires in Descartes, therefore, may not be his idealism, his serenities of mathematical certainty, so much as his bequeathal to England, and thence to America, of the method of radical skepticism. *Nature*'s various idealisms may be more heuristic than primary, for in aiding Emerson's quest to find out what, if anything, lies beyond nature, they indicate his spirit of inquiry, rather than any necessary predisposition against nature on his part. Despite his reputation as an idealist, he is steeped in, and enamored of, the precepts and processes of a clearly Lockean empiricism.

Several of his most characteristic tenets are Lockean in expression, if not in direct origin. Hume hovers near Emerson's principle that "our dealing with sensible objects is a constant exercise in the necessary lesson of difference, of likeness, of order, of being and seeming, of progressive arrangement" (839). (The phrase "constant exercise" recalls Hume's "constant conjunction," which means both that events are merely successive and that the apparent order or causation of events emanates only from mind or imagination.) The empiricism of Emerson, however, is usually less subtle and more robust. A common phrase for Locke's assumptions of tabula rasa and the importance of nurture is "the rise and progress of,"[140] and this eighteenth-century phrase is Emerson's phrase, too: "It were a wise inquiry for the closet to compare, point by point, especially at remarkable crises in life, our daily history, with the rise and progress of ideas in the mind" (858). Thus Emerson's version of tabula rasa reflects the Lockean underpinning of Wordsworth's correlations of external circumstances with internal developments.[141]

The correlation of daily observation with the rise and progress of ideas takes on an especially Lockean character in the exact terminology with which Emerson traces the path from sensation to reflection: "Every property of matter," he writes in chapter 5, "is a school for the understanding,—its solidity or resistance, its inertia, its extension, its figure, its divisibility" (839). "The understanding," he continues, "adds, divides, combines, measures, and finds everlasting nutriment and room for its activity in this worthy scene." Such confidence in correspondence between mind and matter rests on the Lockean subscription to primary qualities as rock-solid reality. Locke said that solidity or resistance, inertia, extension, figure, and divisibility are independent of perceptions and hence something to perceive.

Emerson's understanding of Lockean method as harbinger of and accompaniment to Lockean doctrine informs his sweeping definition of nature: "Nature, in its ministry to man, is not only the material, but is also the process and the result" (828). Emerson, that is, shares the inductive temperament for which Locke is the obvious progenitor. Despite his idealistic animadversions against the painful accumulation of atom after atom, Emerson's "dealing with sensible objects" is a "constant exercise in the necessary lesson of . . . ascent from particular to general" (839). He accordingly declares that man "acts [his condition] as life, before he apprehends it as truth" (825). His truth, like Keats's, is "proved on the pulses."

Experience, in *Nature,* leads to knowledge. Practical knowledge, or science and "the useful arts," inspires this heartfelt rhapsody: "Open any recent journal of science, and weigh the problems suggested concerning Light, Heat, Electricity, Magnetism, Physiology, Geology, and judge whether the interest of natural science is likely to be soon exhausted" (840). Such a thumbnail history of empiricism from Newtonian optics to Lyellian earth science entails particular awareness of Robert Fulton's technology: "[Man] no longer waits for favoring winds, but by means of steam, he realizes the fable of Æolus's bag, and carries the two and thirty winds in the boiler of his boat" (828).

In *Nature* 3, with its description of and meditation on a January sunset, experience is rich, despite, if not because of, its being both preverbal and nonverbal:

> The western clouds divided and subdivided themselves into pink flakes modulated with tints of unspeakable softness; and the air had so much life and sweetness, that it was a pain to come within doors. What was it that nature would say? Was there no meaning in the live repose of the valley behind the mill, and which Homer or Shakespeare would not re-form for me in words? (830)

Such direct contact with, if not immediate impact on, extracultural, fundamental reality, does not completely disappear even after *Nature*'s return to the "artificial" constructs of domesticity and language. In addressing the reader with an all but Marxist understanding of what Marx called "actual life processes,"[142] Emerson exults that "man and woman, and their social life, poverty, labor, sleep, fear, fortune, are known to you" (857). He points out, for good measure, that this paracultural as well as cultural reality exceeds anything expressed in literature, for it amounts to the "true poetry" of a "fact" (857).

The most fully Lockean theme of *Nature*'s experience-philosophy is its emphasis on perception. "The simple perception of natural forms," declares *Nature* 3, "is a delight" (829), but "perception," Emerson knows, is not always "simple." "Ideas," according to Locke, are not only "Perceptions in our Minds" but also "modifications in the Bodies that cause such Perceptions in us."[143] They are not only independent mental entities (Locke scatters Cartesian insights throughout his *Essay*) but also the products of shaping forces. Reality appears to the reader of the *Essay* as a balance between mind and matter or, to borrow from M. H. Abrams's analysis of the "greater Romantic lyric,"[144] as an "interpenetration" or "coalescence" of subject and object, for Lockean ideas are not only objects themselves but also clarifications of the world. Colin Clarke, pointing out that "assumptions about the mind and its place in nature are concealed in every act of perception," adds that "we take it for granted, merely by perceiving or being aware, that the given world both is and is not extrinsic to our selves."[145] It is "implied" in "perceptual experience," Clarke thinks, that "the place of mind in the natural world is equivocal, or a paradox." He argues that "a more or less latent awareness of this paradox, a feeling for the ambiguity and strangeness of perception, a largely unconscious perplexity in fact, was the 'cause' of some of Wordsworth's finest poetry," and some of the finest parts of *Nature,* similarly, derive from that same cause, except that Emerson's perplexity is conscious and his awareness patent.

Consider, for example, his analysis of perceptual strangeness. Any "small alteration in our local position," he observes, "apprizes us of a dualism":

> We are strangely affected by seeing the shore from a moving ship, from a balloon, or through the tints of an unusual sky. The least change in our point of view, gives the whole world a pictorial air. A man who seldom rides, needs only to get into a coach and traverse his own town, to turn the street into a puppet-show. The men, the women,—talking, running, bartering, fighting,—the earnest mechanic, the lounger, the beggar, the boys, the dogs, are unrealized at once, or, at least, wholly detached from all relation to the observer, and seen as apparent, not substantial beings. What new thoughts are suggested by seeing a face of country quite familiar, in the rapid movement of the rail-road car! . . . Turn the eyes upside down, by looking at the landscape through your legs, and how agreeable is the picture, though you have seen it any time these twenty years! (845–46)

Emerson uses these particular cases to suggest "the difference between the observer and the spectacle,—between man and nature" (846). He sometimes responds to the difference by elevating observer over spectacle: "Hence arises a pleasure mixed with awe; I may say, a low degree of the sublime is felt from the fact, probably, that man is hereby apprized, that, whilst the world is a spectacle, something in himself is stable" (846). Another part of the strangeness of perception, however, is the perspective by which the given world is, or appears to be, not only extrinsic to the self but also greater than the self. Emerson's famous announcement that "I become a transparent eye-ball" is in one way an egregious example of the egotistical sublime: "The currents of the Universal Being circulate through *me; I* am part or particle of *God*" (827; my italics). In context, though, the announcement assumes the humble stance by which self subserves perception of not-self: "I am *nothing*. I *see all*" (827; my italics). Thus the transparent eye-ball harks back to Keats's "Negative Capability."

"Emerson's fantastic introjection of the transparent eye-ball as bodily ego," writes Harold Bloom, "seems to make thinking and seeing the same activity."[146] The subjective and objective dimensions of *Nature*'s theme of perception, accordingly, require further attention, both separately and in relation to one another.

Emerson, as one might expect of a Transcendentalist, at times focuses on the subjective dimension alone. "As the eye is the best composer," he writes, "so light is the first of painters" (829); thus, even where speaking of a particular sense, Emerson can be so subjective as to suggest that even sense, to say nothing of imagination, is creative, or that eye projects and extends mind. Although Emerson acknowledges that "we are now so far from the road to truth, that . . . speculative men are esteemed unsound and frivolous," he retains confidence that speculation, the power of mind alone, will "find a theory of nature" (825). In this confidence, he can sound as flatly mentalistic as where he concludes that "whenever a true theory appears, it will be its own evidence" (825).

Whence comes this subjectivity? From Cartesian philosophy? From a rationalism arguably French? Descartes's mentalistic view that sense experience is unreal may indeed inform Emerson's poignant portrait of "man and nature":

> We are as much strangers in nature, as we are aliens from God. We do not understand the notes of birds. The fox and the deer run away from us; the bear and the tiger rend us. We do not know the uses of more than a few

> plants, as corn and the apple, the potato and the vine. . . . Yet this may show us what discord is between man and nature. (853)

The mathematical bent of Descartes's rationalism, moreover, informs Emerson's illustrations of pure theory:

> The astronomer, the geometer, rely on their irrefragable analysis, and disdain the results of observation. The sublime remark of [Leonhard] Euler [1707–83; Swiss mathematician and physicist] on his law of arches, "This will be found contrary to all experience, yet is true;" had already transferred nature into the mind, and left matter like an outcast corpse. (849)

Emerson's subjectivity, however, derives from his empirical tradition as well as from Continental (or ancient) idealistic philosophies, and is closer to Berkeley's subjectivity, if not to Locke's, than to Descartes's. "He that has never doubted the existence of matter," wrote A. R. J. Turgot, "may be assured he has no aptitude for metaphysical inquiries." Although these words of the eighteenth-century French economist sound Cartesian enough (Turgot is the author of a Cartesian proof of the existence of God) and although Emerson quotes these words in *Nature* (849), Emerson, for his part, is acutely aware that such doubt emanates more nearly from Berkeley, for *Nature* 6 argues that what "philosophy does for Berkeley," religion does "for the unschooled," namely, "It puts an affront upon nature" (850). An early reviewer observed that *Nature* denies "the outward and real existence of matter" with the specific, indispensable help of "the Berkeleyan system."[147] Berkeleyan categories, then, abound in *Nature,* but for purposes of entertaining the reconcilability of *Nature*'s subjectivity with its empiricism, it is important to remember that neither Berkeley nor Emerson denies the existence of matter so much as each rejects the esoteric sophistication of science and materialism. Emerson gets this Berkeleyan distinction just right in chapter 7, where he concludes that "idealism saith: matter is a phenomenon, not a substance" (852), that is, accessible, not obscured. For Emerson as for Berkeley, the denial of matter is a starting point, "a useful introductory hypothesis, serving to apprize us of the eternal distinction between the soul and the world" (852).

"Idealism," moreover, "sees the world in God" (851). "The question of the absolute existence of nature, still remains open" so long as "we acquiesce entirely in the permanence of natural laws." Emerson concludes, as does Berkeley, that "God never jests with us," that is, that we can trust the witnesses of our sensation and reflection that nature is solid and real. "So long as the active powers predominate over the reflective," writes Emerson, "we resist with indignation any hint that nature is more short-lived or mutable than spirit" (845). He declares, too, that "day and night, river and storm, beast and bird, acid and alkali, preexist in necessary Ideas in the mind of God, and are what they are by virtue of preceding affections, in the world of spirit" (838). This is to say, in the language of subject-object interaction, that object is present as subject predominates.

At times, subject all but obliterates matter: speaking of any given definition by either Aristotle or Plato, Emerson remarks, boldly, that "a spiritual life has been imparted to nature," that is, that "the solid seeming block of matter has been pervaded and dissolved by a thought" (848). At other times, subject seems to elide nature or brush it off and make short work of it, in haste to merge or claim kinship with the divine Subject: "The intellect searches out the absolute order of things as they stand in the mind of God, and without the colors of affection" (832), that is, without the emotions arising from, or modified by, sense experience. Mind, lest it be overwhelmed by the objective minutiae of experience, must take care in empirical enterprises to preserve its own prerogatives, for "empirical science is apt to cloud the sight, and, by the very knowledge of functions and processes, to bereave the student of the manly contemplation of the whole" (853). A proper relation of subject to object, then, is *S–o,* for as Emerson implies at length, consciousness is not solipsistic, but lordly:

> From the child's successive possession of his several senses up to the hour when he saith, 'thy will be done!' [cf. Matthew 6.10 and 26.42] he is learning the secret that he can reduce under his will, not only particular events, but great classes, nay the whole series of events, and so conform all facts to his character. Nature is thoroughly mediate. It is made to serve. It receives the dominion of man as meekly as the ass on which the Saviour rode [cf. Matthew 21.25]. (841)

Consistent with a more Lockean than Berkeleyan language of empiricism, however, Emerson's relation of subject to object includes, too, a high degree of the objective, and so may be denominated *s–O.* A seemingly subjective formulation, such as "That which was unconscious truth, becomes, when interpreted and defined in an object, a part of the domain of knowledge,—a new amount to the magazine of power" (839), is finally objective in view of the operative phrase, "when interpreted and defined in an object." Mere subjectivity may be impotent and useless apart from contact with an objective world independent of, if not prior to, mind. "Have mountains, and waves, and skies," asks Emerson rhetorically, "no significance but what we consciously give them, when we employ them as emblems of our thoughts?" (837). Quite apart from either how we relate to mountains, waves, and skies or how we force them into our molds, they have significance in themselves. Because of the inviolate autonomy, the identity, and the character of externalities, their reality may precede and reach out to us, for the subject can be shaped, determined, by the object.

Nowhere, perhaps, is this shaping more evident than in the striking series of illustrations by which Emerson suggests that the nonhuman, exclusively inanimate world of nature is the source of all that is best and most human, most spiritual, about us:

> The axioms of physics translate the laws of ethics. Thus, "the whole is greater than its part;" "reaction is equal to action;" "the smallest weight may be made to lift the greatest, the difference of weight being compensated by time;" and many the like propositions, which have an ethical as well as physical sense. These propositions have a much more extensive and universal sense when applied to human life, than when confined to technical use. (837)

The axioms of physics emerge as important or real both in their dimension of vague analogy to human morals and, by their *proportional* analogy to those morals, in themselves.

Besides *s–O* or *S–o,* finally, subject and object in *Nature* may be schematized *s–o* or *S–O.* In this germinative product of Emerson's imagination, subject and object make up more than a one-sided relationship, for they make up, as well, a balance, a fully two-way interpenetration or coalescence. *Nature* acknowledges at once the independence of the objective world and the unreality of sense experience:

> To the senses and the renewed understanding, belongs a sort of instinctive belief in the absolute existence of nature. . . . Things are ultimates, and they

> never look beyond their sphere. . . . [T]he animal eye sees, with wonderful accuracy, sharp outlines and colored surfaces. . . . [But] the first effort of thought tends to relax this despotism of the senses, which binds us to nature as if we were a part of it, and shows us nature aloof, and, as it were, afloat. (845)

Even "the absolute existence of nature" depends, paradoxically enough, on "instinctive belief" and "the renewed understanding," as well as on "the senses." Truth in *Nature,* then, lies neither in the objective alone nor in the subjective alone, but in both perspectives at once and equally. "Man and nature," according to the combined operation of the understanding and the senses, "are indissolubly joined," and "when the eye of Reason opens," that is, when intuition accurately apprehends the apprehensible, then to the "outline and surface" of things are "at once added, grace and expression" (845). "These proceed from imagination and affection," from the subjective faculty and the subjective behavior most mixed with the objective world (845), and this mixture amounts to a synthesis, a third, ultimate reality, a blend or union called not just sense experience or sense perception but, more capaciously, a "more earnest vision" (845).

Perhaps the best single indication of this subject-object blend is an especially inclusive sentence of *Nature* 8: "Nor has science sufficient humanity, so long as the naturalist overlooks that wonderful congruity which subsists between man and world; of which he is lord, not because he is the most subtile inhabitant, but because he is its head and heart, and finds something of himself in every great and small thing, in every mountain stratum, in every new law of color, fact of astronomy, or atmospheric influence which observation or analysis lay open" (854). (Cf. Coleridge's "all things both great and small" in "The Rime of the Ancient Mariner" and Carlyle's frequently iterated view of science-and-the-scientist.) Humans find themselves not by looking within, but by looking outward, and the outside world of cold, hard science, in turn, is humanized. The objective is subjective, the subjective is objective, and all distinction or dualism is collapsed in monistic interpretation of the mind's role in nature.

Precisely in its vigorous empiricism and not just in its subjective indulgences, e.g., "I am part or particle of God," *Nature,* one must admit, can seem foolish at best and, at worst, dangerously wrongheaded. It is one thing for Emerson to indulge his near-positivist, but reasonable and apparently sufficiently grounded, epistemological optimism:

> Undoubtedly we have no questions to ask which are unanswerable. We must trust the perfection of the creation so far, as to believe that whatever curiosity the order of things has awakened in our minds, the order of things can satisfy. (825)

It is quite another, indefensible, thing for him to embrace the definition of nature as "essences unchanged by man; space, the air, the river, the leaf" (825). These very "essences," to say the least, have changed and are indeed at risk of destruction. "For modern readers," writes Herschel Parker, "there is inescapable pain at Emerson's confidence that wild nature is inexhaustible and invulnerable and at the undreamed-of consequences of the belief that nature is created for man's benefit."[148] Richard Poirier's recent comment that "Emerson's proverbial wisdom is an embarrassment to us" is apropos.[149] It reflects two classic demurrers, namely, Yvor Winters's attack on Emerson's "shallow optimism and insufferable smugness" and Quentin Anderson's fulminations against his "individualism" as the "expression of a lamentably infantile and socially retrograde personality."[150] Emerson's perceptually sophisticated, but finally too-untroubled, empiricism seems especially misplaced, if not embarrassing, in the light of William McKibben's powerful recent study of "the end of nature."[151]

Nature, however, holds up at least as well as Emerson's maturer works,[152] for its conception of subject-object interaction is not only sophisticated in its time but also presages the theory of "gene-culture coevolution" developed by Harvard biologist (and former Southern Baptist) E. O. Wilson.[153] "All lower culture," and such higher culture as "religion and ethics," are alike, according to *Nature,* "in degrading nature and suggesting its dependence on spirit" (850), and according to *Nature,* too, "motion, poetry, physical and intellectual science, and religion, all tend to affect our convictions of the reality of the external world" (850). This subjective emphasis, however, is balanced, as in such works of Carlyle's as *On History* and *Signs of the Times,* by *Nature*'s most eloquent, best-sustained passage that heralds objective reality:

> But I own there is something ungrateful in expanding too curiously the particulars of the general proposition, that all culture tends to imbue us with

> idealism. I have no hostility to nature, but a child's love to it. I expand and live in the warm day like corn and melons. Let us speak her fair. I do not wish to fling stones at my beautiful mother, nor spoil my gentle nest. I only wish to indicate the true position of nature in regard to man, wherein to establish man, all right education tends; as the ground which to attain is the object of human life, that is, of man's connexion with nature. (850)

Eric Cheyfitz argues that "Emerson's own thwarted drive to unite with and to put on the eloquent power of the Father" leads him by means of "a violent movement of transgression, reduction, and expulsion" to cast out nature, "the beautiful mother," from his system,[154] but this famous passage seems nonetheless eloquent for Emerson's resistance to transgression of his "beautiful mother," and the appeal of the passage seems timeless, is timely, because Emerson's words anticipate other-than-psychological, other-than-nineteenth-century, for example, sociobiological, concerns.

Nature holds up, too, for its remarkable juxtaposition of subject-object empiricism with experience-theology, that is, with an idealism not so much Berkeleyan, an idea-ism not so much Lockean, as evangelical. (The episcopate of Berkeley evinced proto-evangelical qualities: Berkeley's practical charity was in decided contrast to the negligence of some of his fellow bishops.)[155] Emerson's tone, if I may bracket for the moment the question of whether the juxtaposition results in synthesis, is evangelically homiletical. The former preacher is more Calvinistic than Arminian-Unitarian in his lament over times when "duplicity and falsehood take place of simplicity and truth" and when "simplicity of character and the sovereignty of ideas is broken up by the prevalence of secondary desires, the desire of riches, the desire of pleasure, the desire of power, the desire of praise" (836). Emerson, responding to a fallen world, or at least to a desecrated nature, is fully evangelical in his appeal to conversion-remedy: "The problem of restoring to the world original and eternal beauty, is solved by the redemption of the soul" (857). Even Emerson's most personal, albeit secular, description of his own relation to nature clearly echoes the larger evangelical understanding of conversion as a sudden change wrought in the soul by something greater than the self: "The waving of the boughs in the storm, is new to me and old. It takes me by surprise, and yet is not unknown. Its effect is like that of a higher thought or a better emotion coming over me, when I deemed I was thinking justly or doing right" (827).

The evangelicals emphasized immediate revelation, and *Nature* seems to carry their emphasis to a logical extreme. "Why should not we have . . . a religion by revelation to us," asks Emerson, "and not the history of [foregoing generations]" only? (824–25). His understanding that "the sun shines to-day also" (825) harmonizes with the evangelical understanding that the Holy Spirit operates in the present. Just as the I-felt-my-heart-strangely-warmed formulation of Wesley, despite its reference to time and place, implies direct access to God, so Emerson's belief that "man has access to the entire mind of the Creator" (852) rests on a view of divine experience as explicitly unmediated: "Spirit does not act upon us . . . in space and time, but spiritually, or through ourselves" (852).

Evangelical religion is of the here and now, and an "intercourse with heaven and earth," similarly, becomes part of the "daily food" of Emerson's "lover of nature" (826). Emerson has religious reasons for being interested in the animal kingdom—"How much industry and *providence* and *affection* we have caught from the pantomime of brutes?" (842; my italics)—and for being interested in health—"What a searching *preacher* of self-command is the varying phenomenon of Health!" (842; my italics). His interest in both the animal kingdom and health may derive from such this-worldly evangelical phenomena as Wesley's kindness to animals (he tended to think that they had souls) and Wesley's ministry to the physical needs and welfare of his flock. Emerson's view of intersubjective reality, that is, his faith in friendship as one of life's great blessings, is expressed in the this-worldly evangelical idiom of religious affections, as well as in explicitly theocentric language reminiscent, say, of the emphasis on friendship in the Book of Ecclesiastes:

> We are associated in adolescent and adult life with some friends, who, like skies and waters, are coextensive with our idea; who, answering each to a certain affection of the soul, satisfy our desire on that side; whom we lack power to put at such focal distance from us, that we can mend or even analyze them. We cannot chuse but love them. . . . [M]uch intercourse with a friend has supplied us with a standard of excellence, and has increased our respect for the resources of God who thus sends a real person to outgo our ideal. (844)

"Go out of the house to see the moon," declares Emerson, "an 't is mere tinsel; it will not please as when its light shines upon your necessary journey" (831). Only one who lives actively may read aright such lessons as can ever be known. The evangelical watchword of the here and now implicit in Emerson's metaphor of "your necessary journey" culminates in his elevation of the practical over the intellectual and of action over words:

> Central Unity is . . . conspicuous in actions. Words are finite organs of the infinite mind. They cannot cover the dimensions of what is in truth. They break, chop, and impoverish it. An action is the perfection and publication of thought. A right action seems to fill the eye, and to be related to all nature. (843)

Just as in evangelical parlance a lifetime of such action results in perfection or sanctification, so, in Emerson's view, experiential intensity points to millennial expectations. His idea of perfection is often linked to the ordinary times and places of life's middle journey: "Crossing a bare common, in snow puddles, at twilight, under a clouded sky, without having in my thoughts any occurrence of special good fortune, I have enjoyed a *perfect* exhilaration" (827; my italics). His most rhapsodic, most "evangelical" perfectionism, however, is reserved for the very last sentences of *Nature,* where traditional notions of the kingdom of God yield to a radical, but not less than spiritual, idea of kingdom come:

> As when the summer comes from the south, the snow-banks melt, and the face of the earth becomes green before it, so shall the advancing spirit create its ornaments along its path, and carry with it the beauty it visits, and the song which enchants it; it shall draw beautiful faces, and warm hearts, and wise discourse, and heroic acts, around its way, until evil is no more seen. The kingdom of man over nature, which cometh not with observation [cf. Luke 7.20],—a dominion such as is now beyond his dream of God,—he shall enter without more wonder than the blind man feels who is gradually restored to sight. (858)

What I see as Emerson's millennial/evangelical idea of kingdom come has been seen as the rhapsodic result of his Orphic aesthetic. Bloom's "Emerson: The American Religion" and R. A. Yoder's *Emerson and the Orphic Poet in America* focus on the last chapter of *Nature.*[156] "Orpheus," wrote Emerson in 1849, "is no fable: you have only to sing, and the rocks will crystallize; sing, and the plant will organize; sing, and the animal will be born."[157] Whether Orpheus is understood as both "devoted to Apollo" and "partly turned against Dionysus" or as associated with both Empedocles and Thracian shamanism, Orphism is centered on what Bloom calls a "belief in the latent divinity and immortality of the human soul" and on a necessity for "constant purity, partly achieved through *ekstasis*."[158] As Bloom also points out, however, the Christianized Orpheus emerges from the Florentine Renaissance mythology of Ficino. Robinson, in *Apostle of Culture,* argues that Emerson's "Orphic voice" of "detached authority, tinged with an aura of mysticism," is "closely associated" with his preaching, "taking from the sermon the air of authority and techniques of exposition."[159] Thus the Orphic Emerson and the evangelical Emerson are more complementary than at odds. The "proto-evolutionary implications" of Emerson's Orphic "metamorphosis," moreover, though "often overstated," are "undeniable,"[160] and this particular complexity of *Nature,* the scientifically religious or what I call empirically evangelical complexity of it, is the most inclusive, most defining virtue of it.

Nature's juxtaposition of empiricism with evangelicalism modulates into synthesis. The very sequence of the chapter titles, from "Nature" (narrowly considered), through "Commodity" (or usefulness), "Beauty," "Language," and "Discipline" (or practical rules of conduct), to "Idealism" (or the Berkeleyan denial of matter), "Spirit," and, clearly not least, "Prospects," which attempts to unify all these themes, duplicates the continuum that joins scientific method and rational empiricism to both natural and revealed religion. If the Emersonian, "empirical-evangelical" continuum should seem too sweeping, the Emerson of *Nature* does not shrink from such sweep, for he searches for nothing less than "a true theory" that "will explain all phenomena" (825). Not for him is the timid view that such admittedly difficult topics as "language, sleep, dreams, beasts, sex" are "not only unexplained but inexplicable" (825). Almost nothing would seem to lie outside the purview of America's "primal book," the scope of which is especially evidenced by its ambitious capacity as an empirical-evangelical book.

The natural pole of *Nature*'s natural-spiritual continuum is so refreshingly carefree as completely to lack the evolutionary anxieties that one finds as early as Keats's "Epistle to John Hamilton Reynolds" (1818). Here is the "Epistle":

> . . . '[T]was a quiet eve,
> The rocks were silent, the wide sea did weave
> An untumultuous fringe of silver foam
> Along the flat brown sand; I was at home
> And should have been most happy,—but I saw
> Too far into the sea, where every maw
> The greater on the less feeds evermore.—
> But I saw too distinct into the core
> Of an eternal fierce destruction,
> And so from happiness I far was gone.
> (Lines 89–98)

Here, contrastingly, is *Nature:*

> Therefore is nature glorious with form, color, and motion, that every globe in the remotest heaven; every chemical change from the rudest crystal up to the laws of life; every change of vegetation from the first principle of growth in the eye of a leaf, to the tropical forest and ante-diluvian coal-mine; every animal function from the sponge up to Hercules, shall hint or thunder to man the laws of right and wrong, and echo the Ten Commandments. (841)

(Note the development of Psalm 19.) Such a view is possible for the young Emerson because he does not as yet discover any disjunction between nature and religion, between the world of experience and the realm of traditional, to say nothing, for the moment, of immediate, revelation: "Therefore is nature always the ally of Religion: lends all her pomp and riches to the religious sentiment. Prophet and priest, David, Isaiah, Jesus, have drawn deeply from this source" (841).

Nature's nature, moreover, as well as being proportionate with the Bible, is commensurable with the theism that lies at, or around, the midpoint of its empirical-evangelical continuum. Where Emerson remarks, rather complacently, that "nature always wears the colors of the spirit" (828), *Nature* appears to evince a Platonic view, but where the monograph adds that "there seems to be a necessity in spirit to manifest itself in material forms" (838), Emerson implies that material forms provide much more accessibility to ultimate reality than Plato says they do, and where *Nature* concludes that "spirit is present" both "behind nature" and "throughout nature" (852), Emerson implies the theistic,

Lockean-Wesleyan-Edwardsean compromise between Deism and pantheism. "The foregoing generations," he observes in his introduction, "beheld God and nature face to face; we, through their eyes" (824); but adding what is perhaps the most urgent question in *Nature,* namely, "Why should not we also enjoy an original relation to the universe?" (824), he implies from the outset that God and nature are different but intimately interinvolved, and he calls immediately for the interinvolvement of humankind and Creator/creation.

Nature's nature, finally, is the setting for spiritual encounters of an immediate kind. Emerson speaks of a "general *grace* suffused over nature" (829; my italics). An especially striking counterpart to his intriguing insight that "intense light" and the "infinitude which it hath" "make all matter *gay*" (829; my italics) is found in Charles Wesley's "On the Corpse of a Believer," in which Charles, too, finds the unlikeliest matter unmediating, transparent, revelatory:

Ah! lovely Appearance of Death!
No Sight upon Earth is so fair:
Not all the *gay* pageants that breathe
Can with a dead Body compare.

With solemn Delight I survey
The Corpse, when the Spirit is fled,
In love with the beautiful Clay,
And longing to lie in its stead. (My italics)[161]

These lines may be ghoulish, but Emerson similarly exclaims that "even the corpse hath its own beauty" (829), and both the essayist and the hymn writer are perhaps less morbid than full of beatitude in that their gaiety, their all but comedic illumination, "transfigures all that dread."[162]

Conclusively empirical-evangelical is Emerson's suggestion of radical congruency between natural and spiritual experience: "The stars awaken a certain reverence, because though always present, they are always inaccessible; but all natural objects make a kindred impression, when the mind is open to their influence" (826). *How* the mind is thus open, that is, the burning question of epistemology, nicely complicates Emerson's continuum. Emerson, like Locke, celebrates the senses, but like Locke, too, he recognizes their limitations, their preoccupation with minutiae: recall his warning that "empirical science is apt to cloud the sight" (853). On the other hand, "a distinct but most poetical sense in the mind," built up from the senses and hence related to them, is reliably at work whenever "the wisest man" receives wisdom from "the flowers, the animals, the mountains" (826). On at least three occasions, *Nature* implies that the physical senses are at best only analogues to an exclusively mental kind of spiritual perception:

> We say the *heart* to express emotion, the *head* to denote thought; and *thought* and *emotion* are, in their turn, words borrowed from sensible things, and now appropriated to spiritual nature. . . . [M]an is an analogist, and studies relations in all objects. . . . Meantime, Reason . . . perceives the analogy that marries Matter and Mind. (834, 835, 839)

In one of his most comprehensive apothegms, however, one which allows for the physical senses as windows onto spiritual truth, Emerson implies that the physical senses themselves participate in spiritual experience: "The lover of nature is he" whose spiritual and natural kinds of experience are of a piece, "whose inward and outward senses are still truly adjusted to each other" (826).

An early reviewer of *Nature,* by writing that *Nature*'s main theme is the "spiritual eye," may have meant that Emerson's exclusively sensuous experience either encounters or is proportionally analogous to the noumenon.[163] Where Emerson writes that nature "always speaks of Spirit," always "suggests the absolute," and is "a perpetual effect" (851), and where he observes that "a correspondent revolution in all things will attend the influx of the spirit" ("So fast," he adds, "will disagreeable appearances, swine, spiders, snakes, pests, mad-houses, prisons, enemies vanish" [858]), he teaches that the senses perceive, or apprehend, a Priority in the here and now. Where he writes that "the noblest ministry of nature is to stand as the apparition," the visible state, "of God" (851), or that nature is "the present expositor of the divine mind" (853), or that "the world proceeds from the same spirit as the body of man" (853), he teaches that the senses attend, wait upon, the manifestations of God. Where he writes that "a true theory of nature and of man . . . should contain somewhat progressive" (851), or that "we can see God in the coarse and, as it were, distant phenomena of matter" (851), or that "all things with which we deal, preach to us" ("What is a farm," he asks, "but a mute gospel?" [842]), or that "this moral sentiment which thus scents the air, and grows in the grain, and impregnates the waters of the world, is caught by man and sinks into his soul" (842), he teaches that the senses both manifest spirit and are harbingers of millennium.

This understanding of the correspondence between inner and outer derives in part from the philosophical theology of Swedenborg,[164] for Emerson declares both that "it is not words only that are emblematic; it is things which are emblematic" and that "every natural fact is a symbol of some spiritual fact" (834). One hears here, though, a tone of weary predictability, and hence of Emerson at his least original. The empirical-evangelical, subject-object formulations of *Nature* are distinctive as well as distinct. Empirical advances—e.g., "The economic use of fire, wind, water, and the mariner's needle; steam, coal, chemical agriculture; the repairs of the human body by the dentist and the surgeon"—all constitute only such "resumption of power, as if a banished king should buy his territories inch by inch, instead of vaulting at once into his throne" (856). "Meantime," however, "in the thick darkness, there are not wanting gleams of a better light,—occasional examples of the action of man upon nature with his entire force" (856). These actions spring from "an instantaneous instreaming power" (857), like the power described by testifiers to enabling moments of immediate revelation. The best way for one to "vault" into his or her "throne," to master yet merge with nature, is to invest one's energies of both sense-based reason and spirit in such generally experiential and specifically evangelical goals and phenomena as "the abolition of the Slave-trade," "the miracles of enthusiasm," "prayer," and "religious and political revolutions" (856). As for the especially evangelical cause of abolition, Emerson got on the antislavery bandwagon late, but enthusiastically, for he was "driven out of his study and into moral prophecy" by Daniel Webster's support of the Fugitive Slave Law,[165] but *Nature* strongly prefigures this active support of abolition.

Emerson's list of "empirical"-evangelical goals and phenomena includes, besides "the abolition of the Slave-trade," "the miracles of enthusiasm," "prayer," and "religious and political revolutions," the phrase "the history of Jesus Christ" (*Nature*, 856). This phrase reflects the Higher Criticism's quest for the historical Jesus. Robinson argues, accordingly, that Emersonian Christology is determinedly antisupernatural (this would make it plausibly "empirical").[166] Emerson believes, as Robinson puts it, that "the moral character of Jesus established the supernatural quality of the miracles, rather than vice versa," and Wesley T. Mott, too, de-emphasizes the supernatural in Emerson's understanding of Christ. Emerson believes, as Mott paraphrases him, that Jesus is "not perhaps a savior in the conventional sense," but "the great model of moral growth."[167] Mott admits, however, that Sermon 5 does not quite reject the supernatural nature of Christ, who, as the sermon puts it, "sits at the right hand of God" and "shall acknowledge you before his Father in Heaven." Despite John Michael's emphasis on Emerson's skepticism, even Michael points out that *The Lord's Supper* "preserves the authority" of Jesus as a "glorified friend."[168] This is quite evangelical, so that Emerson's Christology can be understood in the specifically evangelical, as well as the specifically "empirical," context of *Nature*.

The specifically evangelical tenor of *Nature*'s philosophically theological understanding of subject-object interaction looms especially large in the buoyant optimism of the experientialist, and even Arminian, assumptions of *Nature* 4: "This relation between the mind and matter is not fancied by some poet, but stands in the will of God, *and so is free to be known by all men*" (838; my italics). Even where Emerson waxes most Platonic, that is, where he says that we "ascend" into the region of "Ideas" (849), he does not abandon the hope of empirically knowing those "Ideas." "As objects of science," they are "accessible to few men" (849), but they are accessible to some people even *as* objects of science, for by speaking of "*touching* these divine natures" and by claiming that "Ideas" "renew the body" (849; my italics), Emerson discourses more than merely metaphorically. As a result, "we become physically nimble and lightsome": "we tread on air; life is no longer irksome, and we think it will never be so. . . . As it were, for the first time, *we exist*" (849; Emerson's italics). Although this experiential rhapsody is not far from the rarefied evangelical (as well as empirical) realm of Emerson's thought, *Nature* ends on a more tough-minded (yet still empirical-"evangelical") note. "The invariable mark of wisdom," writes Emerson, "is to see the miraculous in the common" (857). Writing, too, that "when a faithful thinker . . . shall . . . kindle science with the fire of the holiest affections, then will God go forth anew into the creation" (857), Emerson offers a sentiment that is Wesleyan-Edwardsean in particular, as well as evangelical in general, and Lockean as well as religious, namely, the triumphantly, faithfully, and epistemologically millennial sentiment.

Nature, then, is resoundingly of a piece. Its empirical themes of the tabula rasa, the physical senses, sense-based reason, the understanding, the waking consciousness, inductive method, radical skepticism, subject-object interaction, and nature-culture coevolution, and its evangelical themes of warm exhortation, personal conversion, immediate revelation, the religious affections, practical charity, moral action, spiritual perfection, and millennial expectation, are joined through its empirical-evangelical themes of Berkeleyan immaterialism, theistical natural religion, the doctrine of proportional analogy, and, clearly not least, the doctrine of the "spiritual sense." Thus experiential perspectives make up a unity of opposing perspectives, an empirical-evangelical synthesis that not only culminates the central dialectic of *Nature* but also anticipates the empirical-evangelical imagination upon which Emerson builds his literary universe.

Anglo-American Ground

Fate implies that England and the United States share a *Zeitgeist*. Emerson notes, first, a tendency within American cities to discuss "the theory of the Age": "By an odd coincidence, four or five noted men were each reading a discourse to the citizens of Boston or New York, on the Spirit of the Times" (330). Second, he points out that "in the same season, the subject had the same prominence . . . in London" (330). *Fate* specifically identifies this perennial Anglo-American sensibility as the "practical question of the conduct of life" (330). Not only *Fate* but also *Experience, The Poet, Self-Reliance, The Over-Soul, The Divinity School Address, The American Scholar,* and *Nature* indicate that concerns in England and the United States indeed run the gamut from the practical, empirical sensibility, to what I have shown is the similarly practical and similarly experiential sensibility of evangelicalism.

Emerson, of course, is far from always entertaining warm feelings toward the British. He complains in *Self-Reliance* that "it is [merely] for want of self-culture" that the "idol" of "England . . . remains for all educated Americans" (905). Such iconoclastic declarations of American independence abound throughout his writings.[169] He is often taken, therefore, as quintessentially, if not exclusively, American. Arguing that he is "the mind of our climate," Harold Bloom wittily observes that Emerson "has the peculiar dialectical gift of being precursor for both the perpetual New Left of student non-students and the perpetual New Right of preacher non-preachers."[170] Emerson's religious thought and influence are especially often understood as distinctively American: Sacvan Bercovitch goes so far as to say that what sets Emerson apart is his American resistance to European excess, that is, that while the Europeans, Carlyle included, are antinomian, Emerson is not.

> Carlyle's hero stands . . . a titan born to master the multitude. He is the Frankenstein's monster of left-wing Protestantism, part of a latter-day antinomian brotherhood that includes Shaw's Superman and Ibsen's Masterbuilder; Nietzsche's Zarathustra and Byron's exiled saint.[171]

Emerson cherishes, by contrast, moral restraint.

Emerson distances himself, however, from any exclusively American religion. Among founders of the relatively few U.S.-originated sects—Ellen Harmon White of the Seventh Day Adventists, Joseph Smith of the Mormons, Alexander Campbell of the Disciples of Christ, and Charles Taze Russell of the Jehovah's Witnesses—Mary Baker Eddy of Christian Science "seized on poor Bronson Alcott for an endorsement" of her "health and harmony" movement, but "the subtle Emerson had evaded her."[172] Thus Emerson keeps as far away as possible from such indigenous, pseudo-Emersonian creeds as "health and harmony" and "positive thinking." Among glaringly pseudo-Emersonian "Positive Thinkers" are Ralph Waldo Trine, author of *In Tune with the Infinite* (1897), and his descendants Harry Emerson Fosdick and Norman Vincent Peale, and the line of descent continues: see Pat Boone and Anita Bryant as themselves in the movie *Roger and Me* (1989). To such a "jumble," Bloom would add the "various Aquarian theosophies."[173]

As for exclusively American philosophy, Bloom, in one mood, declares Emerson "the principal source of the American difference in pragmatic post-philosophy."[174] Sharon Cameron argues that his "essentially physical or bodily ideas of identity" are what place him in a particularly American tradition of writers (her emphasis is on Melville and Hawthorne).[175] "Essentially physical or bodily ideas" and "pragmatic post-philosophy," however, are essentially empirical and hence as Anglo-American as American.

Leon Chai, comparing Emerson with Continental sources, links him to Goethe, Herder, the Schlegels, Schleiermacher, and Mme de Stael (it is odd to see Kant left out).[176] While acknowledging Emerson's differences from Continental figures, Chai emphasizes continuities. He is less concerned with "questions of national identity and the American consciousness" than with the "literary, philosophical, religious, and aesthetic issues" that Emerson shares with many of his distinctively French and German, and even a few of his British, precursors. His prominent place in Chai's general argument that nineteenth-century American literature not only transforms but also assimilates "the cultural legacy of European Romanticism" is both convincing and all too unusual in the current critical climate, which emphasizes Emerson's prominent place in exclusively American studies. Although interested in "Romantic science," however, Chai does not sufficiently stress Romantic religion, and he simply, and uncritically, accepts M. H. Abrams's assumption that such religion is always "secular."

Bloom, in another mood, implies the similarity between Emerson's religious vision and the religious dimension of British Romanticism. Bloom describes British as well as American Romantics as common heirs to "a severely displaced Protestantism," with the difference that while "British poets swerve from their precursors," American poets labor to "complete their fathers."[177] Bloom's last point applies to Emerson-the-Romantic-prose-writer's relation to both the British Wesley and the "poetic faith" of the British Romantics, but neither such American Romantics as Emerson nor the five British Romantic poets whom I treat swerve from their eighteenth-century evangelical precursors so much as they assimilate them into the collective Romantic faith of the Anglo-American world, and the Protestantism of eighteenth-century British and American evangelicals, though in one sense a lateral displacement of Locke's ideas of sensation into the epistemologically efficacious "spiritual sense," remains all the more Protestant, all the more individual-experiential, for that.

Phyllis Cole, in her detailed study of Emerson and England, concludes that his similarity to British sensibility does not significantly emerge until the 1850s, and is then sociological in nature and pessimistic in tone. "Conducting simultaneous and often comparative studies of England and America," Cole writes, "Emerson worked throughout the 1850s toward an understanding of modern society."[178] She shows how he feared that America would share England's fate of mechanization.

It is time, then, for a new look at Emerson's relation to England. What he says about England tends to reflect either one or the other pole of the empirical-evangelical continuum.

As for the empirical pole, *Fate* expresses Emerson's pride in the seafaring technology of his British heritage and implies that this technology is indeed one of England's particular gifts to the world: "Cold and sea will train an imperial Saxon race, which nature cannot bear to lose, and after cooping it up for a thousand years in yonder England, gives a hundred Englands" (344). (Recall Carlyle's *Chartism.*) *Nature,* using the exact terms of empiricism to pay perhaps the highest possible compliment to the mother country, not only divides the day according to nationalities—"The dawn is my America; the sun-set and moon-rise my Paphos . . . ; the night . . . my Germany of mystic philosophy and dreams"—but also decrees that "broad noon shall be my England of the senses and the understanding" (830). Thus the lucidity of sense-based reason boasts a particular national source.

As for the evangelical pole, *The Poet* declares that "the ancient British bards had for the title of their order, 'Those who are free throughout the world'" (937), and *The Poet* repeats the point emphatically: "They are free, and they make free" (937). The context, "I think nothing is of any value in books, excepting the transcendental and extraordinary. . . . [H]ere [i.e., in books] is a new witness" (937), suggests that the kind of freedom uppermost in Emerson's mind is not so much political as Arminian. *Witness* and *extraordinary* constitute distinctively evangelical diction.

Emerson's praise of America, too, employs empirical/evangelical terms. The combination of subject and object, creativity and induction, characterizes, for example, a fully empirical passage from *The American Scholar:* "In silence, in steadiness, in severe abstraction, let him [i.e., the distinctly *American* scholar] hold by himself; add observation to observation; patient of neglect, patient of reproach, and bide his own time,—happy enough if he can satisfy himself alone that this day he has seen something truly" (868). (Recall Teufelsdröckh's view of science in *Sartor Resartus.*) The American scholar must embody experience-philosophy precisely in order to grasp America's vast complexity: "So much only of life as I know by experience, so much of the wilderness have I vanquished and planted" (865). The American scholar's "soul," moreover, should be "free, sovereign, active" (863), that is, describable according to a

Wesleyan and Edwardsean, as well as Lockean, celebration of the spiritual as well as the practical, for "free, sovereign, active" is diction at once Arminian/Calvinist and experiential-empirical.

According to *Experience,* America conduces to conversion, to spiritual rebirth: "I am ready to die out of nature, and be born again into this new yet unapproachable America I have found in the West" (954). According to *Self-Reliance,* the ideal American lives an itinerancy filled with empirical as well as spiritual possibilities:

> A sturdy lad from New Hampshire or Vermont, who in turn tries all the professions, who teams it, farms it, . . . preaches, . . . and always, like a cat, falls on his feet, is worth a hundred of these city dolls. He walks abreast with his days, and feels no shame in not "studying a profession," for he does not postpone his life, but lives already. (903)

Both an "evangelical" SUBJECT and the empirical *object,* finally, coalesce in the conception of American art in *Self-Reliance:* "If the American artist will study WITH HOPE AND LOVE *the precise thing* to be done by him, considering the climate, the soil, the length of the day, the wants of the people, the habit and form of the government, he will create a house in which [beauty, convenience, grandeur of thought, and quaint expression] will find themselves fitted, and taste and sentiment will be satisfied also" (906; my italics and small capital letters).

Emerson thought England as natural a recipient of his empirical-evangelical message as America. He made his "first bid for a national and international reputation" by offering the text of *Nature* to "his circle of American and British friends," and *Nature*'s popularity in England persuaded many Americans to take him seriously "as a force in modern thought."[179] I would only add: and specifically in modern philosophical theology.

Emerson is interested in national character generally. As illustrated by a whole class of his lectures during the 1850s—e.g., *France, or Urbanity* (1854)—he gives weight to the "races" of France and Germany. (Cf. Carlyle's *Sartor Resartus* and *Voltaire.*) Sometimes, even when Emerson has worldly/religious characteristics in mind, he thinks of America in combination with countries other than England. In *Fate,* he writes, "Dante and Columbus were Italians, in their time; they would be Russians or Americans today" (347). In *The Divinity School Address,* he says, "All who hear me, feel, that the language that describes Christ to Europe and America, is not the style of friendship and enthusiasm to a good and noble heart, but is appropriated and formal" (879).

Also in *The Divinity School Address,* however, he remarks that "the Puritans in England and America" found scope not only for "their longings for civil freedom," but also for "their austere piety" (885). In *Fate,* he takes pride in granting privilege to the Anglo-American synthesis, which he, like many others, claims to be the highest result of natural selection.

> The population of the world is a conditional population; not the best, but the best that could live now. . . . We know in history what weight belongs to race. We see the English . . . planting themselves on every shore and market of America. (336)

(Note the disturbing parallel to the ethnocentrism in Carlyle's *Latter-Day Pamphlets.*) Thus, where Emerson mentions England and America together and by the implication of his separate mentions of them, he "perceives" their unity along empirical/evangelical, if not empirical-evangelical, lines.

Intra-Romantic Relationships

The empirical-evangelical perspective from which Emerson views England and the United States, and from which he reads and uses the English language, illuminates his relation to English-language Romanticism. My binational and as much philosophical as theological vantage point makes me swerve against Bloom's theological comment in "Emerson: The American Religion":

> But what if poetry as such is always a counter-theology, or Gentile Mythus, as Vico believed? Abrams, not unlike Matthew Arnold, reads religion as abiding in poetry, as though the poem were a saving remnant. But perhaps the saving remnant *of poetry* is the only force of what we call theology?[180]

The empirical-evangelical prose-poetry of Emerson's prime is Romantic not because it is an English-speaking world's abiding-place of religion alone, but because, like the empirical-evangelical prose-poetry of Carlyle's prime, it is a whole remaining force of that world's philosophical theology. The actual/ideal tension in Emerson's Later Romanticism is not only fully understandable, but also partially reconcilable, along clear lines of the "empirical-evangelical" vision in British High Romanticism, for the high quality of his writing parallels the High Romanticism of England, which is grounded, too, in the twin experiential traditions of empiricism and evangelicalism.

Thus the Romanticism of Emerson is at once late-but-not-belated and Anglo-American. L. J. Swingle's argument about British Romantic philosophy, that it is grounded in the rigorous-yet-constructive methodology of British skeptical tradition, carries theological as well as philosophical implications for my Carlylean-Emersonian view of Anglo-American Romanticism. Swingle's model follows Hume more than Berkeley or Locke, and one even catches a whiff of Derrida's skepticism from Swingle's refreshing interest in immediate historical contexts, for Swingle defines the skeptical component of British empiricism/Romanticism as "the propensity to see . . . polarities as differing so fundamentally at the axiomatic level that each becomes not merely a viable system unto itself but also a nearly unsolvable mystery to systems beyond itself."[181] Swingle's notion of skepticism, however, remains dynamic rather than static and sense-oriented rather than rationalistic, for while he declares that "the specter of enthrallment to single-minded perception haunts Romantic literary art" (49), he adds that "the literary artifact is designed to move the reader, in company with the artist, toward a free mental space beyond or between enthrallments through simultaneous invocations of competing enthrallments" (52). Swingle knows, too, that British Romantic skepticism is consistent with the "mild faith" (Shelley's phrase) of British Romanticism, for Swingle argues that despite the "nagging uneasiness or suspicion" and the "obstinate questionings of sense and outward things" that everywhere abound in British Romantic art,[182] the British Romantics nonetheless are "cautiously supportive of many of our most traditional, fundamental human values" and "inclined to grant or at least explore sympathetically various clusters of provisional truths" (72). Swingle concludes that British Romanticism lets "spirit and inward things emerge" (72), or, as he further paraphrases what may be the greatest discovery by the English Romantics, "It is only by touching the abyss that the soul comes to recognize its power" (77). I seek to explore the widest ramifications of Swingle's view,[183] for to pair representative works by Blake, Wordsworth, Coleridge, Shelley, and Keats with representative works by

Emerson is to link Romantic skepticism with Romantic faith and, by recalling, too, the Romantic *Carlyle's* skeptical faith, to link British with American Romanticism.

Any similarity between Emerson and Blake may add up to less than meets the eye. Although Blake's vow to create his own system sounds like Emerson's boast that "I had better never see a book than to be warped by its attraction clean out of my own orbit, and made a satellite instead of a system" (*The American Scholar,* 862), Emerson's submission to unstructured data—"Light unsystematic, indomitable, will break into my cabin" (*Self-Reliance,* 905)—goes contrary to Blake's well-known reliance on mind as world-conditioner. Blake's conception of the marriage of heaven and hell is perhaps less dismissive of the problem of evil than, say, the raw-Arminian, dualistic conception in Emerson's blunt statement that "of their own volition, souls proceed into heaven, into hell" (*The Divinity School Address,* 877). Neither Blake's conviction in *There Is No Natural Religion* (1788) and *All Religions Are One* (1788) nor Emerson's in *The Over-Soul* that "the spirit of prophecy" is "innate in every man" (911) places either Blake or Emerson in the most Lockean company of evangelicals, which embraces the tenet that nothing is innate.

Emerson and Blake, however, are finally similar, that is, deeply as well as broadly experiential in outlook. Although their mutual admiration for Emanuel Swedenborg may help to account for a certain Continental, abstract tinge to their works, Emerson admires Swedenborg mostly for the imagination with which he endeavors to engraft philosophy on "the popular Christianity of his time"; Swedenborg, according to *The American Scholar,* "saw and showed the connexion between nature and the *affections* of the soul" (873; my italics). This endeavor, as Edwardsean as Swedenborgian, may be said to constitute Emerson's own chief purpose as a writer. Blake's admiration for Swedenborg, short-lived, emphasizes him more as prophet than as philosophical theologian. Blake's purpose in writing, however, is not far from making a connection between the experientially philosophic and the popularly religious, and just as Blake's works seek to cleanse the doors of spiritual as well as natural perception, so Emerson's poet "unlocks our chains, and admits us to a new scene" (*The Poet,* 937).

The Divinity School Address teaches that Jesus "felt respect for Moses and the prophets; but no unfit tenderness at postponing their initial revelations, to the hour and the man that now is; to the eternal revelation in the heart" (879). In Blake's works, similarly, the "new kind of man"[184] is for, and in, the spirit of prophecy, which continues its grand march through him. Just as Blake's doctrine that "mercy has a human heart" ("The Divine Image" [1789]) discovers perhaps the most extreme of all Romantic apotheoses of humankind, so *The Divinity School Address* finds radical interidentifications among humankind, God, and Christ: "Would you see God," declares Emerson's Jesus, "see me; or, see thee, when thou also thinkest as I now think" (879).

The Over-Soul, acknowledging that "the influence of the senses" can overpower the mind, adapts some specific lines from Blake's "Auguries of Innocence" (1803?) to make the argument for a *spiritual* sense: announcing that "time and space are but inverse measures of the force of the soul," Emerson teaches that the human spirit "sports with time" and "can crowd eternity into an hour, / Or stretch an hour to eternity" (912). Even where Emerson and Blake are most spiritual, however, they remain in the world, for as Emerson puts it and as Blake's composite art indicates, the human form is "that singular form which predominates over," is superior to but has contact with, "all other forms," whether spiritual or natural (*Nature,* 843).

Consider the shared subjective mood of Emerson and Wordsworth: "If the Reason be stimulated to more earnest vision," declares Emerson, "outlines and surfaces become transparent, and are no longer seen; causes and spirits are seen through them" (*Nature,* 845). He adds: "The best, the happiest moments of life, are these delicious awakenings of the higher powers, and the reverential withdrawing of nature before its God." This is all but identical to the near-solipsistic subjectivity with which Wordsworth preaches, in book 6 of *The Prelude,* that greatness "make[s] abode" in us only "when the light of sense / Goes out," and "with a flash that has revealed / The invisible world" (lines 600–602).

Wordsworth lends experiential tenor to Emerson. What *Experience* states negatively, that "the pith of each man's genius contracts itself to a very few hours" (943), *Prelude* 12 states positively, that our "spots of time," though few, "retain / A renovating virtue" that "enables us to mount, / When high, more high, and lifts us up when fallen" (lines 208–10, 217–18). "Ode: Intimations of Immortality" (1802–4) renders its soberly experiential point no less tellingly for the familiarity of it:

The Youth, who daily farther from the east
  Must travel, still is Nature's Priest,
  And by the vision splendid
  Is on his way attended;
At length the Man perceives it die away,
And fade into the light of common day.
(Lines 71–76)

Tellingly, too, *Experience* records the same sober point. Natural experience, according to Emerson, tends to neutralize "the promise of genius" in that "we see young men who owe us a new world, so readily and lavishly they promise, but they never acquit the debt; they die young and dodge the account: or if they live, they lose themselves in the crowd" (945).

Emerson can adopt, in the same way as Wordsworth, an elegiac tone of experiential weariness. "Ode: Intimations of Immortality" puts forth the poetic argument that the child's "splendour in the grass" and "glory in the flower," that is, his belief in the external world, yields all too soon to the adult's

obstinate questionings
  Of sense and outward things,
  Fallings from us, vanishings;
  Blank misgivings of a Creature
Moving about in worlds not realized, ...
(Lines 141–45, 178)

Nature, similarly, sharply distinguishes between child and adult. "Children, it is true, believe in the external world," but "the belief that it appears only" will come soon enough "with culture" (850). "This faith," ironically so called, "will as surely arise on the mind as did the first" faith, the open and other-directed, if not kingdom-entering, faith of the child (850).

Neither Emerson nor Wordsworth, of course, is finally upset by growing up, for just as Wordsworth looks upon his childhood experiences as "the hiding-places of [his] power" (*Prelude* 12.279), so Emerson believes that "power keeps quite another road than the turnpikes of choice and will, namely, the subterranean and invisible tunnels and channels of life"

(*Experience,* 952). Just as *The American Scholar* recognizes that "the actions and events of our childhood and youth are now matters of calmest observation" (865), so the preface to *Lyrical Ballads* (1802) emphasizes "emotion recollected in tranquillity" or experience transmogrified by maturity. Just as Wordsworth discovers "abundant recompense" ("Tintern Abbey" [1798], line 88) in "years that bring the philosophic mind" ("Ode: Intimations of Immortality," line 186), so Emerson finds reason for optimism in adulthood.

The Emerson of *Nature,* "in the roar of cities or the broil of politics," does not altogether lose the lesson of country life: "Long hereafter, amidst agitation and terror in the national councils,—in the hour of revolution,—these solemn images [of nature] shall reappear in their morning lustre, as fit symbols and words of the thoughts which the passing events shall awaken" (837). Similarly, "in lonely rooms, and 'mid the din / Of towns and cities," the persona of "Tintern Abbey" owes to the "beauteous forms" of nature "sensations sweet, / Felt in the blood, and felt along the heart; / And passing even into my purer mind, / With tranquil restoration" (lines 22, 25–28).

Just as Wordsworth in "Steamboats, Viaducts, and Railways" (1835) is so far from fearing the Industrial Revolution that he sees in its products additional evidence of the creative imagination, so the Emerson of *The Poet* cautions the readers of his age to see "factory-villages" and "railways" not as the breakup of "the poetry of the landscape" but as part of "the great Order" (931). Emerson's empirical language-theory so closely parallels the well-known theory in Wordsworth's preface to *Lyrical Ballads* as to echo it creatively. Here, at some length, is the preface's justification of experiential subject matter and diction:

> Humble and rustic life was generally chosen, because, in that condition, the essential passions of the heart find a better soil in which they can attain their maturity, one less under restraint, and speak a plainer and more emphatic language; because in that condition of life our elementary feelings co-exist in a state of greater simplicity, and, consequently, may be more accurately contemplated, and more forcibly communicated; because the manners of rural life germinate from those elementary feelings, and, from the necessary character of rural occupations, are more easily comprehended, and are more durable; and lastly, because in that condition the passions of men are incorporated with the beautiful and permanent forms of Nature.

Here, more succinctly, is *Nature*'s similar justification:

> This immediate dependence of language upon nature, this conversion of an outward phenomenon into a type of somewhat in human life, never loses its power to affect us. It is this which gives that piquancy to the conversation of a strong-natured farmer or back-woodsman, which all men relish. (836)

Emerson holds to this view consistently. Witness another, even more succinct, version of the view: "Every man is so far a poet as to be susceptible of enchantments of nature" (*The Poet,* 929).

The empirical-evangelical similarity between Emerson's prose and Wordsworth's works is especially strong. A passage from *The Prelude* constitutes a succinct verse version of a passage from *The Over-Soul.* Compare Emerson's "Always our being is descending into us from we know not whence. The most exact calculator has no prescience that somewhat incalculable may not baulk the very next moment" (910) with Wordsworth's poetic argument, in the stolen boat episode of *The Prelude,* that empirical overconfidence may suddenly be defeated by interventions in the natural world from "unknown modes of being" (1.393).[185] The Wordsworth of "Tintern Abbey" feels "a motion and a spirit, that impels / All thinking things, all objects of all thought, / And rolls through all things," and he is therefore able to "see into the life of things," that is, to enjoy an at once natural and spiritual perception (lines 49, 100–102).[186] Similarly, the Emerson of *Fate* enjoys his perception of theistical/millennial realities:

> The day of days, the great day of the feast of life, is that in which the inward eye opens to the Unity in things, to the omnipresence of law;—sees that what is must be and ought to be, or is the best. This beatitude dips from on high down to us and we see. (341).

According to chapter 14 of Coleridge's *Biographia Literaria* (1817), Wordsworth gives "the charm of novelty to things of every day" and thus excites "a feeling analogous to the supernatural," and this insight fits the Emerson of *The Over-Soul,* who preaches that "the soul that ascendeth to worship the great God . . . dwells in the hour that now is" (921). Where Emerson defines "the institution of preaching" as "the speech of man to men" (*Self-Reliance,* 888), he draws on Wordsworth's definition of the poet as "a man speaking to men," for the Emersonian preacher, no less than the Emersonian poet and no less than Emerson himself, speaks the

Wordsworthian as well as Wesleyan and Edwardsean language of experience. Where *The Poet* states that "the poet . . . traverses *the whole scale* of experience" (925; my italics), Emerson includes spiritual experience along with natural, and as one reads *Nature*'s description of how to "see nature," one thinks of the "spiritual sense" delineated in Wordsworth's great ode:[187]

> The sun illuminates only the eyes of the man, but shines into the eye and heart of the child. The lover of nature is he whose inward and outward senses are still truly adjusted to each other; who has retained the spirit of infancy even into the era of manhood. His intercourse with heaven and earth, becomes part of his daily food. (926)

The empirical-evangelical nature of the philosophical theology that Emerson derives from Coleridge is implicit in Stephen Whicher's point that the young Emerson gradually "groped his way through the thickets of skepticism and self-distrust toward independence and faith, until new lights from 'modern philosophy,' chiefly Coleridge, led him to the 'amazing revelation' of a God within his own heart and released him from the 'yoke of men's opinions.'"[188] *Nature,* in quoting Coleridge's *The Friend* (1818), puts forward the more Platonically than empirically ideal notion that "the problem of philosophy is, for all that exists conditionally, to find a ground unconditional and absolute" (848). But *Nature* quotes, too, Coleridge's evangelical, revivalist comment from his *Lecture on the General Character of the Gothic Mind in the Middle Ages* (1836), namely, that "a Gothic church is a petrified religion" (842). Indeed, *Nature* quotes Coleridge in ways consistent with evangelicalism in combination with empiricism. Coleridge's *Aids to Reflection* (1829) provides *Nature* with what Herschel Parker calls "a basic terminology in [Emerson's] postulation of an intuitive 'Reason,' which is superior to the mere 'Understanding,' or ordinary rationality operating on the materials of sense experience."[189] This terminology is reminiscent of not just Kant but the sixth sense of faith that, as I have previously argued, derives from Coleridge's empirical-evangelical imagination.[190]

In one of Emerson's most rationalistic moods, quoted earlier but worth requoting here, viz., "The astronomer, the geometer, rely on their irrefragable analysis, and disdain the results of observation" (*Nature,* 849), he takes from *Aids to Reflection* another passage worth requoting: "The sublime remark of Euler on his law of arches, 'This will be found contrary to all experience, yet is true' " (*Nature,* 849). In most of what *Nature* owes to Coleridge, however, the mind does not so much supersede as come to terms with nature. Emerson's attempt, quoted earlier, to retain "the spirit of infancy even into the spirit of manhood" (*Nature,* 826) not only reflects the Lockean as well as Wordsworthian theory that "the child is father of the man," that is, that identity and sense experience develop in tandem, but also derives from chapter 4 of *Biographia Literaria,* which "defines the character and privilege of genius as the ability to carry the feelings of childhood into the powers of manhood."[191]

"Our dealing with sensible objects," observes Emerson, "is a constant exercise in the necessary lesson of difference, of likeness, of order, of being and seeming, of progressive arrangement" (*Nature,* 839). This borrowing from *The Friend*[192] indicates how the aesthetics of *Nature,* the conviction that the "standard of beauty" rests on "the entire circuit of natural forms" (*Nature,* 833), comes from the Coleridgean doctrine of unity in multeity, the strange, rich concert of the subjective One with the objective Many.

A contrast between Locke and Coleridge does occur in *The Over-Soul,* which declares that "philosophers like Spinoza, Kant, and Coleridge" speak "*from within,* or from experience," whereas "philosophers like Locke, Paley, Mackintosh and Stewart" speak "*from without,* as spectators merely" (919). But one hears broadly experiential, that is, Lockean as well as experientially spiritual, echoes in Emerson's evident knowledge of not only Coleridge's prose but his poetry as well.

Between Coleridge's "The Nightingale" (1798) and Emerson's *The Poet,* for example, is a particularly Lockean parallel. Here is *The Poet:*

> Even the poets are contented with a civil and conformed manner of living, and to write poems from the fancy, at a safe distance from their own experience. But the highest minds of the world have never ceased to explore the double meaning, or, shall I say, the quadruple, or the centuple, or much more manifold meaning of every sensuous fact. (924)

And here is "The Nightingale," indicting the

> Poet who hath been building up the rhyme
> When he had better far have stretched his limbs

Beside a brook in mossy forest-dell,
By sun or moon-light, to the influxes
Of shapes and sounds and shifting elements
Surrendering his whole spirit, ...
(Lines 24–29)

One finds this Lockean theory, indeed, as early as *Nature,* which declares that "hundreds of writers may be found in every long-civilized nation, who for a short time believe, and make others believe, that they see and utter truths, who do not of themselves clothe one thought in its natural garment, but who feed unconsciously upon the language created by the primary writers of the country, those, namely, who hold primarily on nature" (836).

Too many poets of the 1840s, *The Poet* implies, have only the "genius" of the "landscape garden of a modern house, adorned with fountains and statues, with well-bred men and women standing and sitting in the walks and terraces" (927). Two few get their material from deep, rich, "O Altitudo" experience, since too few "stand out of our low limitations, like a [Mount] Chimborazo under the [equatorial] line, running up from the torrid base through all the climates of the globe, with belts of the herbage of every latitude on its high and mottled sides" (927). This is reminiscent of not only the argument of "The Nightingale" but also the imagery of "Kubla Khan" (1816), in which the "romantic chasm" may have as much to do with the properly inchoate, properly unstructured data base of experience as, say, with the unworldliness of exotic vision.

In both Coleridge's poems and Emerson's essays, finally, one finds the world-orientation of evangelical vision. Coleridge's forgiven, or at least reprieved or shriven, mariner is compelled to share his story of salvation:

I pass, like night, from land to land;
I have strange power of speech;
That moment that his face I see,
I known the man that must hear me:
To him my tale I teach.
("The Rime of the Ancient Mariner" [1798], lines 586–90)

Similarly, the Emersonian preacher, who has received "God himself, into the open soul," "beget[s] a desire and need to impart to others the same knowledge and love" (*The Divinity School Address,* 881). "If utterance is denied," Emerson adds, "the thought lies like a burden on the man." Just as Coleridge's "Frost at Midnight" (1798) speaks of a "secret ministry of frost" (line 72), so the Emerson of *Nature* pleases himself with observing "the *graces* of the wintry scenery" (830; my italics), and thus nature accords with the spiritual vision shared by Coleridge and Emerson.

I turn, now, to the role of second-generation Romanticism in Emerson's intra-Romantic relationships. Emerson's Shelleyan mode can be so antiobjective as to seem antiexperiential. Just as Shelley's "Mont Blanc" (1817) tells of what Earl Wasserman, in his still-magisterial study of the poem, calls "the quality-less essence of experiential qualities,"[193] or what the Bible calls "the peace that passeth understanding," or what T. S. Eliot conveys by "the unstilled world still whirled / About the center of the silent Word,"[194] so *Self-Reliance* speaks of a "new perception" that seems to deliver Emerson from experience:

> When we have new perception, we shall gladly disburthen the memory of its hoarded treasures as old rubbish. . . . We are then in vision. . . . The soul is raised over passion. It seeth identity and eternal causation. It is a perceiving that Truth and Right are. Hence it becomes a Tranquility out of the knowing that all things go well. Vast spaces of nature; the Atlantic Ocean, the South Sea; vast intervals of time, years, centuries, are of no account. (900)

The rather self-loving tone of Shelley's dilation on love, viz., "We dimly see within our intellectual nature a miniature as it were of our entire self, yet deprived of all that we condemn or despise, the ideal prototype of every thing excellent or lovely that we are capable of conceiving as belonging to the nature of man" (*On Love* [1812–14?]), puts one in mind of the extreme subjectivity of *Self-Reliance,* viz., "[every man] must take himself for better, for worse, as his portion" (890).

Just as *Nature* recalls that "as we go back in history, language becomes more picturesque, until its infancy, when it is all poetry" (835), so Shelley's *A Defence of Poetry* (1821) teaches that "in the infancy of society every author is necessarily a poet." This explicit allusion to Shelley, identified by Herschel Parker,[195] suggests that Emerson's rhapsodic estimate of a poet as "the principal event in chronology" (*The Poet,* 928) derives from Shelley's similarly rhapsodic estimate of poets as "the unacknowledged legislators of the world." (I quote the last sentence of *A Defence of Poetry,* but Emerson's estimate may derive, too, from Imlac's in Samuel Johnson's *Rasselas:* "[The poet] must write as the interpreter of nature and the legislator of mankind, and consider himself as presiding over the thoughts and manner of future generations, as a being superior to time and place" [chapter 10].)

Otherwise, however, Emerson's Shelleyan mode follows a paradigm so fully experiential as to be, like Shelley himself, empirical-evangelical.[196] True, *The Over-Soul*'s insistence that even the sun and stars "change and pass" (923) has a Shelleyan-Platonic ring. Compare this insistence with "the many change and pass" from stanza 52 of Shelley's *Adonais* (1821). Emerson's parallels to "Mont Blanc" are so far from *contemptus mundi,* however, as to celebrate the experiential, for the axiom of *The Divinity School Address,* that "one mind is everywhere, in each ray of the star, in each wavelet of the pool, active" (876), serves to gloss, though retroleptically, the careful implication in "Mont Blanc" that the one "mind" or "Power in likeness of the Arve" (lines 2, 16) is knowable only through its effects or acts in the Ravine of Arve. The quite experiential, even evangelical faith of Shelley, "The *breath* whose might I have invoked in song / *Descends* on me" ("Adonais," lines 487–88; my italics), not only harks back to the breathlike "evangelical" interventions in, say, Wordsworth's stolen boat episode[197] but also counterparts Emerson's "evangelical," intensely present-oriented faith that "always our being is descending into us from we know not whence" (*The Over-Soul,* 910).

Emerson's Shelleyan affinities include even the most skeptical, but not for that reason wholly unevangelical, apprehension of the actual. Note, for example, Shelley's vision of modern love in "When the Lamp Is Shattered" (1824):

> When the lips have spoken,
> Loved accents are soon forgot.
> . . . .
> From thy nest every rafter
> Will rot, and thine eagle home
> Leave thee naked to laughter,
> When leaves fall and cold winds come.
> (Lines 7–8, 29–32)

These lines, horrific in their relentless accumulation of harsh detail, find their Emersonian parallel near the deterministically experiential, almost Calvinist beginning of *Experience:* "Every roof is agreeable to the eye, until it is lifted; then we find tragedy and moaning women, and hard-eyed husbands, and deluges of lethe, and the men ask, 'What's the news?' as if the old were so bad" (943).

Emerson's Keatsean affinity, though not fully in accord with Keats's relation to the empirical-evangelical tradition,[198] well illustrates Emerson's intra-Romantic relationships, for although occurring in terms not so much evangelical or theological as empirical and philosophical, his Keatsean affinity participates, nevertheless, in actual/ideal debate. Consider, for example, *Nature*'s jaunty allusion to "Ode on a Grecian Urn" (1820): "The true philosophy and the true poet are one, and a beauty, which is truth, and a truth, which is beauty, is the aim of both" (848). Thus Emerson captures the sloganlike quality, and upbeat rhythm, of the ode's flat declaration that "Beauty is truth, truth beauty" (line 49). Any nice ambiguities in Keats's well-known chiasmus are not of any apparent interest to the young Emerson. *Experience,* however, cannot reconcile opposites so blithely:

> Our love of the real draws us to permanence, but health of body consists in circulation, and sanity of mind in variety or facility of association. We need change of objects. Dedication to one thought is quickly odious. (947)

One thinks, in this connection, of not so much Keats's initial attraction to the permanence of the urn as his increasing, and finally greater, interest in the "little town by river or sea shore" (line 35)—what Emerson would call the "health," the "circulation," and even the "change of objects" of impermanent, but achingly desirable, life.

Experience, then, if Keats's tone is ironic toward the urn, is closer to the ode than *Nature* is. Jack Stillinger's argument that Keats came to "embrace experience and process as his own and man's chief *good*" (my italics)[199] would hardly seem to apply to the Emerson who registers impatience with the muddle of life, as in this passage from *Experience:*

> It is said, all martyrdoms looked mean when they were suffered. Every ship is a romantic object, except that we sail in. Embark, and the romance quits our vessel, and hangs on every other sail in the horizon. (943)

But Emerson is no escapist. For just as Keats enjoins his reader "No, no, go not to Lethe" ("Ode on Melancholy" [1820], line 1), so Emerson advises would-be bards against such artificial stimulants as "wine, mead, narcotics, coffee, tea, opium, the fumes of sandal-wood and tobacco"

(*The Poet,* 935). "The sublime vision," he preaches, "comes to the pure and simple soul in a clean and chaste body" (*The Poet,* 935).

To all people and not just to poets, Emerson recommends, in effect, Keats's doctrine of Negative Capability and his metaphor of Life as a Vale of Soul-Making: "The only mode of obtaining an answer to these questions of the senses," writes Emerson, "is, to forego all low curiosity, and, accepting the tide of being which floats us into the secret of nature, work and live, work and live, and all unawares, the advancing soul has built and forged for itself a new condition, and the question and the answer are one" (*The Over-Soul,* 918). Thus *Nature*'s famous passage on the "transparent eye-ball"—"I am nothing. I see all" (827)—has more to do with Negative Capability than with Egotistical Sublimity.

The Keatsean mode of Emerson's works, though, tends finally to favor the subjective side of the subject-object equation, and so is more tender-minded than tough-minded. Just as *Self-Reliance* enjoins "a man to know his worth, and keep things under his feet" (897), so Keats's "Written upon the Top of Ben Nevis" (1819) overcomes initial skepticism and asserts the lordship of mind: Keats announces, of the stones on the pathway, "I tread on them" (line 12). Both authors, moreover, well earn such headiness, for neither blinks away proto-evolutionary challenges to lordship of mind: while Keats's "Epistle to John Hamilton Reynolds" (1818), quoted earlier, records that "I saw / Too far into the sea, where every maw / The greater on the less feeds evermore" (Lines 93–95), *Fate* expresses the startlingly parallel idea of such "hints of ferocity in the interiors of nature" as the shark, the *labrus,* the sea-wolf, and the grampus (333). Keats works his way through to a disinterested, robust version of evolutionary empiricism in *Hyperion: A Fragment* (1820):

> So on our heels a fresh perfection treads,
> A power more strong in beauty, born of us
> And fated to excel us, as we pass
> In glory that old Darkness.
>
> (2.212–15)

Similarly, *The Poet* proclaims Emerson's view that "within the form of every creature is a force impelling it to ascend into a higher form" (932). Even *Fate,* one recalls, rhapsodizes about evolutionary reality as harmonious mastery, that is, as mind over matter.

"Historically," writes Emerson in *The American Scholar,* "there is thought to be a difference in the ideas which predominate over successive epochs, and there are data for marking the genius of the Classic, of the Romantic, and now of the Reflective or Philosophic age" (871). Emerson sees no reason why his own time should not be as genuinely creative as, and creative in the same way as, the preceding era. "This time, like all times," he writes, "is a very good one, if we but know what to do with it" (871), and he profits from his encounters with High Romanticism. In 1833, he enjoyed hearing Wordsworth recite his poetry and listened to Coleridge "converse with such cogent volubility that he seemed to be reading aloud."[200] Declaring in 1837 that "one design unites and animates the farthest pinnacle and the lowest trench," he implies that the "one design" not only inspires the "genius of Goldsmith, Burns, Cowper, and, in a newer time, of Goethe, Wordsworth, and Carlyle" but also his own genius, which, as I have shown, reflects the unitary design, the blend of actual and ideal, to be found in the native "genius" of both Wordsworth and Carlyle, if not, indeed, of Goldsmith, Burns, and Cowper (*The American Scholar,* 872). An early reviewer of *Nature* was on the right track when he linked *Nature* to both the "Immortality" ode and Coleridge's "Dejection: An Ode" (1802).[201] Another was correct to see the influence of Coleridge and Wordsworth in the "spiritual eye" with which Emerson looks on nature.[202] Emerson brings together, as did Wordsworth and Coleridge, not only poetry and philosophy but also poetry, philosophy, and religion.

This triangle forms such a significant part of Emerson's work that he announces it, however rhetorically, near the beginning of his first important essay. *Nature*'s rhetorical question is worth requoting: "Why should we not have a poetry and philosophy of insight and not of tradition, and a religion by revelation to us?" (*Nature,* 824–25). On a level with such empirical/evangelical, Anglo-American themes surrounding the empirical-evangelical, Anglo-American doctrine of the "spiritual sense" lie the Romantic topoi that Emerson chooses to stress. Consider five representative passages from four of the eight works highlighted in this chapter:

> If a man is at heart just, then in so far is he God.
>
> (*The Divinity School Address,* 877)

> To create,—to create,—is the proof of a divine presence.
>
> (*The American Scholar,* 863)

> Yet I desire, even by profane words, if sacred I may not use, to indicate the heaven of this deity, and to report what hints I have collected of the transcendent simplicity and energy of the Highest Law.
>
> (*The Over-Soul,* 911)

> Fear never but you shall be consistent in whatever variety of actions, so they be each honest and natural in their hour. . . . The voyage of the best ship is a zigzag line of a hundred tacks. This is only microscopic criticism. See the line from a sufficient distance, and it straightens itself to the average tendency.
>
> (*Self-Reliance,* 895)

> That which had been negligently trodden under foot by those who were harnessing and provisioning themselves for long journeys into far countries, is suddenly found to be richer than all foreign parts. The literature of the poor, the feelings of the child, the philosophy of the street, the meaning of household life, are the topics of the time. It is a great stride.
>
> (*The American Scholar,* 872)

This potpourri espouses the sublimity of the commonplace, the criterion of sincerity, the inspiration of language, the divinity of creation, and the apotheosized self. It reflects a philosophically theological sensibility of the Anglo-American world from at least 1772, when Wesley abridged Edwards's *Religious Affections,* to at least 1843, when Carlyle published *Past and Present,* or 1852, when Emerson published *Fate.* The potpourri emerges, like all eight essays studied here and like my sampling of Carlyle, as at once binationally and otherwise broadly, that is, empirically and evangelically, Romantic.

Such experiential themes come together in the young Emerson's romantic estimate of his Romantic calling. In 1835, in a letter to Lydian Jackson (whom he later married), he introduced himself thus:

> I am a poet, of a low class without a doubt yet a poet. That is my nature & vocation. My singing to be sure is very "husky," & is for the most part in prose. Still am I a poet in the sense of a perceiver and dear lover of the harmonies that are in the soul & in matter, & especially of the correspondences between these & those.[203]

This passage, not, it may seem, an auspicious beginning for a romance, clearly impressed Lydian Jackson both emotionally and intellectually.

Anyone else, indeed, who responds to it epistemologically/spiritually, also responds to it in kind, according to its letter and spirit. The "soul & . . . matter" of the passage, to be sure, may pertain to subject/object interaction more than to any empirical-evangelical frame of reference, but the here-and-now of the passage is both empirical and "evangelical," especially in the sense of seeking Lydian as a convert! In the context of Emerson's career, finally, the passage emerges as a fitting focus of my view of his prose, for the passage comes addressed not so much to a Mimi from a Rodolfo or to some hypothetical pantheist from some fellow nature-worshiper: it comes to us as to any hypothetical reader in the Anglo-American world or elsewhere who is similarly, that is, empirically and evangelically, experience-minded, and who is therefore an Anglo-American Romantic by temperament, if not by biography, and it comes from a composite speaker, namely, "Locke," "Wesley," "Edwards," and Emerson, the Anglo-American Romantic writer of belletristic prose.

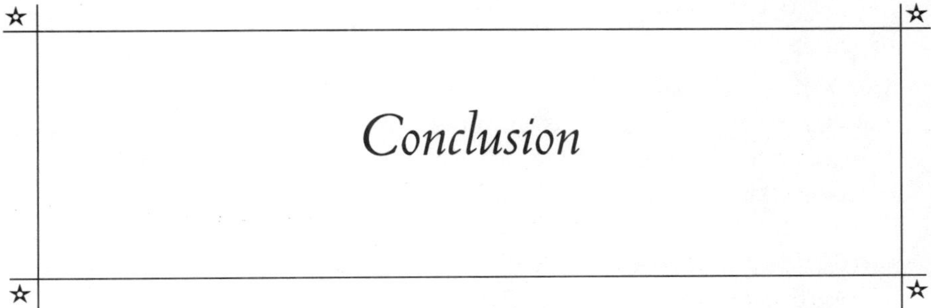

Conclusion

An immediate, more practical than broadly methodological result of this study could be a Romantic-period course on Carlyle and Emerson, who, in their philosophical-theological way, are both coordinators and coordinates of a specifically Anglo-American, because natural-cultural, empirical-evangelical Romanticism. In 1833 and 1847, during two visits to England, Emerson got on well with Carlyle, and their friendship, having much to do with the Anglo-American sensibility shared by Wesley and Edwards, virtually founded Anglo-American literature. "Each helped to publish and create an audience for the other."[1] As early as *Nature*, Emerson quotes Carlyle's translation of Goethe (843); as late as 1860, Carlyle praises Emerson's *The Conduct of Life*.[2] Although Emerson gets from Carlyle a post-Kantian idealism—the Everlasting Yea of *Sartor Resartus* anticipates the "affirmative principle" of *Experience* (942)—and although what one early reviewer found in *Nature* is "an idealistic Pantheism" like that of *Sartor Resartus*[3]—I have contended, in this study, that a theistical, empirical-evangelical imagination is what these two major prose-writers of the Anglo-American world hold most in common. A major basis of their relationship, after all, is the empirical-evangelical, Anglo-American quality of their Romanticism.

Robert Weisbuch, "discovering" American misreadings of Victorian literature, argues (à la Bloom) that Emerson and other major American writers of his age either dodge or transform the various British influences on them.[4] Seeing the relationship between British and American literature as "adversarial," Weisbuch concludes that "American writers refuse the

British limits of possibility for self and world" (193). Weisbuch thinks that the friendship of Carlyle and Emerson, in particular, issues in only "Emerson's reply to Carlyle's *On Heroes* in *Representative Men*" (221). Emerson, Weisbuch declares, "makes his friend representative of the nation that best exemplifies the solid, earthbound, and thus disastrously partial side of dialectical reality" (203). This thesis, although true of the relationship between *On Heroes* and *Representative Men,* does not apply either to the overall relationship between Emerson and Carlyle or to the works of Carlyle in general. In Carlyle's works, after all, the solid and the earthbound form part of a full dialectic.

Weisbuch is often persuasive concerning those times when American literary nationalism arose as a deliberate effort to oppose, and even to rise above, British influence. Melville's "Bartleby the Scrivener," for example, ridicules, mocks, and parodies Dickens's *Bleak House* (221). Weisbuch's contrasts, moreover, are often pleasingly antithetical, for example, while "the world is placed within an expanded American self," "the British self is placed within a world" (221). Although such contrasts may be flattering to virulent forms of American nationalism, however, Weisbuch's view of the American self is not entirely true of even *Self-Reliance,* and the "American" self is found in, say, *Characteristics* by Carlyle. With regard to Carlyle and Emerson, then, Weisbuch, always provocative, is sometimes misleading.

Kenneth Marc Harris, exploring how the works of Carlyle and Emerson continue "the private dialogue" of their letters, acknowledges that in the autumn of their lives they "grew apart in many ways," and that while Carlyle "forces us to admit the truth," Emerson "allows us to entertain the illusions which make the truth endurable."[5] Finally, however, Harris emphasizes that Carlyle and Emerson shared a "Transcendental youth" based on the philosophies of Kant and Fichte, and Harris is at his best in comparing *Sartor Resartus* and *Nature* (8–45). Here, in his view, is the resolution mutually arrived at by Carlyle and Emerson:

> They had abandoned the old religion, they said, not because it was false but because they lacked the "unconscious" state of mind which would have enabled them to believe. Not to fall into skepticism and materialism was for both a point of honor, but there seemed to be no escape. They were imprisoned by their own self-awareness. How could they consciously will them-

> selves to "lose consciousness" and thereby attain faith? . . . A crucial element in their resolution of the dilemma was the conjecture of a dual mode of thought, both "conscious" and "unconscious" at the same time. The distinction was metaphysical as well as psychological, for they hoped to assimilate the supernatural truths that their parents accepted without reflection through the nonreflective portions of the mind, all the while retaining the critical, self-dissecting qualities of intellect which otherwise would render such beliefs incredible. (2)

This statement's blend of philosophy and faith strongly resembles what Carlyle and Emerson indeed share, but I would stress that they manage to entertain both philosophy and faith without having to suppress either. In neither man, moreover, is philosophy necessarily German. Harris's study not only ignores empiricism but also takes almost no notice of evangelicalism. Although acknowledging that Carlyle's "preoccupation with evil" and Emerson's "strain of fatalism" derive ultimately from Calvinist doctrines, Harris merely observes that "those who find such analogies useful are welcome to bear them in mind" (60). He takes no notice whatever of Arminianism.

Christopher Lasch, recently attacking "the Anglo-American idea of progress," finds in the Anglo-American diptych of Carlyle and Emerson an antidote to unbridled economic growth.[6] Lasch's emphasis on them as the central figures in a comprehensive, if too economic, understanding of Anglo-American sensibility is cause for celebration, if not rejoicing. Carlyle and Emerson, Lasch argues, insist on "human limitations" and are thus "latter-day Calvinists without a Calvinist theology" who replace the notion of progress with an almost otherworldly hope. If Lasch had noted that the Lockean-Arminian as well as Calvinist "theology" shared by Carlyle and Emerson allows for spiritual, if not economic, progress in this world, his synthesis of Anglo-American experience would have been even more fully explanatory. *Progress,* after all, is the language not solely of economics but, even more venerably, of such lower-middle-class religious cultures as those of John Bunyan, who wrote *Pilgrim's Progress,* and Philip Doddridge, who wrote *The Rise and Progress of Religion in the Soul.*

Although Lasch's appeals to Edwards as Calvinist and to Locke as both economist and Protestant are especially welcome, a recognition of

Locke's empiricism and the Lockean/Arminian dimension of Edwards's thought are oddly missing from Lasch's analysis. The absence of Wesley from Lasch's otherwise remarkably complete Anglo-American firmament is not quite made up for by his emphasis on William James, despite James's pertinent grasp of the "twice-born" kind of religious experience.

A methodological result of my study could be the application of the empirical-evangelical model to Anglo-American poetry. Alfred, Lord Tennyson, in *In Memoriam A. H. H.* (1850), conceives of experience as both natural and spiritual, for an emblematic conflation of empiricism with Christ-centered faith occurs, auspiciously enough, in the prologue (in which "thee" refers to Christ):

> We have but faith: we cannot know,
> For knowledge is of things we see;
> And yet we trust it comes from thee,
> A beam in darkness: let it grow.
>
> Let knowledge grow from more to more,
> But more of reverence in us dwell;
> That mind and soul, according well,
> May make one music as before,
>
> But vaster.
>
> (Lines 21–29)

Since "it" (lines 23, 24) refers to "knowledge" (line 22), the "things we see" (line 22) are just as much the gift of God as faith itself. Yet "faith" (line 21), even while differing markedly from the "things we see," is dialectically involved with sense experience. Thus, insofar as "it" can refer at once to "knowledge" and to "faith," empirical philosophy and experiential faith form an identity. In the poem as a whole, similarly, empiricism and evangelicalism either follow parallel lines or converge, and the sum of these dual methodologies implies congruency, for they form either a dual perspective or a synthesis. The just-quoted passage exemplifies with particular vividness the mix of empiricism and evangelicalism to be found among mainstream Anglo-American poets in general; Emily Dickinson's irony, telling the truth but telling it slant, is the natural endpoint of the Romantic arc that I describe. Although Karl Keller uses Edwards's theology to trace spiritual residue in her more pre-

Modern than Late Romantic poetry,[7] a broader, more composite means of doing so is at once to bring Wesley, too, into play, and to recognize that Edwards's full utility to literary criticism lies in his philosophical theology.

THE SENSIBILITY SHARED by Wesley, Edwards, Carlyle, and Emerson, then, designates especially well the sense in which British and American cultures merge. Although William McKibben finds in Anglo-American resources only a means of lamenting "the end of nature" and never the means of reaffirming empiricism,[8] and although Garry Wills suggests that TV's "Phallic Pulpit" signals the demise of fundamentalism in America,[9] England and the United States, without sharing absolutely everything,[10] rest even yet on an alternately, or even simultaneously, empirical and evangelical foundationalism. The Lockean and the evangelical understandings of experience persist in the Anglo-American middle class: recall, on the empirical side, the best-selling popularity of Stephen Hawking and Stephen Jay Gould and, on the evangelical side, both the Methodism of the young Margaret Thatcher (née Roberts) and the Calvinist as well as Arminian evangelicalism of preachers at both ends of the 1988 spectrum of American presidential candidates. One thinks, in particular, of a quintessential embodiment of Anglo-American literature, namely, the binational T. S. Eliot, who, though sometimes disclaimed as reactionary, continues, despite his High Church allegiances, to represent the perennially Anglo-American, twofold belief that "history" (including empirical science) "underlies poetry" and that "poetry can be redemptive."[11] Thus, though seemingly dichotomous, empiricism and evangelicalism are antipodal and hence complementary at least in that they influence each other on both sides of, and in both directions across, the Atlantic. The philosophical theology shared by Wesley and Edwards, regardless of whether empiricism and evangelicalism apply to every man, woman, and child, applies to Carlyle and Emerson, who join things and events to words through the grace of ideas, if not through ideal grace. Since each of these codes of experience operates especially in England and the United States, they tend toward the nature-culture synthesis of Anglo-American relations.

Specialists in British and American studies, rather than defending their turfs, would do well to be more open to similarities between their respective subjects. I take the Anglo-American side of the debate between Richard Brodhead, Michael Davitt Bell, and Edgar Dryden, who view "American Romance" as something exclusively American,[12] and Nicolaus Mills, Edwin Eigner, Jonathan Arac, and William C. Spengemann, who see Anglo-American interconnections.[13] As David Van Leer points out, "Comparing the *aesthetic* assumptions of English and American literature has been common since at least Irving and Cooper and lies at the heart of classic statements by D. H. Lawrence, Richard Chase, and especially Harry Levin" (my italics).[14] By adding belletristic prose to the fiction-emphasis shared by Arac, Eigner, and Mills, I, too, am aesthetical, but I add thematic considerations to the aesthetic emphasis shared especially by Spengemann and Mills, and I add philosophically theological considerations to the interdisciplinary approaches of Arac (sociology) and Eigner (philosophy).

Scholars of American literature, in particular, characteristically emphasize its various regional manifestations. A. Carl Bredahl, Jr., establishes a link between Western American narrative and "the surfaces of infinite space"; Bredahl's "new ground" complements the enclosure/disclosure complex of New England and the South.[15] Jack P. Greene argues that the emphasis on individual welfare in the Middle Atlantic and South Atlantic states had more to do with shaping American culture than did the religious emphasis in New England.[16]

New England, however, retains much of its synecdochic power. Many still find New England Puritanism, in particular, crucial to the American sense of self. Sacvan Bercovitch, albeit less optimistically than Perry Miller, embraces New England Puritanism as America's fullest meaning.[17] The American dream, manifest destiny, national mission, the promise of a redemptive future, and "the Biblical myth of exodus and conquest to justify imperialism before the fact," are all, according to Bercovitch, American middle-class goals that derive from America's "Puritan origins."[18]

Yet now there are more Muslims in the United States than Presbyterians or Episcopalians. Andrew Delbanco, while agreeing with Bercovitch that the meaning of America lies in Puritanism, finds in the early Puritans not confident sojourners to millennium but sufferers from the ordeal of emigration.[19] What characterizes America, according to Delbanco, is the feeling of loneliness or abandonment in a hostile or indifferent world.

Theodore Dwight Bozeman points out that the sermon in which occur John Winthrop's conventional words—"As a City upon a Hill, the eyes of all people are upon us"—assumes that the Puritan adventure would not succeed.[20] Winthrop's orthodox establishment had to contend with separatists, Anabaptists, Socinians, Quakers, Gortonists, Seekers, and Ranters.[21] As David D. Hall, contra Miller, points out, the New England Puritans were not so much "intellectual" or continuous with the twentieth century as interested in magic, superstition, monstrous births, witches, abnormalities, and the occult.[22] Thus, insofar as the Puritans were a heterogeneous people with no common purpose, their importance may be greatly overestimated.

Since the migration stopped when the Civil Wars broke out in the 1640s, and since many Puritans then came home, the connection between Puritanism and its British origins remained close. The story of many Puritans' return to England, as Delbanco points out, has been suppressed as incommensurate with American national mythology.[23] The American self, then, especially in its Puritan dimension, originates in England as well as in New England.

Bercovitch assumes that it must be either Puritanism or Lockeanism that fostered the American middle class, and he selects Puritanism.[24] The logic should be "both/and." Since scholars of American literature, American theology, and American history have begun to explore the religious dimension of the partly Locke-derived American national philosophy of pragmatism, philosophically theological, if not partly British, ways of understanding American national character have begun to appear.[25]

Bruce Kuklick, for example, after the anti-Puritanism of Van Wyck Brooks, H. L. Mencken, and Vernon L. Parrington, notably builds on Miller's and Samuel Eliot Morison's reestablishment of early-Puritan intellectual respectability, for Kuklick specifically sees little break between the decline of Protestant moralism and the rise of modern pragmatism.[26] John Dewey, sometime teacher of Congregational Sunday school in Burlington, Vermont, "succeeded in incorporating traditional religious values into a specific conception of man and nature, a naturalistic synthesis that enabled modern philosophy to carry on the ethical obligation of Puritanism by other means."[27] Charley D. Hardwick objects that "for all the boldness" of such "American religious empiricism," it remains "ontologically dangling": "What must reality be like," asks Hardwick, "to warrant the *objective* (yet dynamic, even contingent) religious values the religious empiricists seek in a nonillusory experience?"[28] He answers, in part, that "the ultimate promise of the revival of religious empiricism" must lie in confronting "ontological issues." The old ideas that Dewey thought he was reinvigorating, at any rate, were not just American and ethical but Anglo-American and philosophically theological.

Leonard I. Sweet, in his overview of "the new evangelical historiography," shows how Joel Carpenter, Nathan Hatch, George Marsden, Mark Noll, Harry Stout, Grant Wacker, and other American scholars have advanced to a "front-rank position within scholarship on American religious history generally."[29] These historians, however, are "Calvinist-oriented" (Sweet's phrase). As a means of understanding "the Wesleyan component of evangelicalism" and hence the full "transatlantic influence" on American evangelical tradition, Sweet points to corrective scholarship by Douglas W. Frank and Timothy Smith.[30] While the frontier wilderness in the South forced the Methodists there to develop a theology of experience, experience formed an important part, too, of New England Methodism, which favored the Arminian, and hence as much imported- as indigenous-experiential, side of America's Calvinist/Arminian controversy. (The eventual triumph of Arminianism in England and America was foreshadowed as early as the 1630s, when Arminianism as established thought began to take shape in the works of Archbishop Laud; despite the attempt at the Synod of Dort [1619] to suppress it, Arminianism silently spread until Laud, and even Charles I, embraced it.)[31]

Heart-religion is a term so perennial as to be traceable not just to the "culture of nonconformity" in seventeenth-century England but even to "the discovery of the individual" during the years from 1050 to 1200.[32] Note, for that matter, the heart-religion in Psalm 19. I am interested, however, in an early modern version of the term, namely, the neoapostolic or neoclassically and Romantically evangelical version, which characterized and all but defined the space-time complex of not just England but even America from May 24, 1738, when Wesley's heart was "strangely warmed," to 1860, if no later, when Emerson published *The Conduct of Life*.

The natural as well as cultural uniqueness of the host country, of course, has always helped shape liturgical tradition: witness Augustine in

North Africa, Sidonius in Gaul, Boniface in Germany, Cuthbert in England, and Francis Asbury, the Wesley-ordained Methodist bishop in America.[33] As the twin sources of a bipartite, Anglo-American liturgical tradition, Wesley and Asbury shared a Methodism that makes it feasible, in their cases, to speak of that tradition's relation to the natural or geographical, as well as cultural, uniqueness of a binational entity, namely, Anglo-American sensibility.

Allan Bloom has rightly been taken to task for his assumption that American character derives primarily from German philosophy. To one reviewer's regret that Bloom leaves out British experience, I add that the British experience he leaves out is specifically the alternately, or even simultaneously, philosophical and *religious* British experience.[34]

The experientially philosophical commonality of England and the United States can be inferred from Stephen Jay Gould's response to *Infinite in All Directions* (1988) by Freeman J. Dyson, who was born in Manchester, England, and who compares the Athenians' search for the timeless, general, and universal laws of nature "at the highest level of abstraction" with the "gutsy, hands-on practicality" of the Industrial Revolution.[35] Gould, American biologist that he is, praises the physics of the British-American Dyson for Dyson's preference (despite his genuine respect for "theorists and quantifiers who continue the search for unity and simplification under fully general laws of nature") for the "putterers and historians charged with explaining the inordinately complex particulars that never occur twice in nature's intricacy."[36]

The religious as well as empirical character shared by England and the United States can be inferred from the sum of certain individually various, but not finally disparate, sources and analogues. The "cultural meaning" of the scientific revolution is, according to Margaret C. Jacob, at once English and Protestant,[37] and, according to Frank Burch Brown, Darwin founded his "treasured hope for an ever brighter future" partially on assumptions transcending "purely scientific evidence."[38] Darwin's search for "an elusive God," Brown argues, is just as important to an understanding of Darwin as Darwin's effort to come to terms with a "perplexing world" and an "anxious self." Hamilton Holt's popular edition of a turn-of-the-twentieth-century American Methodist minister's account of his "spiritual sense," a sense informed by both religious and natural knowledge, has been reissued: the nearly blind, anonymous minister writes in his spiritual autobiography that "the world in which I have lived has had more mysteries in it than the world of those who see well, and a larger room for imagination, and for those poetic fancies which give the earth and sky and sun and stars a beauty that is not otherwise their own."[39] John Fowles's epilogue to *A Maggot* (1985), finally, sees John Wesley and Ann Lee, founder of the American Shakers, both as joint Anglo-American revivers of emotion and, through the "wise and decent moderation" of their natural as well as spiritual experience, as joint Anglo-American religious-enlighteners of the early modern world.[40]

CARLYLE AND EMERSON, in sum, although sharing such problematical/elitist ideas as the "great man" theory of history, the Calvinist doctrine of election, and condescension toward the poor, share, too, the fruitful combination of empiricism with evangelicalism, for they signally represent the Anglo-American sensibility for which Wesley and Edwards, following Locke, are dual progenitors. Just as my *Wordsworth's "Natural Methodism"* and my *Locke, Wesley, and the Method of English Romanticism* explore the word *method* and the concept of methodology, so this book plays with *abridgment* and *bridge*. Besides considering Wesley's abridgment of Edwards's *Religious Affections* as an edition, I consider it as linking the study of Great Britain with the young, brash, but hardly isolated discipline of American studies. Although Anglo-American Romanticism can hardly be said to grow from the abridgment alone, the abridgment participates in the transition from the eighteenth century to the nineteenth and even signals a continuity from neoclassic to Romantic. This important British version of an important American work lends its authoritative perspective to an empirical-evangelical vision of intellectual history, religious culture, and literature in the English-speaking world, for common to the sensibilities of England the United States is the single, though twofold, tradition of empirical philosophy and evangelical faith.

Consider, finally, a compendium of the Carlylean-Emersonian expression in which I am interested, a baker's dozen of passages from the Carlyle/Emerson correspondence:[41]

> And so here, looking over the water, let me repeat once more what I believe is already dimly the sentiment of all Englishmen, Cisoceanic and Transoceanic, that we and you are *not* two countries, and cannot for the life of us be; but only two *parishes* of one country, with such wholesome parish hospitalities,

and dirty temporary parish feuds; as we see, both of which brave parishes *vivant! vivant!*

Carlyle to Emerson, August 12, 1834

What is to hinder huge London from being to universal Saxondom what small Mycale was to the tribes of Greece? . . . A meeting of *All the English* ought to be as good as one of All the Ionians; and as Homeric "equal ships" are to Bristol Steamers, so, or somewhat so, may New York and New Holland be to Ephesus and Crete, with their distances, relations, and etceteras!—Few things on this Earth look to me greater than the Future of that Family of Men.

Carlyle to Emerson, August 18, 1841

The engagement of writing & reading 18 lectures on Philosophy to a class of graduates . . . was a task a little more formidable in prospect & in practice than any foregoing one. . . . I doubt the experts in Philosophy will not praise my discourses; but the topics give me room for my guesses, criticism, admirations & experiences with the accepted masters, & also the lessons I have learned from the hidden great. I have the fancy that a realist is a good corrector of formalism, no matter how incapable of syllogism or continuous linked statement. To great results of thought & morals the steps are not many, & it is not the masters who spin the ostentatious continuity.

Emerson to Carlyle, June 17, 1870

I call [*Nature*] rather the Foundation and Ground-plan on which you may build whatsoever of great and true has been given you to build. It is the true Apocalypse this when the "open secret" becomes revealed to a man. I rejoice much in the glad serenity of soul with which you look out on this wondrous Dwelling-place of yours and mine,—with an ear for the *"Ewigen Melodien,"* which pipe in the winds round us, and utter themselves forth in all sounds and sights and things: *not* to be written down by gamut-machinery; but which all right writing is a kind of attempt to write down.

Carlyle to Emerson, February 13, 1837

I hear my Prophet [that is, Carlyle] deplore, as his predecessors did, the deaf ear and the gross heart of his people, and threaten to shut his lips; but, happily, this he cannot do, any more than could they. The word of the Lord *will* be spoken.

Emerson to Carlyle, April 30, 1835

[William Sewall, a leader of the evangelically inspired Oxford Movement] finds me a worthy fellow; "true, most true," . . . .

Carlyle to Emerson, September 26, 1840

James Stephen [of the evangelical Clapham Sect] is of [evangelical philanthropist and abolitionist William] Wilberforce's creed, of Wilberforce's Kin; . . . . In fact I regard the man [Stephen] as standing on the confines of Genius . . . a man of many really good qualities.

Carlyle to Emerson, November 17, 1842

Pantheism, Pottheism, Mydoxy, Thydoxy are nothing at all to me, a weariness the whole jargon, which I avoid speaking of, decline listening to: *Live,* for God's sake, with what Faith thou couldst get; leave off *speaking* about Faith! Thou knowest it not. Be *silent,* do not speak.—As to you, my friend, you are even to go on, giving still harder shocks [than those in *The Divinity School Address*] if need be; and should I come into censure by means of you, there or here, think that I am proud of my company; that, as the boy Hazlitt said after hearing Coleridge, "I will go with that man."

Carlyle to Emerson, November 7, 1838

Speak therefore, while you feel called to do it, and when you feel called. But for yourself, my friend, I prophecy [*sic*] it will not do always, a faculty is in you for a *sort* of speech which is itself *action,* an artistic sort. You *tell* us with piercing emphasis [in *The Divinity School Address*] that man's soul is great; *shew* us a great soul of a man, in some work symbolic of such: this is the seal of such a message, and you will feel by and by that you are called to this. I long to see some concrete thing, some Event, Man's Life, American Forest, or piece of Creation, which this Emerson loves and wonders at, well *Emersonized:* depictured by Emerson, filled with the life of Emerson, and cast forth from him then to live by itself.

Carlyle to Emerson, February 8, 1839

And if I could draw my prophet and his prophetess [Jane Carlyle] to brighten and immortalize my lodge, and make it the window through which for a summer you should look out on a field which Columbus and Berkeley and Lafayette did not scorn to sow, my sun should shine clearer and life would promise something better than peace.

Emerson to Carlyle, March 12, 1835

> The Visible becomes the Bestial when it rests not on the Invisible. Innumerable tumults of Metaphysic must be struggled thro' (whole generations perishing by the way), and at last Transcendentalism evolve itself (if I construe aright), as the *Euthanasia* of Metaphysic altogether. May it be sure, may it be speedy! Thou shalt open thy *eyes,* O Son of Adam; thou shalt *look,* and not forever jargon about *laws* of Optics and the making of spectacles! For myself, I rejoice very much that I seem to be flinging aside innumerable sets of spectacles (could I but *lay* them aside,—with gentleness!) and hope one day actually to see a thing or two. Man *lives* by Belief (as it was well written of old); by Logic he can only at best long to live.
>
> Carlyle to Emerson, May 13, 1835

> Did I tell you that I *saw* Wordsworth this winter? Twice, at considerable length; with almost no disappointment. He is a *natural* man (which means whole immensities here and now); flows like a natural well yielding mere wholesomeness.
>
> Carlyle to Emerson, May 13, 1835

> In the hideous stew of Anarchy in which all English Populations present themselves to my dismal contemplation at this day, it is a solid consolation that there will verily, in another fifty years, be above a hundred million men and women on this Planet who can all read Shakespeare and the English Bible and the (also for a long time biblical and noble) history of their Mother Country,—and proceed again to do, unless the Devil *be* in them, as their forebears did, or better, if they have the heart!
>
> Carlyle to Emerson, April 2, 1872

These conversations, back and forth, like the Lockean works written by Wesley and Edwards, demonstrate empiricism, evangelicalism, the "spiritual sense," and a more experiential than rationalistic idealism. Thus Carlyle's and Emerson's allusions to literature in general, British Romanticism in particular, and even Anglo-Americanism (or what Carlyle disturbingly calls "universal Saxondom") occur in the simultaneously philosophical and theological context that informs their works. During forty years of correspondence, as well as during the mutually creative decades of the 1830s and the 1840s, this premier Anglo-American diptych of nineteenth-century letters exercised an empirical-evangelical imagination, the distinguishing feature of Romanticism in the Anglo-American world.

NOTES

Introduction

1. Thomas McFarland, "Literature and Philosophy," 38.

2. See, e.g., Paul Ricoeur, *Freud and Philosophy.*

3. I refer to Harold Bloom, *The Anxiety of Influence.*

4. See Robert Langbaum, *The Poetry of Experience: The Dramatic Monologue in Modern Literary Tradition;* Langbaum, *The Mysteries of Identity: A Theme in Modern Literature;* and Langbaum, *The Word from Below: Essays on Modern Literature and Culture,* esp. 33–57. See also George Bornstein, *Yeats and Shelley;* Bornstein, *Transformations of Romanticism in Yeats, Eliot, and Stevens;* Bornstein, ed., *Romantic and Modern: Revaluations of Literary Tradition;* and Carlos Baker, *The Echoing Green: Romanticism, Modernism, and the Phenomena of Transference in Poetry.*

5. See, besides Langbaum's work, L. J. Swingle, *The Obstinate Questionings of English Romanticism.*

6. See the discussion in David Lehman, *Signs of the Times: Deconstruction and the Fall of Paul de Man.* See also William Safire, "On Language," *The Gainesville Sun,* March 10, 1991; Safire takes his cue from Paul Goldberger, cultural news editor of *The New York Times,* who does not believe that either Modernism or Romanticism is quite dead.

7. Alvin Kernan, *The Imaginary Library: An Essay on Literature and Society,* esp. 26, 130–31, 156.

8. See, for example, Herbert Tucker, *Tennyson and the Doom of Romanticism;* Joanne Feit Diehl, *Dickinson and the Romantic Imagination;* and Anthony H. Harrison, *Victorian Poets and Romantic Poems: Intertextuality and Ideology.*

9. Richard E. Brantley, *Wordsworth's "Natural Methodism."*

10. Richard E. Brantley, *Locke, Wesley, and the Method of English Romanticism.*

11. Marshall Brown, *Preromanticism.*

12. E. D. Hirsch, Jr., *The Aims of Interpretation,* 140–42. Hirsch paraphrases the view of Edward Dowden, the nineteenth-century biographer of Shelley and Shakespeare.

1. An Anglo-American Nexus

1. I allude to Emerson's *Representative Men* (1850), a collection of essays on Plato, Emanuel Swedenborg, Montaigne, Shakespeare, Napoleon, and Goethe. Some of Emerson's other works, I suggest, add Wesley and Edwards to the list.

2. I adapt the phrase "gene-culture coevolution" to my purposes. The phrase is used throughout Edward O. Wilson, *Sociobiology.*

3. See, e.g., Norman Fiering, *Jonathan Edwards's Moral Thought and Its British Context;* William J. Wainwright, "Jonathan Edwards and the Language of God"; and Nathan O. Hatch and Harry S. Stout, eds., *Jonathan Edwards and the American Experience.*

4. For samples of Perry Miller's argument for Edwards as a Lockean, see Miller's *Jonathan Edwards* and his "Jonathan Edwards and the Sense of the Heart."

5. For Locke's "theocentric framework," see Richard Ashcroft, "Faith and Knowledge in Locke's Philosophy"; David Gauthier, "Why Ought One Obey God? Reflections on Hobbes and Locke"; James Farr, "The Way of Hypotheses: Locke on Method"; and W. M. Spellman, *John Locke and the Problem of Depravity.* Spellman's positioning of Locke on the Latitudinarian *via media* between Calvinism and Deism is especially persuasive. For Locke's empiricism, see, e.g., John W. Yolton, *John Locke and the Compass of Human Understanding,* and Roger Woolhouse, *Locke's Philosophy of Science and Knowledge.*

6. Terrence Erdt, *Jonathan Edwards: Art and the Sense of the Heart.*

7. Roland Delattre, *Beauty and Sensibility in the Thought of Jonathan Edwards: An Essay in Aesthetics and Theological Ethics.*

8. Sacvan Bercovitch, *The American Jeremiad,* 107–8. Edwards's model of mind, according to James Hoopes, is Lockean in that it is unitary, for both Edwards and Locke regard "mind" and "thought" as synonymous, and they do not recognize the unconscious mind. Edwards's commitment to the "way of ideas," however, out-Lockes Locke's, for while Locke's model of soul allows for spiritual substance, Edwards's "soul" is made up of ideas only. See James Hoopes, "Calvinism and Consciousness from Edwards to Beecher."

9. Wallace E. Anderson, "The Development of Edwards' Philosophical Thought," 101–2.

10. See the discussion in Anderson, "The Development of Edwards' Philosophical Thought," 101–2. See also Edward H. Davidson, "From Locke to Edwards"; Claude A. Smith, "Jonathan Edwards and the 'Way of Ideas'"; and Paul Helm, "John Locke and Jonathan Edwards: A Reconsideration." Michael J. Colacurcio's emphasis on Edwards's career after 1750, and especially on *The Great Christian Doctrine of Original Sin Defended,* leads to a perhaps too-narrow focus on his capacity for "idealist imagination": "what makes Edwards everywhere Edwards is some absolutely fundamental bias of imagination in favor of idealism." Edwards's career as a whole includes empiricist as well as idealist elements and is aptly summed up (if again with more idealist bias than the entire career warrants) in this observation by Colacurcio: "A capacity to suspect that reality might be very subtle, and a power to suspend belief long enough to wonder *how* subtle, may tell us more than anything else about the unity and priorities of a mind which saw spiders and thought 'teleology,' which learned of atoms and guessed 'power,' which experienced both nature and grace and leaped to 'idea,' and which ultimately contrived to hand the whole world, including its own consciousness and that of every other man, over to *God Alone.*" See Michael J. Colacurcio, "The Example of Edwards: Idealist Imagination and the Metaphysics of Sovereignty," esp. 96, 98.

11. Robert W. Jenson, *America's Theologian: A Recommendation of Jonathan Edwards,* esp. 3.

12. Charles Rogers, "John Wesley and Jonathan Edwards."

13. See *The Works of the Rev. John Wesley, A.M.*, ed. Thomas Jackson, 10.463, 467, 475.

14. Ibid., 10.460.

15. Albert Outler, *John Wesley,* 16.

16. See Rogers, "John Wesley and Jonathan Edwards," 36.

17. Many thanks to Frederick Dreyer for corresponding with me about his work, which includes his "Faith and Experience in the Thought of John Wesley" and his "Evangelical Thought: John Wesley and Jonathan Edwards."

18. The essay and Harvey G. Townsend's discussion of it are in Townsend, ed., *The Philosophy of Jonathan Edwards from His Private Notebooks,* xi–xiii, 1–20.

19. The other four of Edwards's works abridged by Wesley are *A Faithful Narrative of the Surprising Work of God in the Conversion of many hundred souls in Northampton* (1736); *The Distinguishing Marks of a Work of the Spirit of God* (1741); *Some Thoughts concerning the Present Revival in New England* (1742); and *An Account of the Life of the Late Reverend Mr. David Brainerd*

(1749). Wesley's abridgments of these works are *A Narrative of Many Surprising Conversions in Northampton and Vicinity* (1744); *The Distinguishing Marks of a Work of the Spirit of God* (1744); *Thoughts concerning the Present Revival of Religion* (1745); and *An Extract of the Life of the Late Rev. Mr. David Brainerd* (1768).

20. See John Wesley, ed., *An Extract from a Treatise concerning Religious Affections,* in *The Works of the Rev. John Wesley,* and the discussion in *The Works of Jonathan Edwards,* ed. John E. Smith, vol. 2: *A Treatise concerning Religious Affections,* 79. My quotations of the abridgment are from a widely available reprint of it in the following collection of Wesley's abridgments: John Wesley, ed., *A Christian Library: Consisting of Extracts from and Abridgments of the choicest Pieces of Practical Divinity which have been published in the English Tongue;* see 30.308–76.

21. See Jonathan Edwards, *A Treatise concerning Religious Affections: In Three Parts,* ed. William Gordon.

22. Gregory S. Clapper, "'True Religion' and the Affections: A Study of John Wesley's Abridgment of Jonathan Edwards's Treatise on the Religious Affections," 418.

23. See, e.g., Frank Baker, "A Study of John Wesley's Readings."

24. See, e.g., T. Walter Herbert, *John Wesley as Editor and Author,* 75–79.

25. Many of the alterations are more aesthetically motivated than pursuant to Wesley's fears about whether his readers would follow Edwards's thought. Characteristically, Wesley excises verbiage, thus clarifying Edwards's intentions and enhancing his treatise. The following instance is typical (brackets enclose Wesley's omissions): "The kindling [and raising] of gracious affections is like kindling a flame, the higher it is raised, the more ardent it is [and the more it burns, the more vehemently does it tend and seek to burn]" (Gordon's edition of Edwards, *A Treatise concerning Religious Affections,* 211, and Wesley, "An Extract from a Treatise concerning Religious Affections," in *A Christian Library,* 30.363). See also Edwards, *Treatise,* 50, and Wesley, "Extract," 334; Edwards, 54–55, and Wesley, 336; Edwards, 202, and Wesley, 359; and Edwards, 205, and Wesley, 361. Wesley's omissions of many biblical quotations constitute a major means by which he achieves economy of expression: see Edwards, 39–41, and Wesley, 329; Edwards, 42, and Wesley, 330; Edwards, 43, and Wesley, 330; Edwards, 53, and Wesley, 335; Edwards, 54, and Wesley, 336; Edwards, 79–80, and Wesley, 344; Edwards, 81, and Wesley, 344; Edwards, 82, and Wesley, 344; Edwards, 157, and Wesley, 346; Edwards, 188, and Wesley, 353; Edwards, 199, and Wesley, 358; Edwards, 200, and Wesley, 359; Edwards, 204, and Wesley, 360; Edwards, 255–56, and Wesley, 374; and Edwards, 256–57, and Wesley, 374. Gordon, like Edwards, tolerates repetitiousness; Wesley does not: see Edwards,

17–18, and Wesley, 317; Edwards, 65, and Wesley, 342; Edwards, 74–79, and Wesley, 343; Edwards, 87–155, and Wesley, 346; Edwards, 170–71, and Wesley, 349; Edwards, 192–93, and Wesley, 355; Edwards, 202, and Wesley, 359; Edwards, 214–15, and Wesley, 363; Edwards, 217, and Wesley, 364; Edwards, 225–26, and Wesley, 366; Edwards, 237–53, and Wesley, 367; and Edwards, 244–47, and Wesley, 368. Wesley achieves his combination of brevity and fidelity to the original in part by omitting subtopics of a clearly established line of argument: for an especially notable example, see Edwards, 167–70, and Wesley, 349.

26. I take this epitome of Arminianism from Hymn 17 of the Wesley brothers' *Collection of Hymns, for the Use of the People Called Methodists*. For a characterization of the Wesleys' Arminianism see Richard E. Brantley, "Charles Wesley's Experiential Art."

27. See Edwards, *Religious Affections,* 33, and Wesley, "Extract," 326.

28. See Edwards, *Religious Affections,* 53, and Wesley, "Extract," 335.

29. See Edwards, *Religious Affections,* 55–56, and Wesley, "Extract," 336; and Edwards, *Religious Affections,* 217–21, and Wesley, "Extract," 364.

30. See Edwards, *Religious Affections,* 38, and Wesley, "Extract," 329.

31. See Edwards, *Religious Affections,* 38, and Wesley, "Extract," 329. See also Richard E. Brantley, *Locke, Wesley, and the Method of English Romanticism,* 53, 68, 233 n. 44.

32. See Edwards, *Religious Affections,* 21, and Wesley, "Extract," 319; Edwards, 171–72, and Wesley, 349; Edwards, 179–80, and Wesley, 352; Edwards, 200, and Wesley, 358; Edwards, 201, and Wesley, 359; Edwards, 203, and Wesley, 360; and Edwards, 260–63, and Wesley, 376.

33. See Edwards, *Religious Affections,* 50, and Wesley, "Extract," 334; Edwards, 53, and Wesley, 335; Edwards, 66, and Wesley, 342; and Edwards, 86, and Wesley, 345.

34. See Edwards, *Religious Affections,* 9, and Wesley, "Extract," 314; Edwards, 24, and Wesley, 321; Edwards, 42, and Wesley, 330; Edwards, 60, and Wesley, 340; Edwards, 79, and Wesley, 343; Edwards, 85–86, and Wesley, 345; Edwards, 177, and Wesley, 351; Edwards, 204, and Wesley, 360; Edwards, 211, and Wesley, 363; and Edwards, 223–24, and Wesley, 365.

35. I refer to Blake's "The Mental Traveller" (1801–5?).

36. I refer to Blake's *The Marriage of Heaven and Hell* (1793).

37. Wesley, "Extract," 308.

38. See Clapper, "'True Religion' and the Affections," 417. "Against the encroachments of Arminian liberalism, which emphasized human reason, free will, and a benevolent Deity," wrote John Patrick Diggins (in a statement pointing to the difficulty of irenically reading Arminianism and Calvinism), "Edwards waged a rearguard defense of Calvinism's essential principles: man's utter depravity and

inability to influence salvation through good works; the election of a few by a transforming grace that cannot be resisted; the uncertainty of the state of one's soul, even for the elect, hence the perseverance of the saints; and within this drama of redemption and damnation, the inscrutability of God's nature." See Diggins, "Puritans and Pragmatists," 39.

39. See Edwards, *Religious Affections,* 60–61, and Wesley, "Extract," 340; Edwards, 61–63, and Wesley, 340; and Edwards, 70–73, and Wesley, 343.

40. Clapper, "'True Religion' and the Affections," 418.

41. For a paradoxical argument that Edwards's ontology is finally epistemological, that according to Edwards's thought "dispositions and habits . . . can mediate between being and becoming, permanence and process," see Sang Hyun Lee, *The Philosophical Theology of Jonathan Edwards,* esp. 3, 115–70.

42. See Edwards, *Religious Affections,* 3, and Wesley, "Extract," 311.

43. Ibid. See also Edwards, 2, and Wesley, 310; and Edwards, 189–91, and Wesley, 354.

44. See the discussion in Clapper, "'True Religion' and the Affections," 418–19.

45. See Edwards, *Religious Affections,* 30–31, and Wesley, "Extract," 324; and Edwards, 198, and Wesley, 358. See also Brantley, *Locke, Wesley, and the Method of English Romanticism,* 15, 17, 125.

46. See Edwards, *Religious Affections,* 8, and Wesley, "Extract," 313.

47. Edwards, *Religious Affections,* 48–49.

48. See Wesley, "Extract," 333, where the passage would have appeared.

49. See Brantley, *Locke, Wesley, and the Method of English Romanticism,* 20–21.

50. See Edwards, *Religious Affections,* 18–19, and Wesley, "Extract," 317.

51. See Edwards, *Religious Affections,* 9, and Wesley, "Extract," 315. See also Edwards, 22, and Wesley, 319; Edwards, 26–27, and Wesley, 321–22; and Edwards, 33–34, and Wesley, 326–27.

52. See Brantley, *Locke, Wesley, and the Method of English Romanticism,* 15, 48–49, 61–62, 89, 100, 250 n. 31.

53. For Edwards's most overt "empiricism," and for Wesley's fidelity to it, see Edwards, *Religious Affections,* 13, and Wesley, "Extract," 312–13; Edwards, 17, and Wesley, 317; Edwards, 18, and Wesley, 317–19; Edwards, 33, and Wesley, 325–26; Edwards, 43, and Wesley, 330; Edwards, 48, and Wesley, 333–35; Edwards, 58–60, and Wesley, 338–39; Edwards, 86–87, and Wesley, 345–46; Edwards, 166, and Wesley, 348; Edwards, 221–22, and Wesley, 364–65; Edwards, 224–25, and Wesley, 365; Edwards, 253–55, and Wesley, 372–73; and Edwards, 256, and Wesley, 374–75. Clapper, in "'True Religion' and the Affec-

tions," 419, recognizes "spiritual empiricism" in what the abridgment includes of the treatise's third part, but "spiritual empiricism" is scattered throughout the abridgment.

54. Denis Donoghue, *The Third Voice: Modern British and American Verse Drama,* 18.

55. John Locke, *Essay,* 4.9.3 and 4.10.6 in *An Essay concerning Human Understanding,* ed. Peter H. Nidditch, 618, 621. Subsequent references to this edition are abbreviated "Nidditch."

56. Locke, *Essay,* 4.11.1; Nidditch, 630.

57. Locke, *Essay,* 4.19.5; Nidditch, 698–99.

58. Wesley, "Extract," 333. Cf. Eccles. 11.5.

59. Locke, *Essay,* 4.19.16; Nidditch, 705.

60. "God when he makes the Prophet," Locke observes, "does not unmake the Man," and Locke adds that God "leaves all Man's Faculties in their natural State, to enable him to judge of his Inspirations, whether they be of divine Original or no. . . . We cannot take it for a *Revelation,* or so much as for true, till we have some other Mark that it is a *Revelation,* besides our believing that it is so. . . . *Gideon* was sent by an Angel to deliver Israel from the *Midianites,* and yet he desired a Sign to convince him, that this Commission was from God" (*Essay,* 4.19.14–15; Nidditch, 704).

61. Wesley, "Extract," 325.

62. Ibid., 333.

63. Ibid., 339.

64. Ibid., 346. Cf. Locke, *Essay,* 4.18.10; Nidditch, 696.

65. Wesley, "Extract," 317.

66. For Locke's discussion of "constant impressions" in the mind, see Locke, *Essay,* 1.2.2–5; Nidditch, 49–51.

67. I refer to Wordsworth's "Expostulation and Reply" (1798).

68. See the discussion in Hugh Sykes Davies, "Wordsworth and the Empirical Philosophers." Davies focuses on Wordsworth's objective usage of *impulse,* as in this stanza from "The Tables Turned" (1798): "One *impulse* from a vernal wood / May teach you more of man, / Of moral evil and of good, / Than all the sages can" (my italics).

69. Locke, *Essay,* 4.19.6; Nidditch, 699 (my italics).

70. Wesley, "Extract," 337 (my italics).

71. Locke, *Essay,* 2.9.4; Nidditch, 144 (my italics).

72. Richard Saunders, *A Discourse of Angels: Their Nature and Office, or Ministry; also Something Touching Devils, Apparitions, and Impulses.*

73. Wesley, "Extract," 374.

74. Hymn 280, Wesley and Wesley, *A Collection of Hymns, for the Use of the People Called Methodists* (1780); see the discussion in G. H. Vallins, *The Wesleys and the English Language,* 87.

75. Wesley, "Extract," 340.

76. Ibid., 342.

77. See Brantley, *Locke, Wesley, and the Method of English Romanticism,* 12.

78. See, for example, in Brantley, *Locke, Wesley, and the Method of English Romanticism,* 37–44, how Wesley's definition of faith "delineated, for the first time, revelation's inward as well as outward setting and hence its commensurability with empirical philosophy's subject/object emphasis." The other four of Edwards's works abridged by Wesley are "Lockean," too, but unlike Locke's *Essay,* as well as unlike Edwards's *Religious Affections,* they stress experience to the point of subordinating reason.

79. Wesley, "Extract," 325.

80. Ibid.

81. Ibid.; cf. Locke, *Essay,* 4.19; Nidditch, 697–706.

82. Wesley, "Extract," 326.

83. Ibid., 325.

84. Locke, *Essay,* 4.19.15; Nidditch, 705.

85. Wesley, "Extract," 326.

86. Ibid., 322. Cf. Matt. 6.29, Ps. 73.1, and Heb. 3.16.

87. Wesley, "Extract," 319.

88. This strain of the abridgment's experiential theology, incidentally, finds an illuminating counterpart in another "both/and" permutation of Locke by Wordsworth; here, from "Expostulation and Reply," is the full context of "wise passiveness": "The eye—it cannot choose but see; / We cannot bid the ear be still; / Our bodies feel, where'er they be, / Against or with our will. / Nor less I deem that there are Powers / Which of themselves our minds impress; / That we can feed this mind of ours / In a wise passiveness."

89. Wesley, "Extract," 312.

90. Locke, *Essay,* 2.10.5; Nidditch, 151–52.

91. Wesley, "Extract," 321.

92. Ibid., 312.

93. Although Wordsworth, in the following lines from his "Prospectus" to *The Recluse,* does not address the issue of perception as Wesley and Edwards do, that is, although he does not on this occasion apprehend divine reality through the senses as analogues, tests, and receptors, he otherwise gets this "Wesleyan-Edwardsean," indeed this Lockean, point just right: "My voice proclaims / How exquisitely the individual Mind / (And the progressive powers perhaps no less /

Of the whole species) to the external World / Is fitted;—and how exquisitely, too— / Theme this but little heard of among men— / The external World is fitted to the Mind; / And the creation (by no lower name / Can it be called) which they with blended might / Accomplish:—this is our high argument."

94. Edwards, *A Treatise concerning Religious Affections,* ed. Smith, 46.

95. Wesley, "Extract," 312–13.

96. Ibid., 364–65.

97. Ibid., 313.

98. Edwards, *A Treatise concerning Religious Affections,* ed. Smith, 46.

99. Ibid., 46 (my italics).

100. Wesley, "Extract," 338.

101. Cf. 2 Cor. 3.18; 4.6.

102. Wesley, "Extract," 310 (my italics).

103. Ibid., 339.

104. Ibid., 345–46.

105. One thinks, in this connection, of Wordsworth's "natural piety": "My heart leaps up when I behold / A rainbow in the sky: / So was it when my life began; / So is it now I am a man; / So be it when I shall grow old, / Or let me die! / The child is father of the Man; / And I could wish my days to be / Bound each to each by natural piety." These lines are thoroughly Lockean: see the discussion in Samuel F. Pickering, Jr., *John Locke and Children's Books in Eighteenth-Century England,* 160–68. The abridgment, in its Lockean dimension, is consistent with them. "Natural piety" is secularized piety, or so goes the wisdom about Wordsworth, but the phrase connotes a faith in the God of nature, and as Wordsworth responds to the rainbow, so Wesley and Edwards claim "sense perception" of God's promises.

106. Wesley, "Extract," 373.

107. Ibid.

108. Locke, *Essay,* 4.16.6; Nidditch, 661–62.

109. Wesley, "Extract," 335 (my italics).

110. Edwards, *A Treatise concerning Religious Affections,* ed. Smith, 17.

111. Wesley, "Extract," 375.

112. John Wesley, *The Appeals to Men of Reason and Religion,* ed. Gerald R. Cragg, 57.

113. See the discussion in Brantley, *Locke, Wesley, and the Method of English Romanticism,* 48–53, 99–100, 109, 113, 116, 144, 221–23.

114. Peter Browne, *The Procedure, Extent, and Limits of Human Understanding,* 141–42.

115. See Locke, *Essay,* 4.16.12; Nidditch, 667.

116. See, for example, the discussion in Leopold Damrosch's review of Brantley,

Locke, Wesley, and the Method of English Romanticism in *Eighteenth-Century Studies* 19 (1986): 438–41.

117. Anders Jeffner, *Butler and Hume on Religion: A Comparative Analysis,* 185.

118. Wesley, "Extract," 313.

119. Ibid., 346.

120. I refer to W. B. Yeats's "The Fascination of What's Difficult" (1910).

121. I refer to H. J. Zelley's hymn, "Heavenly Sunshine" (1898). See William J. Reynolds, ed., *Baptist Hymnal,* 472.

122. For Wesley's account of his conversion, see *The Journal of the Rev. John Wesley, A. M.,* ed. Nehemiah Curnock, 1.475–76.

123. See Kenneth MacLean, *John Locke and English Literature of the Eighteenth Century,* and Hans Aarsleff, *From Locke to Saussure: Essays on the Study of Language and Intellectual History.*

124. I refer to Wordsworth's "Lines, Written a Few Miles Above Tintern Abbey" (1798).

125. For a full study of Wesley's intellectual influence, see esp. chapter 3 of Brantley, *Locke, Wesley, and the Method of English Romanticism,* 103–28. The Christian movement, the Methodists, the Baptists, the black churches, and the Mormons illustrate what Nathan O. Hatch calls "The Democratization of American Christianity": Hatch studies "the democratic character of the early republic's insurgent religious movements." Methodists and Baptists, however (if not Mormons, the black churches, and the Christian movement), all had access to Arminian-democratic, and hence imported, religious thought. Democratization, perhaps, was not quite so indigenous a process as Hatch implies. See Hatch, *The Democratization of American Christianity,* esp. 9.

126. Frank Baker, "John Wesley and America," esp. 124.

127. As quoted ibid., 121 (my italics).

128. For an especially readable discussion of the range and nature of Wesley's abridgments, see Herbert, *John Wesley as Editor and Author,* 25–31. See also Reginald Doidge, *John Wesley's* Christian Library.

129. Clapper, "'True Religion' and the Affections," 417.

130. G. S. Rousseau, "John Wesley's *Primitive Physick* (1747)."

131. *The Letters of the Rev. John Wesley, A. M.,* ed. John Telford, 6.201.

132. Alan Heimert, *Religion and the American Mind, from the Great Awakening to the Revolution;* Peter Shaw, *American Patriots and the Rituals of Revolution;* Philip Greven, *The Protestant Temperament: Patterns of Child-rearing, Religious Experience, and the Self in Early America;* and Bercovitch, *The American Jeremiad,* 133.

133. Jay Fliegelman, *Prodigals and Pilgrims: The American Revolution against Patriarchal Authority, 1750–1800.*

134. See the discussion in Edwards, *A Treatise concerning Religious Affections,* ed. Smith, 75–80. *Religious Affections,* according to William Breitenbach, was the chief Edwardsean influence on such early nineteenth-century "New Divinity" theologian-preachers (of western Massachusetts and Connecticut) as Jonathan Edwards, Jr., Samuel Hopkins, and Joseph Bellamy, but Breitenbach confines his emphasis to *Religious Affections*'s "piety and moralism." See Breitenbach, "Piety and Moralism: Edwards and the New Divinity."

135. Richard Carwardine, *Transatlantic Revivalism: Popular Evangelicalism in Britain and America, 1790–1865,* 6, 9, 40, 123–24, 146.

136. David Hempton, *Methodism and Politics in British Society, 1750–1850,* esp. 22. Hempton's awareness of a religious dimension to the political common ground between England and the United States provides a corrective to the narrow, negative view of Christopher Hitchens in *Blood, Class, and Nostalgia: Anglo-American Ironies.*

137. Frederick Dreyer, "A 'Religious Society Under Heaven': John Wesley and the Identity of Methodism."

138. Carwardine, *Transatlantic Revivalism,* 10. On December 24, 1784, at the Lovely Lane Chapel in Baltimore, Methodism was organized as an American denomination, with eighty preachers and a membership of 14,988. By 1790, the membership was 57,631. From 1773 to 1790, the American population increased 75 percent. During the same period, Methodism increased 5,500 percent. See Edmund W. Robb, Jr., "American Methodism at 200: The Case for Hope," 21.

139. Hempton, *Methodism and Politics in British Society, 1750–1850,* 12.

140. T. W. Laquer, *Religion and Respectability: Sunday Schools and Working-Class Culture, 1780–1850,* esp. 44.

2. The Empirical/Evangelical Dialectic of Thomas Carlyle

1. *Thomas Carlyle: Selected Writings,* ed. Alan Shelston, 15.

2. Eloise M. Behnken, *Thomas Carlyle: "Calvinist without the Theology,"* 3. See also Albert J. LaValley, *Carlyle and the Idea of the Modern: Studies in Carlyle's Prophetic Literature and Its Relation to Blake, Nietzsche, Marx, and Others.*

3. George P. Landow, *Elegant Jeremiahs: The Sage from Carlyle to Mailer,* esp. 132–53. G. B. Tennyson describes Carlyle not as secularized, Fascist, and Marxist, but as "obsessed with the idea of God" and with "the reality of the transcendent." See G. B. Tennyson, "Carlyle: Beginning with the Word," esp. 18–19.

4. For a subtle study of radical skepticism in both British empiricism and Cartesian methodology, see L. J. Swingle, *The Obstinate Questionings of English Romanticism,* esp. chapter 1, "The Romantic Situation: The Ground of Romantic Questioning."

5. Michael Timko, *Carlyle and Tennyson,* esp. 7–23.

6. See the accounts in A. Abbott Ikeler, *Puritan Temper and Transcendental Faith: Carlyle's Literary Vision,* 61–71; and Timko, *Carlyle and Tennyson,* 7–23.

7. Thomas Carlyle, *Sartor Resartus: The Life and Opinions of Herr Teufelsdröckh,* ed. Charles Frederick Harrold, vi–vii.

8. Ian Campbell, "Thomas Carlyle (1795–1881)," 48.

9. David J. DeLaura, "Carlyle and Arnold: The Religious Issue."

10. Behnken, *Thomas Carlyle: "Calvinist without the Theology",* 2.

11. For the relationship between Carlyle and Edward Irving, see, for example, Fred Kaplan, *Thomas Carlyle: A Biography,* 94, 147–49, 155, 172–74.

12. See the discussions in Landow, *Elegant Jeremiahs: The Sage from Carlyle to Mailer,* esp. 132–53; and G. Robert Stange, "Refractions of *Past and Present,*" 110.

13. The phrase is that of Behnken in *Thomas Carlyle,* 5–6.

14. See the discussion in *Thomas Carlyle: Selected Writings,* ed. Shelston, 7–30, esp. 15. In the early 1820s, Carlyle produced more than four volumes of translations and biographical and critical notices of German authors and philosophers, including a translation of Goethe's *Wilhelm Meister's Apprenticeship* (1824) and a biography of Schiller (1825). The fullest overviews of Carlyle's relation to the Germans are still to be found in Louis Cazamian, *Carlyle;* and Carlyle, *Sartor Resartus: The Life and Opinions of Herr Teufelsdröckh,* ed. Harrold.

15. Ikeler, *Puritan Temper and Transcendental Faith: Carlyle's Literary Vision,* 102. Carlyle, according to Wendell V. Harris, is exclusively transcendental and not empirical or religious at all; see Harris, *The Omnipresent Debate: Empiricism and Transcendentalism in Nineteenth-Century English Prose,* esp. 180–93, 201–10, 261, 265.

16. Campbell, "Thomas Carlyle (1795–1881)," 51–52.

17. Ruth apRoberts, *The Ancient Dialect: Thomas Carlyle and Comparative Religion.*

18. See George Steiner, "Ecstasies, Not Arguments," a review of the journals of Mircea Eliade, in *TLS* (September 28–October 4, 1990) 1015–16.

19. *Thomas Carlyle: Selected Writings,* ed. Shelston, 52. Subsequent references to Shelston's edition will be by page number alone. Shelston's edition, based on H. D. Traill's *The Works* (30 volumes; 1898–1901), is both widely available and fully representative, but the University of California Press will soon publish new

editions of Carlyle's major works under the general editorship of Murray Baumgarten.

20. As quoted in Ikeler, *Puritan Temper and Transcendental Faith*, 6–7.

21. Ikeler, *Puritan Temper and Transcendental Faith*, 5.

22. I refer to line 49 of Wordsworth's "Tintern Abbey."

23. Landow is the exception; see *Elegant Jeremiahs*, 21, 29n, 33, 61, 71n.

24. Carlisle Moore, "Carlyle: Mathematics and 'Mathesis.'"

25. See *Thomas Carlyle: Selected Writings*, ed. Shelston, 87. See also G. B. Tennyson, *Sartor Called Resartus: The Genesis, Structure, and Style of Thomas Carlyle's First Major Work*.

26. *Thomas Carlyle: Selected Writings*, ed. Shelston, 87.

27. Campbell, "Thomas Carlyle," 52.

28. See the discussion in *Thomas Carlyle: Selected Writings*, ed. Shelston, 87.

29. See the discussion ibid., 113.

30. George Levine, *The Boundaries of Fiction: Carlyle, Macaulay, Newman*.

31. Mark Cumming, *A Disimprisoned Epic: Form and Vision in Carlyle's French Revolution*.

32. See John D. Rosenberg, *Carlyle and the Burden of History*.

33. Ibid., passim.

34. Landow, *Elegant Jeremiahs*, 33, 41, 43, 67, 92, 162.

35. See also *Thomas Carlyle: Selected Writings*, ed. Shelston, 166, 178, 179, 190, 204.

36. Ibid., 160, 162, 164, 172, 176, 223–24.

37. See, for example, Carlyle's *Characteristics* (1831).

38. Rosenberg, *Carlyle and the Burden of History*.

39. Stange, "Refractions of *Past and Present*," 110.

40. Campbell, "Thomas Carlyle," 62–63. See also Campbell's *Thomas Carlyle*.

41. As quoted in Campbell, "Thomas Carlyle," 60.

42. Ikeler, *Puritan Temper and Transcendental Faith*, 137, 146.

43. See, for example, Philip Rosenberg, *The Seventh Hero: Thomas Carlyle and the Theory of Radical Activism*, and John D. Rosenberg, *Carlyle and the Burden of History*.

44. See the discussion in Campbell, "Thomas Carlyle," 51.

45. Ibid.

46. See Timko, *Carlyle and Tennyson*, 116–39 ("Carlyle and the Romantic Poets").

47. *Thomas Carlyle: Selected Writings*, ed. Shelston, 14.

48. See the discussion ibid.

49. Chris R. Vanden Bosshe, *Carlyle and the Search for Authority,* vii. See also viii–ix, 1, 14, and passim.

3. The Empirical/Evangelical Dialectic of Ralph Waldo Emerson

1. A good introduction to American Transcendentalism remains that of Octavius Brooks Frothingham, *Transcendentalism in New England.*

2. Francis Murphy and Herschel Parker, eds., *The Norton Anthology of American Literature: Second Edition* 1.821. For the historical context of Emerson's scientific views, see, for example, Charles Singer, *A Short History of Scientific Ideas to 1900;* Charles Gillespie, *The Edge of Objectivity;* Harold Sharlin, *The Convergent Century: The Unification of Science in the Nineteenth Century;* and Edward Lurie, *Nature and the American Mind: Louis Aggasiz and the Culture of Science.*

3. For Emerson's knowledge of Plato, see Stuart Gerry Brown, "Emerson's Platonism."

4. Murphy and Parker, eds., *The Norton Anthology of American Literature: Second Edition* 1.822.

5. See, e.g., the discussion in Arthur O. Wlecke, *Wordsworth and the Sublime,* esp. 155. See also Frederick J. Copleston, *A History of Philosophy* 8.176–81.

6. See, e.g., Richard Ashcroft, "Faith and Knowledge in Locke's Philosophy." See also James Farr, "The Way of Hypotheses: Locke on Method."

7. Harold Bloom, ed., *Modern Critical Views: Ralph Waldo Emerson,* 5.

8. *Selections from Ralph Waldo Emerson: An Organic Anthology,* ed. Stephen E. Whicher, 350. Subsequent citations of this edition are by page number alone.

9. Bloom, ed., *Modern Critical Views: Ralph Waldo Emerson,* 5.

10. David Van Leer, *Emerson's Epistemology: The Argument of the Essays,* xiii.

11. Van Leer focuses on *Nature, An Address Delivered before the Senior Class in Divinity College, Cambridge, Sunday Evening 15 July, 1838* (hereafter *The Divinity School Address*), *Self-Reliance,* and *Experience.*

12. Van Leer, *Emerson's Epistemology,* xiv.

13. Witness, for example, the centrality of *The Lord's Supper* in both David Robinson's *Apostle of Culture: Emerson as Preacher and Lecturer* and John Michael's *Emerson and Skepticism: The Cipher of the World.* Michael, focusing on Emerson's early career, offers close readings of just three essays: *The Lord's Supper, Nature,* and *The Divinity School Address.*

14. Van Leer, *Emerson's Epistemology,* esp. 2–3.

15. *The Collected Works of Ralph Waldo Emerson,* ed. Robert Spilka, Albert

Ferguson, et al., 1.201, 206–7, as quoted in Van Leer, *Emerson's Epistemology,* 2–3.

16. Van Leer, *Emerson's Epistemology,* 222.

17. See René Wellek, "Emerson and German Philosophy." See also Joel Porte, *Emerson and Thoreau: Transcendentalists in Conflict,* 45–92.

18. Van Leer, *Emerson's Epistemology,* x.

19. See the discussion ibid., 211. See also Norman Fiering's two volumes, *Moral Philosophy at Seventeenth-Century Harvard: A Discipline in Transition* and *Jonathan Edwards's Moral Thought and Its British Context.* See also Hans Aarsleff, *From Locke to Saussure: Essays on the Study of Language and Intellectual History.*

20. Michael, *Emerson and Skepticism,* xi. For pertinent introductions to the skeptical background, see Richard H. Popkin's two volumes, *The History of Skepticism: From Erasmus to Spinoza* and *The High Road to Pyrrhonism.*

21. See Michael, *Emerson and Skepticism,* 169; Evan Carton, *The Rhetoric of American Romance: Dialectic and Identity in Emerson, Dickinson, Poe, and Hawthorne.*

22. Michael, *Emerson and Skepticism,* 169.

23. Ibid., xii–xiii.

24. Ibid.

25. Ibid., 168.

26. As quoted in ibid.

27. Cameron Thompson, "John Locke and New England Transcendentalism."

28. *The Journals and Miscellaneous Notebooks of Ralph Waldo Emerson,* ed. William Gilman et al., hereafter *Journals.*

29. Stephen E. Whicher, *Freedom and Fate: An Inner Life of Ralph Waldo Emerson,* 17.

30. Michael, *Emerson and Skepticism,* 169.

31. Bloom, ed., *Modern Critical Views: Ralph Waldo Emerson,* 1.

32. Perry Miller, "From Edwards to Emerson."

33. Bloom, ed., *Modern Critical Views: Ralph Waldo Emerson,* 5.

34. See Robinson, *Apostle of Culture,* and Lawrence Buell, *Literary Transcendentalism: Style and Vision in the American Renaissance.*

35. See David Robinson's introduction to *The Complete Sermons of Ralph Waldo Emerson,* edited by Albert J. von Frank, 1.3.

36. Robinson, *Apostle of Culture,* 4.

37. Ibid.

38. See Leonard Neufeldt, *The House of Emerson,* 47–74; and Sacvan Bercovitch, "Emerson the Prophet: Romanticism, Puritanism, and Auto-American-Biography."

39. As quoted in Bloom, ed., *Modern Critical Views: Ralph Waldo Emerson,* 11.

40. See Robinson's discussion of Sermon 38 in his introduction to *The Complete Sermons of Ralph Waldo Emerson,* ed. von Frank, 1.27–28.

41. Bloom, ed., *Modern Critical Views: Ralph Waldo Emerson,* 11.

42. See Robinson's introduction to *The Complete Sermons of Ralph Waldo Emerson,* ed. von Frank, 1.27–29; Karen Kalenevitch, "Turning from the Orthodox: Emerson's Gospel Lectures"; and Barbara L. Packer, "Origin and Authority: Emerson and the Higher Criticism." It is well worth pointing out, in this connection, that many Unitarians continued to believe in the Bible as "the very word of God": see, for example, Sydney Ahlstrom and Jonathan S. Carey, eds., *An American Reformation: A Documentary History of Unitarian Christianity,* esp. 33. For the larger context of the Higher Criticism, see Jerry W. Brown, *The Rise of Biblical Criticism in America, 1800–1870: The New England Scholars.*

43. See Robinson's introduction to *The Complete Sermons of Ralph Waldo Emerson,* ed. von Frank, 1.3.

44. Phyllis Cole, "From the Edwardses to the Emersons: Four Generations of Evangelical Family Culture."

45. MSS Houghton Library, as quoted in Cole, "From the Edwardses to the Emersons," 73.

46. See Robinson's introduction to *The Complete Sermons of Ralph Waldo Emerson,* ed. von Frank, 1.3.

47. MSS Houghton Library, as quoted in Cole, "From the Edwardses to the Emersons," 75.

48. For a study of similar Arminian diction, see Richard E. Brantley, "Charles Wesley's Experiential Art."

49. *Journals* 5.323–24, as quoted in Cole, "From the Edwardses to the Emersons," 70.

50. Cole, "From the Edwardses to the Emersons," 71.

51. Daniel Walker Howe, *The Unitarian Conscience: Harvard Moral Philosophy, 1805–1861,* 161.

52. Robinson, *Apostle of Culture,* 29.

53. As quoted ibid., 26.

54. William G. McLoughlin, *Revivals, Awakenings, and Reform: An Essay on Religion and Social Change in America, 1607–1977,* esp. 103.

55. See Robinson's introduction to *The Complete Sermons of Ralph Waldo Emerson,* ed. von Frank, 1.4.

56. See the discussion of Lyman Beecher in Robinson's introduction to *The Complete Sermons of Ralph Waldo Emerson,* ed. von Frank, 1.5.

57. See the discussion of Henry Ware, Jr., and Lyman Beecher in Robinson's

introduction to *The Complete Sermons of Ralph Waldo Emerson,* ed. von Frank, 1.5–6.

58. See the discussion in Robinson's introduction to *The Complete Sermons of Ralph Waldo Emerson,* ed. von Frank, 1.6.

59. Ibid.

60. Philip Gura, *The Wisdom of Words: Language, Theology, and Literature in the New England Renaissance,* esp. 77–78.

61. See especially chapters 4 and 5 of Teresa Toulouse, *The Art of Prophesying: New England Sermons and the Shaping of Belief;* and see Robinson's introduction to *The Complete Sermons of Ralph Waldo Emerson,* ed. von Frank, esp. 1.7, 21, and 27.

62. See Robinson's introduction to *The Complete Sermons of Ralph Waldo Emerson,* ed. von Frank, 1.7.

63. Michael, *Emerson and Skepticism,* 165.

64. Robinson, *Apostle of Culture,* 184–85.

65. *Journals* 1.56n.

66. "Hill" was either Joseph Bancroft Hill (1796–1864) or his twin brother John Boynton Hill (1796–1886). See *Journals* 1.58.

67. *Journals* 3.339.

68. *Journals* 1.26n.

69. *Journals* 1.13.

70. *Journals* 1.343.

71. Van Leer, *Emerson's Epistemology,* 15–16.

72. For supplementary views of Cartesian idealism, see Bernard Williams, *Descartes: The Project of Pure Inquiry;* Richard Rorty, *Philosophy and the Mirror of Nature,* 54–69; and Colin McGinn, *The Character of Mind.*

73. *Journals* 1.202 (my italics).

74. *Journals* 1.202.

75. *Journals* 2.231.

76. *Journals* 3.139. See also "Fencing" in *The Educational Writings of John Locke,* ed. John W. Adamson, 127.

77. *Journals* 3.197–98.

78. *Journals* 3.212–13.

79. *Journals* 5.250.

80. Murphy and Parker, eds., *The Norton Anthology of American Literature: Second Edition* 1.871. Subsequent references to this volume are by page number alone. This edition is based on *The Complete Works of Ralph Waldo Emerson: Centenary Edition,* ed. Edward Waldo Emerson. Edward Waldo Emerson's edition is being superseded by *The Collected Works of Ralph Waldo Emerson,* ed. Robert Spiller, Alfred Ferguson, et al. (3 volumes to date).

81. *Journals* 5.383.
82. *Journals* 8.67.
83. *Journals* 11.167.
84. *Journals* 5.13.
85. *Journals* 5.255.
86. See *The Norton Anthology of English Literature: Fifth Edition,* ed. M. H. Abrams et al., 2.962–63.
87. *Journals* 3.210.
88. *Journals* 13.228. Cf. Blake's "With Happiness Stretchd Across the Hills" (1801).
89. *Journals* 13.255.
90. *Journals* 13.354, 356.
91. *Literature* appears in *English Traits;* see the discussion in Neufeldt, *The House of Emerson,* 66.
92. *Journals* 10.507.
93. *Journals* 13.354.
94. Miller, "From Edwards to Emerson," esp. 192, 195. For a discerning assessment of Miller's essay, see William L. Hedges, "From Franklin to Emerson."
95. *Journals* 2.159.
96. *Journals* 2.227.
97. *The Complete Sermons of Ralph Waldo Emerson,* ed. von Frank, 1.219–24. See also the discussion in Robinson's introduction, 1.25.
98. See Herschel Parker's discussion in Murphy and Parker, eds., *The Norton Anthology of American Literature: Second Edition* 1.820.
99. *Journals* 4.257.
100. *Journals* 2.197.
101. Ibid.
102. As quoted by David Levin at the National Conference on Franklin and Edwards, Yale Divinity School, February 22–24, 1990.
103. *Journals* 4.381 (my italics).
104. Leonard Neufeldt, "'The Fields of My Fathers' and Emerson's Literary Vocation."
105. See Robinson's introduction to *The Complete Sermons of Ralph Waldo Emerson,* ed. von Frank, 1.14.
106. See the discussion in Douglas Percy Brayton, *The History of the Follen Church,* 7–8.
107. As quoted in Robinson's introduction to *The Complete Sermons of Ralph Waldo Emerson,* ed. von Frank, 1.11–12.
108. Ibid.
109. Ibid., 12.

110. See Brantley, "John Wesley (1703–1791)."

111. See the discussion in Robinson's introduction to *The Complete Sermons of Ralph Waldo Emerson,* ed. von Frank, 1.15.

112. Robinson, *Apostle of Culture,* 31.

113. *Journals* 3.115.

114. *Journals* 7.397.

115. *Journals* 11.286.

116. *Journals* 2.35.

117. *Journals* 4.282.

118. See A. M. Baumgartner, "'The Lyceum Is My Pulpit': Homiletics in Emerson's Early Lectures."

119. "I look upon all the world," said the itinerant Wesley, "as my parish." See *The Journal of the Rev. John Wesley, A. M.,* ed. Nehemiah Curnock, 2.218.

120. See William Hazlitt, "My First Acquaintance with Poets," 280–81.

121. *Journals* 2.238.

122. *Journals* 2.244–45.

123. *Journals* 3.207 (my italics).

124. *Journals* 7.359.

125. *Journals* 7.360.

126. *Journals* 8.219.

127. *Journals* 2.388n91.

128. *Journals* 11.53. Compare Emerson's tribute to Tarbox with Wordsworth's description of a leech-gatherer:

> As a huge stone is sometimes seen to lie
> Couched on the bald top of an eminence;
> Wonder to all who do the same espy,
> By what means it could thither come, and whence;
> So that it seems a thing endued with sense:
> Like a sea beast crawled forth, that on a shelf
> Of rock or sand reposeth, there to sun itself;
>
> Such seemed this Man, ...
>
> (Lines 57–64)

For my discussion of "natural methodism" in "Resolution and Independence" (1802), see Richard E. Brantley, *Wordsworth's "Natural Methodism,"* 127–32.

129. As quoted in Murphy and Parker, eds., *The Norton Anthology of American Literature: Second Edition,* 1.825n. For a range of source materials for the study of *Nature,* see Alfred R. Ferguson, and Merton M. Sealts, Jr., eds., *Emerson's* Nature: *Origin, Growth, Meaning.*

130. Gay Wilson Allen, *Waldo Emerson: A Biography,* 259.

131. Porte, *Emerson and Thoreau: Transcendentalists in Conflict,* 63.

132. Buell, *Literary Transcendentalism: Style and Vision in the American Renaissance,* 4–54.

133. Neufeldt, *The House of Emerson,* 16.

134. See Warner Berthoff's facsimile edition of the first edition of Emerson's *Nature,* xi. See also *Selections from Ralph Waldo Emerson,* ed. Whicher, 13; Bloom, "Emerson: The American Religion," 112; and Jonathan Bishop, *Emerson on the Soul,* 9.

135. Barbara L. Packer, *Emerson's Fall: A New Interpretation of the Major Essays,* passim.

136. Roland Barthes, *S/Z,* passim.

137. Michael, *Emerson and Skepticism,* 36.

138. See the discussion in Murphy and Parker, eds., *The Norton Anthology of American Literature: Second Edition* 1.835n, 839.

139. See the discussion in Murphy and Parker, eds., *The Norton Anthology of American Literature: Second Edition* 1.840n.

140. See, for example, a work reprinted often: Philip Doddridge, *The Rise and Progress of Religion in the Soul.* Doddridge's partly Lockean theory of education was embodied in his school at Harborough, and both his school and his theory influenced Wesley's partly Lockean experiment at the Kingswood School.

141. See Colin Clarke, *The Romantic Paradox: An Essay on the Poetry of Wordsworth,* and Hugh Sykes Davies, "Wordsworth and the Empirical Philosophers."

142. I have in mind *Die Deutsche Ideologie,* in Hazard Adams, ed., *Critical Theory Since Plato,* 632.

143. Locke, *Essay,* 2.8.7; Nidditch, 134.

144. M. H. Abrams, "Structure and Style in the Greater Romantic Lyric."

145. Clarke, *Romantic Paradox,* 1–2.

146. Bloom, ed., *Modern Critical Views: Ralph Waldo Emerson,* 6. For studies of the linguistic tensions in this famous passage, see Sherman Paul, *Emerson's Angle of Vision: Man and Nature in American Experience,* 71–102; Richard Poirier, *A World Elsewhere: The Place of Style in American Literature,* 56–70; and Kenneth Burke, "I, Eye, Ay—Emerson's Early Essay 'Nature': Thoughts on the Machinery of Transcendence," esp. 13–14.

147. As quoted in Murphy and Parker, eds., *The Norton Anthology of American Literature: Second Edition* 1.821.

148. Murphy and Parker, eds., *The Norton Anthology of American Literature: Second Edition* 1.824.

149. Richard Poirier, "The Question of Genius: The Challenge of Emerson," 168.

150. See Quentin Anderson, *The Imperial Self: An Essay in American Literary and Cultural History,* and Yvor Winters, *Maule's Curse: Some Studies in the History of American Obscurantism.*

151. William McKibben, *The End of Nature.*

152. For admiring accounts of Emerson's work as a whole, see (besides Whicher's *Freedom and Fate* and Bishop's *Emerson on the Soul*) R. W. B. Lewis, *The American Adam: Innocence, Tragedy, and Tradition in the Nineteenth Century;* Harold Bloom, *The Ringers in the Tower: Studies in Romantic Tradition,* 217–26, 291–304; Harold Bloom, *Figures of Capable Imagination;* Julie Ellison, *Emerson's Romantic Style;* and even Poirier, *A World Elsewhere,* 50–92.

153. See (besides Edward O. Wilson's *Sociobiology: The New Synthesis*) Wilson, *On Human Nature,* and Charles J. Lumsden and Edward O. Wilson, *Promethean Fire: Reflections on the Origin of Mind.* See also the reference to sociobiology in Leonard I. Sweet, *Quantum Spirituality: A Postmodern Apologetic,* 4.

154. Eric Cheyfitz, *The Trans-Parent: Sexual Politics in the Language of Emerson,* 110–14.

155. See the discussion in Richard Mant, *A History of the Church of England, from the Reformation to the Union of the Churches of England and Ireland Jan. 1, 1801,* 2.156.

156. See R. A. Yoder, *Emerson and the Orphic Poet in America;* and Bloom, "Emerson: The American Religion," 111.

157. As quoted in Bloom, ed., *Modern Critical Views: Ralph Waldo Emerson,* 108.

158. See the discussion in Bloom, ed., *Modern Critical Views: Ralph Waldo Emerson,* 108–10.

159. Robinson, *Apostle of Culture,* 177.

160. See Van Leer, *Emerson's Epistemology,* 263, and the overview in Daniel B. Shea's "Emerson and the American Metamorphosis."

161. See the discussion of Charles Wesley's Hymn 64 in Brantley, "Charles Wesley's Experiential Art," esp. 9–10.

162. I allude to "Lapis Lazuli" (1938) by William Butler Yeats.

163. As quoted in Murphy and Parker, eds., *The Norton Anthology of American Literature: Second Edition* 1.821.

164. For the influence of Swedenborg on Emerson, see, for example, Paul, *Emerson's Angle of Vision,* 60–70.

165. Bloom, ed., *Modern Critical Views: Ralph Waldo Emerson,* 3.

166. See Robinson's introduction to *The Complete Sermons of Ralph Waldo Emerson,* ed. von Frank, 1.29–30.

167. Wesley T. Mott, "'Christ Crucified': Christology, Identity, and Emerson's Sermon No. 5," esp. 29.

168. Michael, *Emerson and Skepticism,* xi.

169. See, for example, *The American Scholar,* 859, 863; *Self-Reliance,* 901; *The Over-Soul,* 915; *The Poet,* 939; *Experience,* 951; and *Fate,* 349–50, in Murphy and Parker, eds., *The Norton Anthology of American Literature: Second Edition* 1.

170. Bloom, ed., *Modern Critical Views: Ralph Waldo Emerson,* 1, 9.

171. Bercovitch, "Emerson the Prophet," in Bloom, ed., *Modern Critical Views: Ralph Waldo Emerson,* 29. See also Bloom's introduction, 5.

172. See the discussion in Bloom's "Emerson: The American Religion" in Bloom, ed., *Modern Critical Views: Ralph Waldo Emerson,* 99.

173. Ibid., 98–99.

174. Ibid., 1.

175. Sharon Cameron, *The Corporeal Self,* 3.

176. Leon Chai, *The Romantic Foundations of the American Renaissance.*

177. Harold Bloom, *The Anxiety of Influence,* 152.

178. See Phyllis Cole's study of *English Traits* (1856) and *The Conduct of Life* (1860) in her "Emerson, England, and Fate."

179. Murphy and Parker, eds., *The Norton Anthology of American Literature: Second Edition* 1.824.

180. See Bloom, ed., *Modern Critical Views: Ralph Waldo Emerson,* 102.

181. L. J. Swingle, *The Obstinate Questionings of English Romanticism,* 39. Subsequent references to this book appear by page number alone.

182. Swingle refers to Wordsworth's "Ode: Intimations of Immortality," lines 142–43.

183. See my review of L. J. Swingle, *The Obstinate Questionings of English Romanticism,* in *ANQ: A Quarterly Journal of Short Articles, Notes, and Reviews* 3 (July 1990): 142–45. See also the admiring review by David Punter in *Studies in Romanticism* 30 (Summer 1991): 305–11.

184. See Michael Davis, *William Blake: A New Kind of Man.*

185. See the discussion in Brantley, *Wordsworth's "Natural Methodism,"* 50–53.

186. See the discussion in Brantley, *Locke, Wesley, and the Method of English Romanticism,* 138–44.

187. Ibid., 149–53.

188. *Selections from Ralph Waldo Emerson,* ed. Whicher, 2. See also Whicher's *Freedom and Fate.*

189. See the discussion in Murphy and Parker, eds., *The Norton Anthology of American Literature: Second Edition* 1.820.

190. Brantley, *Locke, Wesley, and the Method of English Romanticism,* 160–68.

191. See the discussion in Murphy and Parker, eds., *The Norton Anthology of American Literature: Second Edition* 1.826n.

192. See the discussion in Murphy and Parker, eds., *The Norton Anthology of American Literature: Second Edition* 1.839n.

193. Earl Wasserman, *The Subtler Language: Critical Readings of Neoclassic and Romantic Poems,* 236.

194. I refer to T. S. Eliot's "Ash Wednesday."

195. Murphy and Parker, eds., *The Norton Anthology of American Literature: Second Edition* 1.835n.

196. Brantley, *Locke, Wesley, and the Method of English Romanticism,* 168–85.

197. Brantley, *Wordsworth's "Natural Methodism,"* 50–53.

198. Brantley, *Locke, Wesley, and the Method of English Romanticism,* 185–200.

199. Jack Stillinger, "Imagination and Reality in the Odes of Keats," 2.

200. See the discussion in Murphy and Parker, eds., *The Norton Anthology of American Literature: Second Edition* 1.820–21.

201. See the discussion in Murphy and Parker, eds., *The Norton Anthology of American Literature: Second Edition* 1.821.

202. Ibid.

203. As quoted in Murphy and Parker, eds., *The Norton Anthology of American Literature: Second Edition* 1.821.

Conclusion

1. Francis Murphy and Herschel Parker, eds., *The Norton Anthology of American Literature: Second Edition* 1.821.

2. See *Selections from Ralph Waldo Emerson: An Organic Anthology,* ed. Stephen E. Whicher, 302.

3. As quoted in Murphy and Parker, eds., *The Norton Anthology of American Literature: Second Edition* 1.821.

4. Robert Weisbuch, *Atlantic Double-Cross: American Literature and British Influence in the Age of Emerson.* Subsequent references to this study appear by page number alone.

5. Kenneth Marc Harris, *Carlyle and Emerson: Their Long Debate,* 5, 171. Subsequent references to this study appear by page number alone.

6. Christopher Lasch, *The True and Only Heaven: Progress and Its Critics,* esp. 13–17, 226–95.

7. Karl Keller, *The Only Kangaroo among the Beauty: Emily Dickinson and America,* 67–96.

8. William McKibben's *The End of Nature* draws upon British as well as American culture—and notably includes the hymns of Charles Wesley—as it develops its movingly elegiac tone.

9. See Garry Wills, "The Phallic Pulpit."

10. It is well to temper any comparison of England and the United States, of course, with such diverting but suggestive comments as those by Paul Theroux:

> Once from behind a closed door, I heard an Englishwoman exclaim with real pleasure, "They are *funny,* the Yanks!" And I crept away and laughed to think that an English person was saying such a thing. And I thought: They wallpaper their ceilings! They put little knitted bobble-hats on their soft-boiled eggs to keep them warm! They don't give you bags in supermarkets! They say sorry when you step on their toes! Their government makes them get a hundred-dollar license every year for watching television! They issue drivers' licenses that are valid for thirty or forty years—mine expires in the year 2011! They charge you for matches when you buy cigarettes! They smoke on buses! They drive on the left! They spy for the Russians! They say "nigger" and "Jewboy" without flinching! They call their houses Holmleigh and Sparrow View! They sunbathe in their underwear! They don't say "You're welcome!" They still have milk bottles and milkmen, and junk dealers with horse-drawn wagons! They love candy and Lucozade and left-overs called bubble-and-squeak! They live in Barking and Dorking and Shellow Bowells! They have amazing names, like Mr. Eatwell and Lady Inkpen and Major Twaddle and Miss Tosh! And they think *we're* funny?

See Theroux, *The Kingdom by the Sea: A Journey around Great Britain,* 4. Perhaps even more to the point, here, are the numerous differences between British and American English.

11. Cynthia Ozick, "A Critic at Large (T. S. Eliot)," esp. 154.

12. See Edgar A. Dryden, *The Form of American Romance;* Michael Davitt Bell, *The Development of American Romance;* and Richard Brodhead, *Hawthorne, Melville, and the Novel.*

13. See William C. Spengemann, "American Writers and English Literature"; Jonathan Arac, *Commissioned Spirits: The Shaping of Social Motion in Dickens, Carlyle, Melville, and Hawthorne;* Edwin Eigner, *The Metaphysical Novel in England and America;* and Nicolaus Mills, *American and English Fiction in the Nineteenth Century.*

14. David Van Leer, *Emerson's Epistemology: The Argument of the Essays,* 208.

15. A. Carl Bredahl, Jr., *New Ground: Western American Narrative and the Literary Canon,* esp. 7–48. According to Charles H. Adams, in his review of *New Ground,* Bredahl tends to perpetuate "the binary stance of East/West," and so "contributes finally to continued sectionalism rather than to an understanding of collective cultural dynamics"; see Adams, "Versions of Revision: Conflict and

Community in the American Canon." Bredahl, however, realizes that not just Western American narrative, but also the literature of other American regions, "grows out of the common experience with the physical environment."

16. Jack P. Greene, *Pursuits of Happiness: The Social Development of Early Modern British Colonies and the Formation of American Culture.*

17. See Sacvan Bercovitch, *The Puritan Origins of the American Self,* and Bercovitch, *The American Jeremiad.*

18. For an especially helpful recent overview of scholarship on the Puritans, see Gordon S. Wood, "Struggle over the Puritans."

19. Andrew Delbanco, *The Puritan Ordeal.*

20. Theodore Dwight Bozeman, *To Live Ancient Lives: The Primitivist Dimension in Puritanism.*

21. See David Grayson Allen, *In English Ways: The Movement of Societies and the Transfer of English Local Law and Custom to Massachusetts Bay, 1600–1690;* David Cressy, *Coming Over: Migration and Communication between England and New England in the Seventeenth Century;* and Philip F. Gura, *A Glimpse of Sion's Glory: Puritan Radicalism in New England, 1620–1660.*

22. David D. Hall, *Worlds of Wonder, Days of Judgment: Popular Religious Belief in Early New England.*

23. Delbanco, *The Puritan Ordeal,* 184–214.

24. Bercovitch, *The American Jeremiad,* 107–8.

25. For explorations of John Dewey's pragmatism as a means of restoring religious values, see Giles Gunn, *The Culture of Criticism and the Criticism of Culture;* William Shea, *The Naturalists and the Supernatural;* and William Dean, *American Religious Empiricism.* For the centrality of William James's "flowing experientialism," or "stream-of-consciousness," see Bruce Kuklick, ed., *William James: Writings, 1902–1910.*

26. Bruce Kuklick, *Churchmen and Philosophers: From Jonathan Edwards to John Dewey.*

27. See John Patrick Diggins, "Puritans and Pragmatists," a review of Bruce Kuklick, *Churchmen and Philosophers,* in *The New Republic,* April 28, 1986, 38–41.

28. Charley D. Hardwick, "New Openings for Religious Empiricism," esp. 549–50.

29. Leonard I. Sweet, "Wise as Serpents, Innocent as Doves: The New Evangelical Historiography," esp. 400. For "the new evangelical historiography," see, for example, Grant Wacker, "The Demise of Biblical Civilization"; Harry S. Stout, *The New England Soul: Preaching and Religious Culture in Colonial New England;* Mark A. Noll, "Scientific History in America: A Centennial Observation from a Christian Point of View"; Noll, ed., *The Princeton Theology, 1812–1921:*

Scripture, Science, Theological Method from Archibald Alexander to Benjamin Breckinridge Warfield; Noll, "Evangelicalism and the Study of the Bible"; Noll, *Between Faith and Criticism: Evangelicals, Scholarship, and the Bible in America;* George M. Marsden, "Fundamentalism as an American Phenomenon: A Comparison with English Evangelicalism"; Marsden, "America's 'Christian' Origins: Puritan New England as Case Study"; Marsden, "Evangelicals, History, and Modernity"; Marsden, *Reforming Fundamentalism: Fuller Seminary and the New Evangelicalism;* Nathan O. Hatch, *The Sacred Cause of Liberty: Republican Thought and the Millennium in Revolutionary New England;* and Joel A. Carpenter, "Fundamentalist Institutions and the Rise of Evangelical Protestantism, 1929–1942." See also Leonard I. Sweet, ed., *The Evangelical Tradition in America.*

30. Sweet refers, specifically, to Douglas W. Frank, *Less than Conquerors: How Evangelicals Entered the Twentieth Century,* and Timothy Smith, *Revivalism and Social Reform in Mid-Nineteenth-Century America.* See Sweet, "Wise as Serpents, Innocent as Doves: The New Evangelical Historiography," 400.

31. Nicholas Tyacke, *Anti-Calvinists: The Rise of English Arminianism, c. 1590–1640.*

32. See Colin Morris, *The Discovery of the Individual, 1050–1200,* and Neil Keeble, *The Literary Culture of Nonconformity in Later Seventeenth-Century England.*

33. See Charles Norris Cochrane, *Christianity and Classical Culture,* and R. A. Markus, *Saeculum: History and Society in the Theology of St. Augustine.*

34. See the anonymous review, and the resulting controversy, in the 1987 volume of *TLS* (786, 950, 1047, 1109); see also Allan Bloom, *The Closing of the American Mind.*

35. Freeman J. Dyson, *Infinite in All Directions.*

36. See Stephen Jay Gould's review of Freeman J. Dyson, *Infinite in All Directions,* in *The New York Review of Books* 35 (October 27, 1988): 32–34.

37. Margaret C. Jacob, *The Cultural Meaning of the Scientific Revolution.*

38. Frank Burch Brown, *The Evolution of Darwin's Religious Views.*

39. Hamilton Holt, ed., with a new introduction by Werner Sollors, *The Life Stories of Undistinguished Americans: As Told by Themselves,* as quoted in Edmund Morris's review of the reissue in *The New Yorker,* June 11, 1990, 100–102.

40. John Fowles, *A Maggot,* 449–55.

41. Joseph Slater, ed., *The Correspondence of Emerson and Carlyle,* 102, 120, 122, 130, 132, 157, 200, 215, 281, 305, 335, 570, 588.

WORKS CITED

Aarsleff, Hans. *From Locke to Saussure: Essays on the Study of Language and Intellectual History.* Minneapolis: University of Minnesota Press, 1982.

Abrams, M. H. "Structure and Style in the Greater Romantic Lyric." In *From Sensibility to Romanticism,* edited by F. W. Hilles and Harold Bloom. New York: Oxford University Press, 1965.

——— et al., eds. *The Norton Anthology of English Literature: Fifth Edition.* 2 vols. New York: W. W. Norton & Company, 1986.

Adams, Charles H. "Versions of Revision: Conflict and Community in the American Canon." Review of *New Ground: Western American Narrative and the Literary Canon,* by A. Carl Bredahl, Jr. *Kenyon Review* 13 (Spring 1991): 193–99.

Ahlstrom, Sydney, and Jonathan S. Carey, eds. *An American Reformation: A Documentary History of Unitarian Christianity.* Middletown: Wesleyan University Press, 1986.

Allen, David Grayson. *In English Ways: The Movement of Societies and the Transfer of English Local Law and Custom to Massachusetts Bay, 1600–1690.* Chapel Hill: University of North Carolina Press, 1981.

Allen, Gay Wilson. *Waldo Emerson: A Biography.* New York: Viking Press, 1981.

Anderson, Quentin. *The Imperial Self: An Essay in American Literary and Cultural History.* New York: Knopf, 1971.

Anderson, Wallace E. "The Development of Edwards' Philosophical Thought." In *Scientific and Philosophical Writings.* Vol. 6 of *The Works of Jonathan Edwards.* New Haven: Yale University Press, 1980.

Anonymous. Reviews of *The Closing of the American Mind,* by Allan Bloom. *TLS* 4370–4421 (1987): 786, 950, 1047, 1109.

apRoberts, Ruth. *The Ancient Dialect: Thomas Carlyle and Comparative Religion.* Berkeley: University of California Press, 1988.

Arac, Jonathan. *Commissioned Spirits: The Shaping of Social Motion in Dickens, Carlyle, Melville, and Hawthorne.* New Brunswick: Rutgers University Press, 1979.

Ashcroft, Richard. "Faith and Knowledge in Locke's Philosophy." In *John Locke: Problems and Perspectives,* edited by John W. Yolton, 194–223. Cambridge: Cambridge University Press, 1969.

Baker, Carlos. *The Echoing Green: Romanticism, Modernism, and the Phenomena of Transference in Poetry.* Princeton: Princeton University Press, 1984.

Baker, Frank. "John Wesley and America." *Proceedings of the Wesley Historical Society* 44 (September 1984): 117–29.

———. "A Study of John Wesley's Readings." *The London Quarterly and Holborn Review* 168 (May 1943): 237–49.

Barthes, Roland. *S/Z.* New York: Hill and Wang, 1974.

Baumgarten, A. M. "'The Lyceum Is My Pulpit': Homiletics in Emerson's Early Lectures." *American Literature* 34 (January 1963): 47–86.

Behnken, Eloise M. *Thomas Carlyle: "Calvinist without the Theology."* Columbia: University of Missouri Press, 1978.

Bell, Michael Davitt. *The Development of American Romance.* Chicago: University of Chicago Press, 1980.

Bercovitch, Sacvan. *The American Jeremiad.* Madison: University of Wisconsin Press, 1978.

———. "Emerson the Prophet: Romanticism, Puritanism, and Auto-American-Biography." 1975. In *Modern Critical Views: Ralph Waldo Emerson,* edited by Harold Bloom, 29–44. New York: Chelsea House, 1985.

———. *The Puritan Origins of the American Self.* New Haven: Yale University Press, 1975.

———, ed. *Reconstructing American Literary History.* Cambridge: Harvard University Press, 1986.

Bishop, Jonathan. *Emerson on the Soul.* Cambridge: Harvard University Press, 1964.

Blake, William. *The Poetry and Prose of William Blake.* Edited by David V. Erdman. With commentary by Harold Bloom. Garden City, N.Y.: Doubleday, 1965.

Bloom, Allan. *The Closing of the American Mind.* New York: Simon and Schuster, 1987.

Bloom, Harold. *The Anxiety of Influence.* New York: Oxford University Press, 1973.

———. "Emerson: The American Religion." 1982. In *Modern Critical Views: Ralph Waldo Emerson,* edited by Harold Bloom. New York: Chelsea House, 1985.

———. *Figures of Capable Imagination.* New York: Seabury Press, 1976.

———. *The Ringers in the Tower: Studies in Romantic Tradition.* Chicago: University of Chicago Press, 1971.

———, ed. *Modern Critical Views: Ralph Waldo Emerson.* New York: Chelsea House, 1985.

Bornstein, George. *Transformations of Romanticism in Yeats, Eliot, and Stevens.* Chicago: University of Chicago Press, 1976.

———. *Yeats and Shelley.* Chicago: University of Chicago Press, 1970.

———, ed. *Romantic and Modern: Revaluations of Literary Tradition.* Pittsburgh: University of Pittsburgh Press, 1977.

Bozeman, Theodore Dwight. *To Live Ancient Lives: The Primitivist Dimension in Puritanism.* Chapel Hill: University of North Carolina Press, 1988.

Brantley, Richard E. "Charles Wesley's Experiential Art." *Eighteenth-Century Life* 11 (May 1987): 1–11.

———. "John Wesley (1703–1791)." In *British Prose Writers, 1660–1800: Second Series,* edited by Donald T. Siebert, 338–49. Vol. 104 of *The Dictionary of Literary Biography.* Detroit: Gale Research, 1991.

———. *Locke, Wesley, and the Method of English Romanticism.* Gainesville: University of Florida Press, 1984.

———. Review of *The Obstinate Questionings of English Romanticism,* by L. J. Swingle. *ANQ: A Quarterly Journal of Short Articles, Notes, and Reviews* 3 (July 1990): 142–45.

———. *Wordsworth's "Natural Methodism."* New Haven: Yale University Press, 1975.

Brayton, Douglas Percy. *The History of the Follen Church.* N.p., 1939.

Bredahl, A. Carl, Jr. *New Ground: Western American Narrative and the Literary Canon.* Chapel Hill: University of North Carolina Press, 1989.

Breitenbach, William. "Piety and Moralism: Edwards and the New Divinity." In *Jonathan Edwards and the American Experience,* edited by Nathan O. Hatch and Harry S. Stout, 177–204. New York: Oxford University Press, 1988.

Brodhead, Richard. *Hawthorne, Melville, and the Novel.* Chicago: University of Chicago Press, 1976.

Brown, Frank Burch. *The Evolution of Darwin's Religious Views.* Macon: Mercer University Press, 1986.

Brown, Jerry W. *The Rise of Biblical Criticism in America, 1800–1870: The New England Scholars.* Middletown: Wesleyan University Press, 1969.

Brown, Marshall. *Preromanticism.* Stanford: Stanford University Press, 1991.

Brown, Stuart Gerry. "Emerson's Platonism." *New England Quarterly* 18 (September 1945): 325–45.

Browne, Peter. *The Procedure, Extent, and Limits of Human Understanding.* 2d ed. London: W. Innys, 1729.

Buell, Lawrence. *Literary Transcendentalism: Style and Vision in the American Renaissance.* Ithaca: Cornell University Press, 1973.

Burke, Kenneth. "I, Eye, Ay—Emerson's Early Essay 'Nature': Thoughts on the Machinery of Transcendence." In *Transcendentalism and Its Legacy,* edited by Myron Simon and Thornton H. Parsons. Ann Arbor: University of Michigan Press, 1966.

Cameron, Sharon. *The Corporeal Self.* Baltimore: Johns Hopkins University Press, 1980.

Campbell, Ian. *Thomas Carlyle.* New York: Charles Scribner's Sons, 1974.

———. "Thomas Carlyle (1795–1881)." In *Victorian Prose Writers Before 1867,* edited by William B. Thesing. Vol. 55 of *The Dictionary of Literary Biography.* Detroit: Gale Research Company, 1987.

Carlyle, Thomas. *Critical and Miscellaneous Essays.* Edited by H. D. Traill. 30 vols. New York: Charles Scribner's Sons, 1898–1901.

———. *Sartor Resartus: The Life and Opinions of Herr Teufelsdröckh.* Edited by Charles Frederick Harrold. New York: Odyssey, 1937.

———. *Thomas Carlyle: Selected Writings.* Edited by Alan Shelston. 1971. Reprint. Harmondsworth, England: Penguin Books, 1986.

Carpenter, Joel A. "Fundamentalist Institutions and the Rise of Evangelical Protestantism, 1929–1942." *Church History* 49 (March 1980): 62–75.

Carton, Evan. *The Rhetoric of American Romance: Dialectic and Identity in Emerson, Dickinson, Poe, and Hawthorne.* Baltimore: Johns Hopkins University Press, 1985.

Carwardine, Richard. *Transatlantic Revivalism: Popular Evangelicalism in Britain and America, 1790–1865.* Westport, Conn.: Greenwood Press, 1978.

Cazamian, Louis. *Carlyle.* Translated by E. K. Brown. 1932. Reprint. Hamden, Conn.: Archon Books, 1966.

Chai, Leon. *The Romantic Foundation of the American Renaissance.* Ithaca: Cornell University Press, 1987.

Cheyfitz, Eric. *The Trans-Parent: Sexual Politics in the Language of Emerson.* Baltimore: Johns Hopkins University Press, 1981.

Clapper, Gregory S. "'True Religion' and the Affections: A Study of John Wesley's Abridgment of Jonathan Edwards's Treatise on the Religious Affections." In *Wesleyan Theology Today,* edited by Theodore Runyon. Nashville: Abingdon Press, 1985.

Clarke, Colin. *The Romantic Paradox: An Essay on the Poetry of Wordsworth.* New York: Barnes & Noble, 1963.

Cochrane, Charles Norris. *Christianity and Classical Culture.* London: Oxford University Press, 1957.

Colacurcio, Michael J. "The Example of Edwards: Idealist Imagination and the Metaphysics of Sovereignty." In *Puritan Influences in American Literature,* edited by Emory Elliott, 55–106. Urbana: University of Illinois Press, 1979.

Cole, Phyllis. "Emerson, England, and Fate." In *Critical Essays on Ralph Waldo Emerson,* edited by Robert E. Burkholder and Joel Myerson, 448–61. Boston: G. K. Hall & Company, 1983.

———. "From the Edwardses to the Emersons: Four Generations of Evangelical Family Culture." *College English Association Critic* 49 (1986–87): 70–78.

Coleridge, Samuel Taylor. *Poetical Works of Coleridge, including poems and versions of poems, herein published for the first time.* Edited by Ernest Hartley Coleridge. 1912. Reprint. London and New York: Oxford University Press, 1969.

Copleston, Frederick J. *A History of Philosophy.* Garden City, N.Y.: Doubleday, 1966.

Cressy, David. *Coming Over: Migration and Communication between England and New England in the Seventeenth Century.* Cambridge: Cambridge University Press, 1987.

Cumming, Mark A. *A Disimprisoned Epic: Form and Vision in Carlyle's French Revolution.* Philadelphia: University of Pennsylvania Press, 1988.

Damrosch, Leopold, Jr. Review of *Locke, Wesley, and the Method of English Romanticism,* by Richard E. Brantley. *Eighteenth-Century Studies* 19 (Spring 1986): 438–41.

Davidson, Edward H. "From Locke to Edwards." *Journal of the History of Ideas* 24 (July–September 1963): 355–72.

Davies, Hugh Sykes. "Wordsworth and the Empirical Philosophers." In *The English Mind: Studies in the English Moralists Presented to Basil Willey,* edited by Hugh Sykes Davies and George Watson. Cambridge: Cambridge University Press, 1964.

Davis, Michael. *William Blake: A New Kind of Man.* Berkeley: University of California Press, 1977.

Dean, William. *American Religious Empiricism.* Stony Brook: State University of New York Press, 1986.

Delattre, Roland. *Beauty and Sensibility in the Thought of Jonathan Edwards: An Essay in Aesthetics and Theological Ethics.* New Haven: Yale University Press, 1968.

DeLaura, David J. "Carlyle and Arnold: The Religious Issue." In *Carlyle Past and*

Present, edited by K. J. Fielding and Rodger L. Tarr, 127–54. New York: Barnes & Noble, 1976.

Delbanco, Andrew. *The Puritan Ordeal.* Cambridge: Harvard University Press, 1989.

Diehl, Joanne Feit. *Dickinson and the Romantic Imagination.* Princeton: Princeton University Press, 1981.

Diggins, John Patrick. "Puritans and Pragmatists." Review of *Churchmen and Philosophers,* by Bruce Kuklick. *New Republic* 194 (April 28, 1986): 38–41.

Doddridge, Philip. *The Rise and Progress of Religion in the Soul.* London: J. Waugh, 1745.

Doidge, Reginald. *John Wesley's Christian Library.* London: Epworth, 1938.

Donoghue, Denis. *The Third Voice: Modern British and American Verse Drama.* Princeton: Princeton University Press, 1959.

Dreyer, Frederick. "Evangelical Thought: John Wesley and Jonathan Edwards." *Albion* 19 (Summer 1987): 177–92.

———. "Faith and Experience in the Thought of John Wesley." *American Historical Review* 88 (February 1983): 12–30.

———. "A 'Religious Society Under Heaven': John Wesley and the Identity of Methodism." *Journal of British Studies* 25 (January 1986): 62–83.

Dryden, Edgar A. *The Form of American Romance.* Baltimore: Johns Hopkins University Press, 1988.

Dyson, Freeman J. *Infinite in All Directions.* New York: Harper & Row, 1988.

Edwards, Jonathan. *An Account of the Life of the Late Reverend Mr. David Brainerd.* Boston: D. Henchman, 1749.

———. *The Distinguishing Marks of a Work of the Spirit of God.* Boston: S. Kneeland and T. Green, 1741.

———. *The Distinguishing Marks of a Work of the Spirit of God.* Edited by John Wesley. London: W. Strahan, 1744.

———. *An Extract of the Life of the Late Rev. Mr. David Brainerd.* Edited by John Wesley. Bristol: William Pine, 1768.

———. *An Extract from a Treatise concerning Religious Affections.* Edited by John Wesley. In vol. 23 of *The Works of the Rev. John Wesley.* 32 vols. Bristol: J. Paramore, 1771–74.

———. *A Faithful Narrative of the Surprising Work of God in the Conversion of many hundred souls in Northampton.* Edinburgh: J. Oswald, 1736.

———. *A Narrative of Many Surprising Conversions in Northampton and Vicinity.* Edited by John Wesley. Boston: Felix Farley, 1744.

———. *Some Thoughts concerning the Present Revival in New England.* Boston: S. Kneeland and T. Green, 1742.

———. *Thoughts concerning the Present Revival of Religion.* Edited by John Wesley. London: W. Strahan, 1745.

———. *A Treatise concerning Religious Affections*. In vol. 2 of *The Works of Jonathan Edwards*. Edited by John E. Smith. New Haven: Yale University Press, 1959.

———. *A Treatise concerning Religious Affections: In Three Parts*. Edited by William Gordon. London: T. Field, 1762.

Eigner, Edwin. *The Metaphysical Novel in England and America*. Berkeley: University of California Press, 1978.

Ellison, Julie. *Emerson's Romantic Style*. Princeton: Princeton University Press, 1984.

Emerson, Ralph Waldo. *The Collected Works of Ralph Waldo Emerson*. Edited by Robert Spiller, Albert Ferguson, et al. Cambridge: Harvard University Press, 1971–.

———. *The Complete Sermons of Ralph Waldo Emerson*. Vol. 1. Edited by Albert J. von Frank. With an introduction by David Robinson. Columbia: University of Missouri Press, 1989.

———. *The Complete Works of Ralph Waldo Emerson: Centenary Edition*. Edited by Edward Waldo Emerson. 12 vols. Boston and New York: Houghton Mifflin Company, 1903–4.

———. *The Journals and Miscellaneous Notebooks of Ralph Waldo Emerson*. Edited by William Gilman, et al. 16 vols. Cambridge: Harvard University Press, 1960–82.

———. *Nature*. Edited by Warner Berthoff. 1836. Reprint. San Francisco: Chandler Publishing Company, 1968.

———. *Selections from Ralph Waldo Emerson: An Organic Anthology*. Edited by Stephen E. Whicher. Boston: Houghton Mifflin Company, 1957.

Erdt, Terrence. *Jonathan Edwards: Art and the Sense of the Heart*. Amherst: University of Massachusetts Press, 1980.

Farr, James. "The Way of Hypotheses: Locke on Method." *Journal of the History of Ideas* 48 (January-March 1987): 51–72.

Ferguson, Alfred R., and Merton M. Sealts, Jr., eds. *Emerson's* Nature: *Origin, Growth, Meaning*. 2d ed. Carbondale: Southern Illinois University Press, 1979.

Fiering, Norman. *Jonathan Edwards's Moral Thought and Its British Context*. Chapel Hill: University of North Carolina Press, 1981.

———. *Moral Philosophy at Seventeenth-Century Harvard: A Discipline in Transition*. Chapel Hill: University of North Carolina Press, 1981.

Fliegelman, Jay. *Prodigals and Pilgrims: The American Revolution against Patriarchal Authority, 1750–1800*. Cambridge: Cambridge University Press, 1982.

Fowles, John. *A Maggot*. Boston and Toronto: Little, Brown and Company, 1985.

Frank, Douglas W. *Less than Conquerors: How Evangelicals Entered the Twentieth Century*. Grand Rapids: Eerdmans, 1986.

Frothingham, Octavius Brooks. *Transcendentalism in New England.* Reprint. Gloucester, Mass.: Peter Smith, 1965.

Gauthier, David. "Why Ought One Obey God? Reflections on Hobbes and Locke." *Canadian Journal of Philosophy* 7 (September 1977): 425–46.

Gillespie, Charles. *The Edge of Objectivity.* Princeton: Princeton University Press, 1960.

Gould, Stephen Jay. Review of *Infinite in All Directions,* by Freeman J. Dyson. *The New York Review of Books* 35 (October 27, 1988): 32–34.

Greene, Jack P. *Pursuits of Happiness: The Social Development of Early Modern British Colonies and the Formation of American Culture.* Chapel Hill: University of North Carolina Press, 1988.

Greven, Philip. *The Protestant Temperament: Patterns of Child-Rearing, Religious Experience, and the Self in Early America.* New York: Knopf, 1977.

Gunn, Giles. *The Culture of Criticism and the Criticism of Culture.* New York: Oxford University Press, 1987.

Gura, Philip F. *A Glimpse of Sion's Glory: Puritan Radicalism in New England, 1620–1660.* Middletown: Wesleyan University Press, 1984.

———. *The Wisdom of Words: Language, Theology, and Literature in the New England Renaissance.* Middletown: Wesleyan University Press, 1981.

Hall, David D. *Worlds of Wonder, Days of Judgment: Popular Religious Belief in Early New England.* New York: Knopf, 1989.

Hardwick, Charley D. "New Openings for Religious Empiricism." *Journal of the American Academy of Religion* 56 (Fall 1988): 545–51.

Harris, Kenneth Marc. *Carlyle and Emerson: Their Long Debate.* Cambridge: Cambridge University Press, 1978.

Harris, Wendell V. *The Omnipresent Debate: Empiricism and Transcendentalism in Nineteenth-Century English Prose.* De Kalb: Northern Illinois University Press, 1981.

Harrison, Anthony H. *Victorian Poets and Romantic Poems: Intertextuality and Ideology.* Charlottesville: University Press of Virginia, 1990.

Hatch, Nathan O. *The Democratization of American Christianity.* New Haven: Yale University Press, 1989.

———. *The Sacred Cause of Liberty: Republican Thought and the Millennium in Revolutionary New England.* New Haven: Yale University Press, 1977.

———, and Harry S. Stout, eds. *Jonathan Edwards and The American Experience.* New York: Oxford University Press, 1988.

Hazlitt, William. "My First Acquaintance with Poets." 1823. In *Prose of the Romantic Period,* edited by Carl R. Woodring. Boston: Houghton Mifflin Company, 1961.

Hedges, William L. "From Franklin to Emerson." 1976. In *Critical Essays on*

Ralph Waldo Emerson, edited by Robert E. Burkholder and Joel Myerson, 462–78. Boston: G. K. Hall & Company, 1983.

Heimert, Alan. *Religion and the American Mind, from the Great Awakening to the Revolution.* Cambridge: Harvard University Press, 1966.

Helm, Paul. "John Locke and Jonathan Edwards: A Reconsideration." *Journal of the History of Philosophy* 7 (April 1969): 51–61.

Hempton, David. *Methodism and Politics in British Society, 1750–1850.* Stanford: Stanford University Press, 1984.

Herbert, T. Walter. *John Wesley as Editor and Author.* Princeton: Princeton University Press, 1940.

Hirsch, E. D., Jr. *The Aims of Interpretation.* Chicago: University of Chicago Press, 1975.

Hitchens, Christopher. *Blood, Class, and Nostalgia: Anglo-American Ironies.* New York: Farrar, Straus & Giroux, 1990.

Holt, Hamilton, ed. *The Life Stories of Undistinguished Americans: As Told by Themselves.* 1906. Reprinted with a new introduction by Werner Sollors. New York: Routledge, 1990.

Hoopes, James. "Calvinism and Consciousness from Edwards to Beecher." In *Jonathan Edwards and the American Experience,* edited by Nathan O. Hatch and Harry S. Stout. New York: Oxford University Press, 1988.

Howe, Daniel Walker. *The Unitarian Conscience: Harvard Moral Philosophy, 1805–1861.* Cambridge: Harvard University Press, 1970.

Ikeler, A. Abbott. *Puritan Temper and Transcendental Faith: Carlyle's Literary Vision.* Columbus: Ohio State University Press, 1977.

Jacob, Margaret C. *The Cultural Meaning of the Scientific Revolution.* New York: Knopf, 1988.

Jeffner, Anders. *Butler and Hume on Religion: A Comparative Analysis.* Stockholm: Diakonistyrelsense bokförlog, 1966.

Jenson, Robert W. *America's Theologian: A Recommendation of Jonathan Edwards.* New York: Oxford University Press, 1988.

Kalenevitch, Karen. "Turning from the Orthodox: Emerson's Gospel Lectures." In *Studies in the American Renaissance: 1986,* edited by Joel Myerson, 69–112. Charlottesville: University Press of Virginia, 1986.

Kaplan, Fred. *Thomas Carlyle: A Biography.* Ithaca: Cornell University Press, 1983.

Keats, John. *Keats: Selected Poems and Letters.* Edited by Douglas Bush. New York: Riverside Editions, 1959.

Keeble, Neil. *The Literary Culture of Nonconformity in Later Seventeenth-Century England.* Leicester: University of Leicester Press, 1987.

Keller, Karl. *The Only Kangaroo among the Beauty: Emily Dickinson and America.* Baltimore: Johns Hopkins University Press, 1979.

Kernan, Alvin. *The Imaginary Library: An Essay on Literature and Society.* Princeton: Princeton University Press, 1982.

Kuklick, Bruce. *Churchmen and Philosophers: From Jonathan Edwards to John Dewey.* New Haven: Yale University Press, 1985.

———, ed. *William James: Writings, 1902–1910.* New York: Library of America, 1987.

Landow, George P. *Elegant Jeremiahs: The Sage from Carlyle to Mailer.* Ithaca: Cornell University Press, 1986.

Langbaum, Robert. *The Mysteries of Identity: A Theme in Modern Literature.* New York: Oxford University Press, 1977.

———. *The Poetry of Experience: The Dramatic Monologue in Modern Literary Tradition.* London: Chatto & Windus, 1957.

———. *The Word from Below: Essays on Modern Literature and Culture.* Madison: University of Wisconsin Press, 1987.

Laquer, T. W. *Religion and Respectability: Sunday Schools and Working-Class Culture, 1780–1850.* New Haven: Yale University Press, 1976.

Lasch, Christopher. *The True and Only Heaven: Progress and Its Critics.* New York: W. W. Norton and Company, 1991.

LaValley, Albert J. *Carlyle and the Idea of the Modern: Studies in Carlyle's Prophetic Literature and Its Relation to Blake, Nietzsche, Marx, and Others.* New Haven: Yale University Press, 1968.

Lee, Sang Hyun. *The Philosophical Theology of Jonathan Edwards.* Princeton: Princeton University Press, 1988.

Lehman, David. *Signs of the Times: Deconstruction and the Fall of Paul de Man.* New York: Poseidon Press, 1991.

Levine, George. *The Boundaries of Fiction: Carlyle, Macaulay, Newman.* Princeton: Princeton University Press, 1968.

Lewis, R. W. B. *The American Adam: Innocence, Tragedy, and Tradition in the Nineteenth Century.* Chicago: University of Chicago Press, 1955.

Locke, John. *The Educational Writings of John Locke.* Edited by John W. Adamson. Cambridge: Cambridge University Press, 1922.

———. *An Essay concerning Human Understanding.* Edited by Peter H. Nidditch. Oxford: Clarendon Press, 1975.

Lumsden, Charles J., and Edward O. Wilson. *Promethean Fire: Reflections on the Origin of Mind.* Cambridge: Harvard University Press, 1983.

Lurie, Edward. *Nature and the American Mind: Louis Aggasiz and the Culture of Science.* New York: Science History Publications, 1974.

McFarland, Thomas. "Literature and Philosophy." In *Interrelations of Literature.* Edited by Jean-Pierre Barricelli and Joseph Gibaldi. New York: Modern Language Association of America, 1982.

McGinn, Colin. *The Character of Mind*. Oxford: Clarendon Press, 1982.
McKibben, William. *The End of Nature*. New York: Random House, 1989.
MacLean, Kenneth. *John Locke and English Literature of the Eighteenth Century.* 1936. Reprint. New York: Russell & Russell, 1962.
McLoughlin, William G. *Revivals, Awakenings, and Reform: An Essay on Religion and Social Change in America, 1607–1977*. Chicago: University of Chicago Press, 1978.
Mant, Richard. *A History of the Church of England, from the Reformation to the Union of the Churches of England and Ireland Jan. 1, 1801*. 2 vols. London: J. W. Parker, 1840.
Markus, R. A. *Saeculum: History and Society in the Theology of St. Augustine*. Cambridge: Cambridge University Press, 1970.
Marsden, George M. "America's 'Christian' Origins: Puritan New England as Case Study." In *John Calvin: His Influence in the Western World,* edited by W. Stanford Reid. Grand Rapids: Zondervan, 1982.
———. "Evangelicals, History, and Modernity." In *Evangelicalism and Modern America,* edited by George M. Marsden. Grand Rapids: Eerdmans, 1984.
———. "Fundamentalism as an American Phenomenon: A Comparison with English Evangelicalism." *Church History* 46 (June 1977): 215–32.
———. *Reforming Fundamentalism: Fuller Seminary and the New Evangelicalism*. Grand Rapids: Eerdmans, 1987.
Marx, Karl. *Die Deutsche Ideologie*. In *Critical Theory Since Plato,* edited by Hazard Adams. New York: Harcourt Brace Jovanovich, 1971.
Michael, John. *Emerson and Skepticism: The Cipher of the World*. Baltimore: Johns Hopkins University Press, 1988.
Miller, Perry. "From Edwards to Emerson." 1940. In *Errand Into the Wilderness,* by Perry Miller, 184–203. Cambridge: Harvard University Press, 1956.
———. *Jonathan Edwards*. New York: W. Sloane, 1949.
———. "Jonathan Edwards and the Sense of the Heart." *Harvard Theological Review* 41 (April 1948): 123–45.
Mills, Nicolaus. *American and English Fiction in the Nineteenth Century.* Bloomington: Indiana University Press, 1973.
Moore, Carlisle. "Carlyle: Mathematics and 'Mathesis.'" In *Carlyle Past and Present,* edited by K. J. Fielding and Rodger L. Tarr, 61–95. New York: Barnes & Noble, 1976.
Morris, Colin. *The Discovery of the Individual, 1050–1200*. 1972. Reprint. Toronto: University of Toronto Press, 1987.
Morris, Edmund. Review of *The Life Stories of Undistinguished Americans,* edited by Hamilton Holt. *The New Yorker,* June 11, 1990, 100–102.
Mott, Wesley T. "'Christ Crucified': Christology, Identity, and Emerson's Sermon

No. 5." In *Emerson Centenary Essays,* edited by Joel Myerson, 17–40. Carbondale: Southern Illinois University Press, 1982.

Murphy, Francis, and Herschel Parker, eds. *The Norton Anthology of American Literature: Second Edition.* 2 vols. New York: W. W. Norton & Company, 1985.

Neufeldt, Leonard. "'The Fields of My Fathers' and Emerson's Literary Vocation." *American Transcendental Quarterly* 31 (Summer 1976): 3–9.

———. *The House of Emerson.* Lincoln: University of Nebraska Press, 1982.

Noll, Mark A. *Between Faith and Criticism: Evangelicals, Scholarship, and the Bible in America.* San Francisco: Harper & Row, 1986.

———. "Evangelicalism and the Study of the Bible." In *Evangelicalism and Modern America,* edited by George M. Marsden. New York: Oxford University Press, 1984.

———. "Scientific History in America: A Centennial Observation from a Christian Point of View." *Fides et Historia* 14 (January 1981): 21–37.

———, ed. *The Princeton Theology, 1812–1921: Scripture, Science, Theological Method from Archibald Alexander to Benjamin Breckinridge Warfield.* Grand Rapids: Baker Book House, 1983.

Outler, Albert. *John Wesley.* New York: Oxford University Press, 1964.

Ozick, Cynthia. "A Critic at Large (T. S. Eliot)." *The New Yorker,* November 20, 1989, 117–54.

Packer, Barbara L. *Emerson's Fall: A New Interpretation of the Major Essays.* New York: Continuum, 1982.

———. "Origin and Authority: Emerson and the Higher Criticism." In *Reconstructing American Literary History,* edited by Sacvan Bercovitch, 76–82. Cambridge: Harvard University Press, 1986.

Paul, Sherman. *Emerson's Angle of Vision: Man and Nature in American Experience.* Cambridge: Harvard University Press, 1952.

Pickering, Samuel F., Jr. *John Locke and Children's Books in Eighteenth-Century England.* Knoxville: University of Tennessee Press, 1981.

Poirier, Richard. "The Question of Genius: The Challenge of Emerson." 1985. In *Modern Critical Views: Ralph Waldo Emerson,* edited by Harold Bloom. New York: Chelsea House, 1985.

———. *A World Elsewhere: The Place of Style in American Literature.* New York: Oxford University Press, 1966.

Popkin, Richard H. *The High Road to Pyrrhonism.* San Diego: Austin Hill, 1980.

———. *The History of Skepticism: From Erasmus to Spinoza.* Berkeley: University of California Press, 1979.

Porte, Joel. *Emerson and Thoreau: Transcendentalists in Conflict.* Middletown: Wesleyan University Press, 1966.

Punter, David. Review of *The Obstinate Questionings of English Romanticism,* by L. J. Swingle. *Studies in Romanticism* 30 (Summer 1991): 305–11.

Reynolds, William J., ed. *Baptist Hymnal.* Nashville: Convention Press, 1975.

Ricoeur, Paul. *Freud and Philosophy.* Cambridge: Cambridge University Press, 1970.

Robb, Edmund W., Jr. "American Methodism at 200: The Case for Hope." *Christianity Today* 28 (December 14, 1984): 21–25.

Robinson, David. *Apostle of Culture: Emerson as Preacher and Lecturer.* Philadelphia: University of Pennsylvania Press, 1982.

Rogers, Charles. "John Wesley and Jonathan Edwards." *Duke Divinity School Review* 31 (January 1966): 20–38.

Rorty, Richard. *Philosophy and the Mirror of Nature.* Princeton: Princeton University Press, 1979.

Rosenberg, John D. *Carlyle and the Burden of History.* Oxford: Clarendon Press, 1985.

Rosenberg, Philip. *The Seventh Hero: Thomas Carlyle and the Theory of Radical Activism.* Cambridge: Harvard University Press, 1974.

Rousseau, G. S. "John Wesley's *Primitive Physick* (1747)." *Harvard Library Bulletin* 16 (July 1968): 242–56.

Safire, William. "On Language." *The Gainesville Sun,* March 10, 1991.

Saunders, Richard. *A Discourse of Angels: Their Nature and Office, or Ministry; also Something Touching Devils, Apparitions, and Impulses.* London: Thomas Parkhurst, 1701.

Sharlin, Harold. *The Convergent Century: The Unification of Science in the Nineteenth Century.* New York: Abelard-Schuman, 1966.

Shaw, Peter. *American Patriots and the Rituals of Revolution.* Cambridge: Harvard University Press, 1981.

Shea, Daniel B. "Emerson and the American Metamorphosis." In *Emerson: Prophecy, Metamorphosis, Influence,* edited by David Levin, 38–53. New York: Columbia University Press, 1975.

Shea, William. *The Naturalists and the Supernatural.* Macon: Mercer University Press, 1984.

Shelley, Percy Bysshe. *The Complete Works of Percy Bysshe Shelley.* Edited by Roger Ingpen and Walter E. Peck. 10 vols. London: Ernest Benn, 1965.

Singer, Charles. *A Short History of Scientific Ideas to 1900.* New York: Oxford University Press, 1959.

Slater, Joseph, ed. *The Correspondence of Emerson and Carlyle.* New York and London: Columbia University Press, 1964.

Smith, Claude A. "Jonathan Edwards and the 'Way of Ideas.'" *Harvard Theological Review* 59 (April 1966): 153–73.

Smith, Timothy. *Revivalism and Social Reform in Mid-Nineteenth-Century America.* New York: Abingdon Press, 1957.

Spellman, W. M. *John Locke and the Problem of Depravity.* Oxford: Clarendon Press, 1988.

Spengemann, William C. "American Writers and English Literature." *ELH* 52 (Spring 1985): 209–38.

Stange, G. Robert. "Refractions of *Past and Present.*" In *Carlyle Past and Present,* edited by K. J. Fielding and Rodger L. Tarr. New York: Barnes & Noble, 1976.

Steiner, George. "Ecstasies, Not Arguments." *TLS* (September 28–October 4, 1990): 1015–16.

Stillinger, Jack. "Imagination and Reality in the Odes of Keats." In *Twentieth-Century Interpretations of Keats's Odes,* edited by Jack Stillinger. Englewood Cliffs, N.J.: Prentice-Hall, 1968.

Stout, Harry S. *The New England Soul: Preaching and Religious Culture in Colonial New England.* New York: Oxford University Press, 1986.

Sweet, Leonard I. *Quantum Spirituality: A Postmodern Apologetic.* Dayton, Ohio: Whaleprints, 1991.

———. "Wise as Serpents, Innocent as Doves: The New Evangelical Historiography." *Journal of the American Academy of Religion* 56 (Fall 1988): 397–416.

———, ed. *The Evangelical Tradition in America.* Macon: Mercer University Press, 1984.

Swingle, L. J. *The Obstinate Questionings of English Romanticism.* Baton Rouge: Louisiana State University Press, 1987.

Tennyson, G. B. "Carlyle: Beginning With the Word." In *The Victorian Experience: The Prose Writers,* edited by Richard A. Levine, 1–21. Athens: Ohio University Press, 1982.

———. *Sartor Called Resartus: The Genesis, Structure, and Style of Thomas Carlyle's First Major Work.* Princeton: Princeton University Press, 1965.

Theroux, Paul. *The Kingdom by the Sea: A Journey around Great Britain.* New York: Washington Square Press, 1983.

Thompson, Cameron. "John Locke and New England Transcendentalism." *New England Quarterly* 35 (December 1962): 435–57.

Timko, Michael. *Carlyle and Tennyson.* Iowa City: University of Iowa Press, 1988.

Toulouse, Teresa. *The Art of Prophesying: New England Sermons and the Shaping of Belief.* Athens: University of Georgia Press, 1987.

Townsend, Harvey G., ed. *The Philosophy of Jonathan Edwards From His Private Notebooks.* Eugene: University of Oregon Monographs, 1955.

Tucker, Herbert. *Tennyson and the Doom of Romanticism.* Cambridge: Harvard University Press, 1988.

Tyacke, Nicholas. *Anti-Calvinists: The Rise of English Arminianism, c. 1590–1640*. New York: Oxford University Press, 1987.

Vallins, G. H. *The Wesleys and the English Language*. London: Epworth, 1957.

Vanden Bosshe, Chris R. *Carlyle and the Search for Authority*. Columbus: Ohio State University Press, 1991.

Van Leer, David. *Emerson's Epistemology: The Argument of the Essays*. Cambridge: Cambridge University Press, 1986.

Wacker, Grant. "The Demise of Biblical Civilization." In *The Bible in America: Essays in Cultural History*, edited by Nathan O. Hatch and Mark A. Noll, 121–38. New York: Oxford University Press, 1982.

Wainwright, William J. "Jonathan Edwards and the Language of God." *Journal of the American Academy of Religion* 48 (December 1980): 519–30.

Wasserman, Earl. *The Subtler Language: Critical Readings of Neoclassic and Romantic Poems*. Baltimore: Johns Hopkins University Press, 1959.

Weisbuch, Robert. *Atlantic Double-Cross: American Literature and British Influence in the Age of Emerson*. Chicago: University of Chicago Press, 1986.

Wellek, René. "Emerson and German Philosophy." In *Confrontations: Studies in the Intellectual and Literary Relations between Germany, England, and the United States during the Nineteenth Century*, edited by René Wellek, 187–212. Princeton: Princeton University Press, 1965.

Wesley, Charles, and John Wesley. *Collection of Hymns, for the Use of the People Called Methodists*. London: J. Paramore, 1780.

Wesley, John. *The Appeals to Men of Reason and Religion*. Edited by Gerald R. Cragg. Oxford: Clarendon Press, 1975.

———. *The Journal of the Rev. John Wesley, A. M., Sometime Fellow of Lincoln College, Oxford, Enlarged from Original MSS., With Notes from Unpublished Diaries, Annotations, Maps, and Illustrations*. Edited by Nehemiah Curnock. 8 vols. London: Robert Culley, 1909.

———. *The Letters of the Rev. John Wesley, A. M.* Edited by John Telford. London: Epworth, 1931.

———. *The Works of the Rev. John Wesley, A. M.* Edited by Thomas Jackson. 14 vols. London: Wesleyan-Methodist Book-Room, n.d.

———. ed. *A Christian Library: Consisting of Extracts from and Abridgments of the choicest Pieces of Practical Divinity which have been published in the English Tongue*. 50 vols. Philadelphia: Jonathan Pounder, 1819–27.

———, ed. *The Distinguishing Marks of a Work of the Spirit of God*, by Jonathan Edwards. London: W. Strahan, 1744.

———, ed. *An Extract of the Life of the Late Rev. Mr. David Brainerd*, by Jonathan Edwards. Bristol: William Pine, 1768.

———, ed. *An Extract from a Treatise concerning Religious Affections*, by

Jonathan Edwards. In vol. 23 of *The Works of the Rev. John Wesley.* 32 vols. Bristol: J. Paramore, 1771–74.

———, ed. *A Narrative of Many Surprising Conversions in Northampton and Vicinity,* by Jonathan Edwards. Boston: Felix Farley, 1744.

———, ed. *Thoughts Concerning the Present Revival of Religion,* by Jonathan Edwards. London: W. Strahan, 1745.

Whicher, Stephen E. *Freedom and Fate: An Inner Life of Ralph Waldo Emerson.* 1953. Reprint. Philadelphia: University of Pennsylvania Press, 1979.

Williams, Bernard. *Descartes: The Project of Pure Inquiry.* Harmondsworth, England: Penguin Books, 1978.

Wills, Garry. "The Phallic Pulpit." *The New York Review of Books* 36 (December 21, 1989): 20–26.

Wilson, Edward O. *On Human Nature.* Cambridge: Harvard University Press, 1978.

———. *Sociobiology: The New Synthesis.* Cambridge: Harvard University Press, 1980.

Winters, Yvor. *Maule's Curse: Some Studies in the History of American Obscurantism.* Norfolk, Conn.: New Directions, 1936.

Wlecke, Arthur O. *Wordsworth and the Sublime.* Berkeley: University of California Press, 1973.

Wood, Gordon S. "Struggle Over the Puritans." *The New York Review of Books* 36 (November 9, 1989): 26–43.

Woolhouse, Roger. *Locke's Philosophy of Science and Knowledge.* Oxford: Clarendon Press, 1971.

Wordsworth, William. *The Poetical Works of William Wordsworth.* Edited by Ernest de Selincourt. 5 vols. 2d ed. of vol. 2 (1952) and vol. 3 (1954) revised by Helen Darbishire. Oxford: Clarendon Press, 1940–49.

———. *The Prelude; or, Growth of a Poet's Mind.* Edited by Ernest de Selincourt. 2d ed. revised by Helen Darbishire. Oxford: Clarendon Press, 1959.

Yoder, R. A. *Emerson and the Orphic Poet in America.* Berkeley: University of California Press, 1978.

Yolton, John W. *John Locke and the Compass of Human Understanding.* Cambridge: Cambridge University Press, 1970.

INDEX